Roots and Rituals

Insights into Hebrew, Holidays, and History

Mitchell First

KODESH PRESS

Roots and Rituals
Insights into Hebrew, Holidays, and History

© Mitchell First, 2018

PB ISBN: 978-1-947857-06-3
HC ISBN: 978-1-947857-18-6

The publisher extends its gratitude to
Mr. Laurence Goldstein for his help editing this work.

Published and Distributed Exclusively by
Kodesh Press L.L.C
New York, NY
www.kodeshpress.com
kodeshpress@gmail.com

Table of Contents

III. Hebrew Language

A. Particular Hebrew Words and Phrases

Preface

I started writing short columns weekly for the *Jewish Link of New Jersey* newspaper in 2014. This book consists of my favorite sixty of these columns. Actually, sixty-two. I threw in two extra for free! I also improved many of these columns with additional material. This book also includes an appendix with two longer articles. These were well-received articles that were previously published online at seforim.blogspot.com.

First and foremost, I would like to thank Moshe Kinderlerher, co-founder and co-publisher of the *Jewish Link of New Jersey*, for giving me the opportunity to write regularly for this paper. When I started, I had no idea that I would learn so much from writing these columns and that they would end up as my third book. This book is the direct result of his faith in me as a writer.

After many months, I learned the secret to writing good weekly columns: Do not start on Monday and finish on Wednesday. Rather, write the columns a few weeks in advance. This way, there is no rush each week. There is time to think out each topic carefully, and do the additional research that may be necessary, and to consult with others when necessary. My goal was always not only to produce interesting columns but to produce accurate ones as well.

Writing for the *Jewish Link of New Jersey* was the third time that I was fortunate enough to find a regular place for my writings. My first two opportunities came with the founding of the print journal *Ḥakirah*, and the online site seforim.blogspot.com. With each of these, I had the opportunity to publish relatively long scholarly articles, and these articles ended up forming the basis for my second book, *Esther Unmasked: Solving Eleven Mysteries of the Jewish Holidays and Liturgy*

(Kodesh Press, 2015).[1] Now, in recent years, just when I needed it, along came the *Jewish Link of New Jersey* newspaper, giving me the opportunity to write shorter articles on a wider variety of topics.

Acknowledgements

In the introduction to *Esther Unmasked*, I particularly thanked **Sam Borodach, Rabbi Ezra Frazer, Allen Friedman, Rabbi Avrohom Lieberman, Meylekh Viswanath and Rabbi Moshe Yasgur** for their many years of extensive discussions and sharing of sources with me.

I then added the following:

I would also like to acknowledge some of the many others who contributed over the years towards my efforts, either by sharing particular ideas and sources, or by encouraging me in my research. First and foremost is my *chavruta* Josh Teplow. In addition: Ze'ev Atlas, David Barach, Lazer Borgen, Menachem Butler, Myron Chaitovsky, Ben Cooper, Yisrael Dubitsky, David Fisher, Howard Friedman, Rabbi Mordy Friedman, Rachel Friedman, David Gertler, Jeff Glazer, Binyamin Goldstein, Azriel Haimowitz, Dick Harris (of blessed memory), Ziggy Hirsch, Rabbi Aryeh Kaplan, Daniel Klein, Heshie Klein, Rabbi Stephen Knapp, Steve and Abby Leichman, Ari Leifer, Arvin Levine, Josh Levy, Yehiel Levy, Moshe Markovitz, Rabbi Michael Pariser, Lenny Presby, Rabbi Baruch Price, Michael Rapoport, Chanani Sandler, Eli Schaap, David Schachter, Steve Schaffer, Richie Schiffmiller, Fred Schulman, Mark Siletski, Kal Staiman, Zalman Suldan, Zvi Weissler, Rabbi Richard Wolpoe, Rabbi Benjamin Yablok, Neal Yaros, Joshua Zakheim, Rabbi Alan Zelenetz, and Ariel Zell.

I would now like to add a few more names to the above list (again in alphabetical order): Joey Adler, Avi-Gil Chaitovsky, Joel Chudow, Mollie Fisch, Ira Friedman, Aharon Gal, Richard Gertler, Rabbi Jay Goldmintz, Shulamis Hes, Rabbi Reuven Chaim Klein, Rabbi Ariel Kopitnikoff, Yaacov Metzger, Jeff Neugroschl, Moshe Rosenberg,

---

1. My first book, *Jewish History in Conflict: A Study of the Major Discrepancy Between Rabbinic and Conventional Chronology*, published in 1997, was based on my M.A. paper at the Bernard Revel Graduate School of Yeshiva University.

Menachem Shapiro, Rob Sperber, Nati Sulimanoff, Rabbi Chaim Sunitsky, Rabbi Simcha Weinberg, and Barry Weissman.

I would particularly like to thank Michael Rapoport and Rabbi Simcha Weinberg for their wonderful and unique feedback and encouragement to me on my weekly columns. Also, Mollie Fisch, Abby Leichman, and Jesse Schwartzman provided regular encouragement.

Additionally, Moshe Schapiro and Mary Ann Linahan saved me dozens of trips to the Yeshiva University library by graciously responding to my requests for copies of sources, enabling me to keep my day job as an attorney.

I gained much over the years from the *shiurim* of the rabbis at Congregation Beth Aaron in Teaneck, N.J: Rabbi Ephraim Kanarfogel and Rabbi Laurence Rothwachs. I would like to thank them for the many opportunities they gave me to deliver *shiurim* in Congregation Beth Aaron. These *shiurim* helped lay the groundwork for many of these articles.

I would also like to thank Daniel A. Klein whose 1998 edition of S.D. Luzzatto's commentary on Genesis introduced me to the world of close analysis of the meanings and subtleties of Hebrew roots.

I have benefited much from exchanging ideas over many years with my children Shaya, Daniel and Rachel.

Special thanks to Alec Goldstein of Kodesh Press for his second tremendous job of publishing for me. (Kodesh Press also published *Esther Unmasked*.) Alec has always been a pleasure to work with. Moreover, he has contributed many scholarly insights as well.

I would like to thank my beloved wife Sharon for allowing me to live this additional life as a Jewish history scholar, outside my legal career, and pursue my research and writing interests. My mother, Judge Lee Blech First, has also provided me with continued encouragement.

I dedicate this book to my beloved father Harry First, Esq., זכרונו לברכה, who passed away in 2017. He loved history. He also introduced me to a field of law that was not all-consuming and that enabled me to have time to pursue my scholarly interests. The book includes an article that I wrote about him.

I would also like to thank my good friends for several decades, Allen and Rachel Friedman, and Dr. Elliot Goldofsky, for contributing dedication pages that helped fund the publication of this book.

Please feel free to contact me with insights or additional material on any of the topics that I have addressed. I can be reached at MFirstAtty@aol.com. (I still use AOL as it helps me relate to the ancient world!)

Mitchell First
Teaneck, N.J.
September 2018

P.S. Regarding the title of the book, *Roots and Rituals*, a google search revealed that there is a company in the United Kingdom that sells **hair care** products that goes by this name. I hope that my using this title for the book will not lead to too much confusion for consumers between our products!

A Tribute to my Father, Harry First (אהרו בן שלמה הכהן ז"ל)[1]

My father passed away on September 2, 2017, at the age of 91. I wanted to share his life story.

He was born in Brooklyn in 1925. His mother died when he was 17. Shortly after his mother's death, he enlisted in the US army. In the summer of 1944, at age 18, he was sent to France and served as a machine gunner. A few months later, his division was overtaken by the Nazis in Alsace-Lorraine and he was captured.

How did he survive in captivity? One of the first things he did was throw away his dog tag, so his captors would not know he was Jewish and give him "special treatment." Because he knew Yiddish, he understood much of what his captors were saying and could even speak some German. But he had to avoid using certain Hebrew words that made their way into Yiddish that might give away his Jewish identity. He made sure to listen more than he spoke.

He remembers that the German guards were very anti-Semitic. Once a German guard showed him a picture of Hitler and said: "Do you know who this is? He is the man who took everything from the Jews and gave it to us." And when President Roosevelt died in April 1945, they came into the barracks shouting that "Rosenfeld" was dead. To them, the U.S. President was a Jew named "Rosenfeld!"

He often had to think fast. When a Nazi guard wondered where he had learned German, he told him that he was a student. The guard got suspicious. "If you are a student," he asked, "why are you not an officer?" My father says that he looked down at the ground as though ashamed and came up with the following response: "Because I drank too much." The guard was satisfied with this answer. (My father later wondered whether the guard might also have had the same problem!)

---

1. This is all adapted from my eulogy at my father's funeral and from an article I wrote about him in the *Jewish Link of New Jersey* on the occasion of his *sheloshim*.

While in captivity, he bartered his cigarettes for bread and potatoes. He also bartered his milk rations with captured Indian prisoners who had been serving in the British army. They would not eat the meat rations and wanted the milk.

My father initially hid his Jewish identity from both his captors and fellow soldiers. But after several months an American soldier approached him and said that the prisoners would probably be dead within three days. What type of burial did he want? My father recalled that the question really jarred him. The thought of a cross over his grave hit him so hard that for the first time he risked his life and admitted that he was Jewish. But it turned out that this soldier was working for the Germans. My father and the other captive soldiers who admitted to being Jewish were then singled out for harsher treatment.

When the war was over, he went to Brooklyn College and Law School on the GI Bill. The government paid for the education of its former soldiers.

He became a lawyer and encouraged my mother Lee to become a lawyer as well. They practiced law together for 20 years. After lawyers begin practicing, many have the urge to become judges. My father encouraged my mother to achieve this goal. In 1975, New York Governor Hugh Carey appointed her a Judge in the Workers' Compensation court. She held this position for 12 years. (Her accomplishment was especially impressive since she had come to this country from Switzerland at age thirteen, not knowing any English.) My father retired from the practice of law in 2005, at the age of 80.

My father was always very optimistic. One of his favorite sayings was "when life gives you a lemon, you should turn it into lemonade." After having being a teenager in the army with bullets and death all around him, nothing in any courtroom ever scared him. Also, his ability to think well on his feet, nurtured while in captivity, helped him when he was in court.

One time, my father was trying a case in Staten Island. A statement he made offended the judge, and the judge ordered him put in handcuffs. My father responded to the judge that he had fought the Nazis as a teenager in World War II and nothing that the judge did would scare him.

My father and mother were among the founding families of the Riverdale Jewish Center. My parents came to Riverdale in the 1950's when there was practically nothing there. My parents were also very involved in the founding of S.A.R. Academy.

How did my parents meet? My mother's father was an Orthodox rabbi and educator, Rabbi Benzion Blech. He always wanted my mother to marry someone Orthodox and very learned. But my mother had other ideas. While attending Brooklyn College, she saw my father from afar, while he was working as a librarian in Brooklyn College. He was attending Brooklyn Law School at the time. It was love at first sight for my mother. She won my father over, but then came the harder challenge: convincing her father. My father was not Orthodox and had never met an Orthodox person before. He did not at all fit her father's image of a son-in-law.

An old friend of my mother's, "Chayele," now advanced in years, recently told one of my sons the following story: My mother and father had been dating, but Rabbi Blech did not know that they were dating. Chayele came up with an idea. She told my father to sit in the front of the room where Rabbi Blech was giving *shiur*. Every time Rabbi Blech finished a thought, my father should nod his head approvingly and mutter: "a gut vort." My father did this and then after the shiur, as Chayele hoped, Rabbi Blech walked over to one of his *talmidim* and asked "who is this new *illui* in the front row? Maybe he's a *shidduch* for my daughter!"

I am sure that this story is not true! Nevertheless, in retelling this story, I see myself in the role of the ancient Greek historian Herodotus (5th century B.C.E.). In a famous passage (VII, 152), he explains that his role is to transmit the ancient stories that are told, even when he does not believe them. Sometimes entertainment value trumps truth!

The true story, as my mother relates in her book, *Justice is Blonde*, is that her father eventually realized that my mother was not going to marry any of the learned Torah scholars that he had hoped for and was set on marrying the handsome law student she had met in the library. Thus, she gradually won her father over to this *shidduch* with my father, who was willing to become Orthodox.

One time a friend of my father's warned him that by marrying my mother, he would not be able to eat in restaurants again. My father was thrilled with the thought. Having lost his mother at age 17 and been eating out since then, he was looking forward to a life of eating at home.

My father put his life on the line to fight Hitler. God rewarded him with *arikhat yamim*. May his memory be a blessing.

לזכר נשמות

אבי מורי יעקב בן אליעזר ורחל ז"ל
ואמי מורתי דבורה בת הרב חיים וחנה מלכה ז"ל
Dr. Jack & Devorah Friedman

who passed on to us their love of Jewish scholarship and learning

Allen & Rachel Friedman & Family

In Recognition of:
Dr. Philip Wilner, Ramaz H.S., Class of 1975

In Appreciation of:
Mitchell First, Esq., Ramaz H.S., Class of 1975

In Memory of:
Rabbi Joseph Klausner z"l, Ramaz H.S., Class of 1975

In Honor of:
Rabbi Shaya First, former rabbinic intern, Young Israel of
Jamaica Estates

Submitted with much gratitude by:

Elliot Goldofsky, M.D., Ramaz H.S., Class of 1976

SPONSORS

The author would like to express his appreciation to the following individuals for their generous donations which helped fund the publication of this book:

Dr. Atara Berliner, in memory of her parents Rabbi Albert Berliner and Marilyn Berliner, z"l, who devoted their lives to Torah education

Patty and Sam Borodach, in memory of Sam's father Dr. Gerold Borodach, z"l

Michele and Dr. Ben Cooper

Roz and Ira Friedman, in memory of their parents Abe and Charlotte Remer, and David J. and Rose Anne Friedman, z"l

Amy and Ziggy Hirsch

Ellen and Dr. Richard Gertler

Rabbi Avrohom Lieberman

Mitch Morrison, in memory of his parents Ruben and Helen Morrison, z"l

Pearl Neuman and David Schachter in honor of their children and grandchildren: Ariel, Chana, Eitan and Livvy

Aliza and Kal Staiman

Drs. Dora and Zalman Suldan, in honor of our friend Mitch First and the light he shines on Torah and Jewish scholarship

Rebecca and Josh Teplow: in honor of our dear children, Joe, Avery and Tamara; in honor of our mother, Miriam Teplow; and in memory of our parents, Elaine and Leonard Wacholder and Josef Teplow, all of blessed memory

Rabbi Simcha Weinberg in honor of Dr. Heshie Klein, who introduced him to the author

Dr. Barry Weissman in honor of the Aug. 19, 2018 marriage of Lara H. Weissman to Stuart Jaffee

Barbara and Neal Yaros in honor of their grandchildren: Gavriel, Tzvi, Tamar, Liana, Shoshana, and Calev

The Zell Family

Guide to Reading this Book by *Parashah*

Since many people today focus their learning and *divrei Torah* by *parashah*, I thought it would be helpful to make a list suggesting articles that were relevant in some major or minor way to each *parashah*. I did not do this for the entire *Chumash*. But I am presenting suggestions from *Bereshit* through *Mishpatim*. (Of course, the list below only includes a small portion of the sixty-four articles in this book.)

Bereshit:	The Origin of the Jewish Count from Creation
	The Longevity of the Ancients Recorded in Genesis
	The Multiple Meanings of the Word שָׁנָה
	What is the Origin of the Words עֶרֶב and בֹּקֶר?
Noach:	The Root of the Word מַבּוּל: A Flood of Possibilities
Lekh Lekha:	What is the Origin of the Word בְּרִית (Covenant)?
Va-Yera:	לחם and מלחמה: Is There a Connection?
	What is the Origin of the Word נביא?
Chayey Sarah:	What is the Meaning of the Word מִשְׁתָּאֵה (Gen. 24:21)?
Toledot:	ארמי אבד אבי: Uncovering the Interpretation Hidden in the Mishnah
Va-Yetze:	What is the Meaning of the Word כֶּסֶף?
Va-Yishlach:	Searching for Omitted *Nuns*
Miketz:	Some Interesting Words in *Parashat Miketz*
	What is the Origin of the Word חֲלוֹם (Dream)?
Va-Yigash:	What is the Origin of the Word שְׁאוֹל (Netherworld)?
Va-Yechi:	The Meaning of the Word הִתְפַּלֵּל
Shemot:	Did Moses Have a Speech Impediment?
Va-Era:	John Lennon and the Plague of עָרֹב (*Arov*)
Bo:	Nevuchad**n**ezzar or Nevuchad**r**ezzar?
Be-Shalach:	Some Interesting Words in אָז יָשִׁיר
	Males and Memory: The Meanings of the Root זכר
Yitro:	What is the Origin of the Words חָתָן and כַּלָּה?
Mishpatim:	An Insight into the Text of *Birkat Ha-Mazon:* הקדושה or הגדושה?

Abbreviations of Frequently Cited Sources

Ernest Klein, *A Comprehensive Etymological Dictionary of the Hebrew Language for Readers of English* (1987). Cited as "E. Klein."

Ludwig Koehler and Walter Baumgartner, *The Hebrew & Aramaic Lexicon of the Old Testament* (1995, revised edition). Cited as "Koehler-Baumgartner."

Marcus Jastrow, *A Dictionary of the Targumim, the Talmud Babli and Yerushalmi, and the Midrashic Literature* (1903). Cited as "M. Jastrow."

Hayim ben Yosef Tawil, *An Akkadian Lexical Companion For Biblical Hebrew* (2009). Cited as "H. Tawil."

Solomon Mandelkern, *Heikhal Ha-Kodesh* (1896). Cited as "S. Mandelkern."

Francis Brown, S.R. Driver, and Charles A. Briggs, *A Hebrew and English Lexicon of the Old Testament* (1906). Cited as "Brown-Driver-Briggs."

I also frequently cited to *Theological Dictionary of the Old Testament*. This is a 15 volume work which spanned the years 1974-2006. Each article is by a separate author.

All citations to *The Complete ArtScroll Siddur* are to the third edition (1990).

All citations to the *Encylopaedia Judaica* are to the 1972 edition.

I. Jewish Liturgy

1. Insights into the History of the *Haftarah*

1. Although there are many theories, no one knows when and why the practice of the *haftarah* was instituted.

The Complete ArtScroll Siddur includes the following statement: "The practice of reading from the Prophets… was introduced during the reign of the infamous Syrian-Greek king Antiochus…. [He] forbade the public reading of the Torah. Unable to refresh their spiritual thirst from the Torah itself, the people resorted to readings from the Prophets…" (p. 445).

There is little basis for this explanation of the origin of the *haftarah*. The persecution by Antiochus took place in 167-164 B.C.E. This explanation is merely a conjecture first made by R. David Abudarham in the 14th century.[1] (He does not name the particular persecution he had in mind. It is R. Elijah Levita of the 15th century who first suggests the persecution of Antiochus.) Most scholars have trouble accepting the idea that Antiochus or any persecutor would have made a distinction between a reading from the Torah and a reading from the Prophets.

2. With regard to the earliest references to the practice of reading a *haftarah*, the practice is mentioned several times in the fourth chapter of Mishnah *Megillah*. But we cannot tell from these references whether the practice existed already before the destruction of the Temple in 70 C.E.[2]

Fortunately, the New Testament helps us with regard to dating the practice of reading from the *Neviim* in some form. Acts 13:15 states

---

1. The persecution explanation should have been presented by *The Complete ArtScroll Siddur* as a mere late conjecture. A much fairer presentation is made in *The Pentateuch and Haftorahs* of Dr. J.H. Hertz (p. 20).This work states at the outset: "We possess no historical data concerning the institution of these Lessons." It then mentions the persecution explanation and properly describes it as a statement by a "medieval author on the Liturgy."
2. See also the story at *Megillah* 25a involving a *haftarah* read in front of R. Eliezer ben Hyrcanus. This story could have occurred before 70 C.E., but it cannot be precisely dated. R. Eliezer ben Hyrcanus was an early Tanna who was a teacher of R. Akiva.

that "after the reading of the law and the prophets" on the Sabbath, Paul was invited to deliver an exhortation. (See similarly Acts 13:27.) Paul died around 67 C.E.

A few decades earlier than this, we have a reference to Jesus reading two verses from Isaiah out loud in synagogue. See Luke 4:17. This also seems to be a reference to a *haftarah* reading in its earliest form.

3. The earliest reference in rabbinic literature to specific *haftarah* selections is at Tosefta *Megillah*, 3rd chapter. Here, the selections for the four special *Shabbatot* are given (*Shekalim, Zakhor, Parah,* and *Ha-Chodesh*). Also, a *baraita* at *Megillah* 31a gives the selections for Hanukkah and for all the festivals, and for other special occasions. All of this does not mean that the practice of reading *haftarot* on holidays preceded the practice of reading *haftarot* on a regular *Shabbat*. Rather, it only means that the idea of a **fixed reading** for the holiday *haftarot* preceded the idea of a fixed reading for the *haftarot* on a regular *Shabbat*.

Nowhere in the Talmud are specific *haftarot* assigned to the *parashah* of ordinary *Shabbatot*. Very likely, there was no fixed *haftarah* for each ordinary *Shabbat* in talmudic times. A fixed *haftarah* for each ordinary *Shabbat parashah* was a later development and, as we all know, has only been partially accomplished. Variations in custom still exist between Ashkenazim and Sephardim, and within each of these communities.

It is well-documented that in the Amoraic and Geonic periods in Palestine, the widespread practice was to read the Torah on a cycle that took approximately 3½ years (loosely referred to as the "triennial cycle"). Accordingly, in Palestine they had over 150 different Torah reading sections. As a consequence, many more *haftarot* were in use in Palestine in those periods than are in use today. From documents discovered in the Cairo Genizah, scholars have made much progress in reconstructing the *haftarot* that were being read on the triennial cycle. See, e.g., Yosef Ofer, "Ha-Haftarot Al Pi Ha-Minhag Ha-Telat Shenati," *Tarbitz* 58 (1989), pp. 173-185.

It is interesting that the *haftarah* that we read today on *Shabbat Ha-Gadol*, "*ve-arvah… minchat Yehudah*," started out as a *haftarah* on the triennial cycle. It was a *haftarah* for a section of *Parashat Tzav* that had to do with a *minchah* offering.[3] When the triennial cycle began to fall out of use in the period of the later Geonim and early Rishonim, "*ve-arvah*" managed to survive as a *haftarah* because it evolved into a *haftarah* for *Shabbat Ha-Gadol*.[4] (As evolutionists will tell you, adaptation is the key to survival!)

4. Now I would like to engage in some speculation about the origin of the practice of reading a *haftarah*.

One possibility is that the *haftarah* reading was originally enacted to exhort us to improve our conduct. The *Neviim* were perhaps a better fit for this than the *Ketuvim*. Another possibility is that the goal of the enactment was simply to increase our study of *Nakh*. But since it was also felt that the readings should match the *parashah*, the readings were limited to the *Neviim*; there were more opportunities for such matchings in the *Neviim*. An alternative idea is that the primary goal of the enactment to read the *Neviim* was to provide honor to the deceased individual prophets.

Another theory is that the *haftarah* was instituted after some act of persecution or other disaster in which Torah scrolls were destroyed or ruined. It was forbidden to read the Torah portion from any but a ritually fit parchment scroll, but there was no such requirement about a reading from the *Nakh*. The temporary substituted practice then remained. (Again, perhaps the *Neviim* were chosen, rather than the *Ketuvim*, due to the better matches to the Torah portion.)   All of these theories have been suggested, and many more.[5]

But a different theory that has been suggested sounds the most reasonable to me. Today, we have a formal reading of a large section with a special *haftarah* blessing. But the practice perhaps started as part of a sermon or homily after the Torah reading, where the sermon or homily began with a reading or discussion of a few verses from the *Neviim* that were connected to the *parashah*.[6] (As suggested earlier, the

---

3. I am referring to the section that commences at Lev. 6:12. See Ofer, p. 180.

4. See S. Katz, *The Haftarah* (2000), p. 178, n. 9.

5. For collections of various theories, see, e.g., S. Weingarten, "*Reishitan Shel Ha-Haftarot*," *Sinai* 83 (1978), pp. 107-36 and S. Rosenberg, *The Haphtara Cycle* (2000), pp. xxi-xxiv.

6. One scholar who suggests this is Rosenberg. See his *The Haphtara Cycle*, pp. xxviii -xxxii. (His discussion here is very interesting but includes much speculation.)

Ketuvim do not match the *parashah* in the same way that the *Neviim* do.[7]) Over time, the practice slowly evolved into a formal reading of a larger section from the *Neviim*, with an introductory blessing.

Until the time of the early Rishonim, there was no distinction between the *Neviim* and the *Ketuvim* in terms of degree of sanctity and level of inspiration. See Sid Z. Leiman, *The Canonization of Hebrew Scripture* (1991, 2nd edition), pp. 64-66.

5. As to the meaning of the words *haftarah* and the related word *maftir*, most likely they mean something like "conclusion."[8] Theoretically, the reference could be to the conclusion of the *shacharit* service, the conclusion of the reading sections (Torah and *haftarah*), or the conclusion of the entire synagogue service. But the meaning "conclusion of the entire synagogue service" is the most likely one. The practice of reading a *haftarah* originated in the pre-70 C.E. period. Scholars now understand that, in this early period, synagogues were usually places of studying and reading of the Torah, and not places of formal prayer. Moreover, according to most scholars, there was no *Amidah* at all in the pre-70 C.E. period, neither *shacharit* nor *musaf*.[9] Alternatively, if there was an *Amidah* in the pre-70 C.E. period, it was for Rosh Hashanah and *Yom Tov* only (and probably recited only in limited circles).[10] Thus, in the pre-70 C.E. period, after the reading of the Torah and whatever limited reading of the *Neviim* took place, the "service" in the synagogue was typically concluded.[11]

---

7. It has been suggested that the *haftarah* was not drawn from the *Ketuvim* because there was no widely accepted official Aramaic translation of the *Ketuvim* (see *Megillah* 3a). But if the practice of reading from the *Neviim* began with the reading of only a few verses, the lack of an accepted official Aramaic translation should not have been a factor in preventing readings from the *Ketuvim*. Rather, the reason the readings were chosen from the *Neviim* was likely because they had more of a connection to the *parashah*.

8. See similarly the Mishnaic passage (*Pesachim* 10:8): *ve-ein maftirin achar ha-pesach afikoman.*

9. See A. Friedman, "The *Amida*'s Biblical and Historical Roots: Some New Perspectives," *Tradition* 45:3 (2012), pp. 21-34.

10. See Tosefta *Rosh Hashanah* 2:16 and Tosefta *Berakhot* 3:13. See also my *Esther Unmasked* (2015), pp. 91-92. But note that many scholars make the argument that these Tosefta passages are anachronistic and cannot be relied upon. See, e.g., L. Levine, *The Ancient Synagogue* (2000), p. 549.

11. This is also evident from Acts chap. 13.

Many other interpretations of the words *haftarah* and *maftir* have been offered.[12] But they are all much less likely than the one I just described.

*

Mitchell First is a personal injury attorney and Jewish history scholar. He looks forward to the discovery of a new Dead Sea Scroll that might shed some light on the origin of the *haftarah*.

2. The Blessing "Who Has Not Made Me A Woman"

There has been much scholarly research on this blessing and on the *she-asani kirtzono* blessing. I would like to share some of the findings.

1. The blessing *she-lo asani ishah* is found in the Tosefta and in the Talmud. But the blessing *she-asani kirtzono* is first recorded only in the 14th century (in the *Tur* and the Abudarham). What did women recite before this?

The language in the *Tur* is **nahagu nashim** le-varekh she-asani *kirtzono*. It has been suggested that this language implies that this blessing was an innovation by women themselves, not something suggested by rabbinic leaders. Perhaps this innovation did not occur until the 14th century. But it is also possible that some version appropriate to females arose well before the 14th century, just that no remnants of it have survived.

2. Other formulations of the blessing for women have been found in the 14th and 15th centuries:

A. A *siddur* from 14th or 15th century Provence (southern France) has the formulation "**who has made me a woman.**" It is written in Shuadit (the Jewish-French language of the area), utilizing Hebrew characters. (The actual text is: פנה מי פיס קי.)

B. Two *siddurim* written by R. Abraham Farisol of Italy, one written in 1471 and the other in 1480, have *she-asitani ishah ve-lo ish*, "**who has made me a woman, not a man.**" The males in Italy at

---

12. Many are collected in Weingarten and Rosenberg.

this time were reciting "who has made me a man, not a woman." The version by R. Farisol is just the mirror image, for females.[13]

It is important to point out that all three of the above *siddurim* were manuscripts that were privately commissioned for specific women. These were not manuscripts that had both the male and female versions of the blessing. These manuscripts may not necessarily reflect what other women in their regions were reciting, praying by heart or using a typical *siddur* written for males.

C. The *Leket Yosher* reports that his teacher R. Israel Isserlein (15th century, Austria, author of *Terumat Ha-Deshen*) was of the view that women should recite *she-lo asani behemah.* (Some males were reciting such a text as part of their liturgy. This made it a candidate for the third blessing for women.)

3. Diogenes Laertius, 3rd century C.E., wrote that either Socrates (5th century B.C.E) or another early Greek philosopher is reported to have said: "there were three blessings for which he was grateful to Fortune: "first, that I was born a human being and not one of the brutes; next that I was born a man and not a woman; thirdly a Greek and not a Barbarian."

Did this line of thought of the ancient Greeks lead to our three daily blessings? Many scholars have been willing to take this position, but it is obviously only a conjecture. Note that our three blessings were originally: who has not made me a *goy*, who has not made me a woman, and who has not made me a *bor* (an uncultured, mannerless person). See *Menachot* 43b, Tosefta *Berkahot*, chapter 6, and the Jerusalem Talmud *Berkahot*, chapter 9.

Our three blessings are brought down in *Menachot* 43b in the name of R. Meir (2nd century C.E.). In the other two sources, they are brought down in the name of his contemporary, R. Judah. Most likely, the author of the statement was R. Judah, and the attribution to R. Meir at *Menachot* 43b is the result of a scribal error. This is the conclusion of Joseph Tabory, the scholar who has written the leading article on this subject. But does the fact that the blessings are brought

---

13. D. Sperber, *On Changes in Jewish Liturgy: Options and Limitations* (2010), p. 41, describes the first manuscript as reading "*she-asani ishah.*" But this is an error.

down in the name of R. Judah mean that they originated with him? Perhaps he is merely reporting an earlier tradition. As always, we do not know. (One reason it is interesting to determine whether the statement was made by R. Judah or by R. Meir is that the wife of R. Meir was the very knowledgeable Beruriah.)

4.   An Iranian prayer in a 2nd or 3rd century C.E. source expressed gratitude to their divinity, Hormiz: "O Creator, I thank Thee for that Thou hast made me an Iranian, and of the true religion... Thanks to Thee, O Creator, for this, that Thou hast made me of the race of men... for this, that Thou hast created me free and not a slave; for this, that Thou hast created me a man and not a woman." It has been suggested that this prayer was influenced by our Jewish prayer. Of course, this too is only conjecture.

5. Although the reasons for the three blessings are not stated in the passage in *Menachot*, they are stated in the passage in the Tosefta and the Jerusalem Talmud. The explanation given for *she-lo asani ishah* is that women are not obligated in the commandments. Men are here being thankful that they are obligated. Admittedly, it does not sound appropriate to our contemporary ears for women to be mentioned alongside these other two groups. But in Tannaitic and Amoraic literature, statements were often oversimplified and stated in groups like this so that they could be easily memorized and passed down.

6. There is a general principle that blessings that are not found in the Talmud are not to be recited with *shem* and *malkhut*. Most Sephardic *poskim* and *siddurim* have adopted this limitation in the case of *she-asani kirtzono* and instructed women to recite only the words: *barukh she-asani kirtzono*. In contrast, in the Ashkenazic world, the prevalent practice is to recite the blessing *she-asani kirtzono* with *shem* and *malkhut*. (But a few Ashkenazic sources do argue for the limitation. See, e.g., Isaac Baer, *Avodat Yisrael* [1868], p. 41, and R. Barukh Epstein, *Barukh She-amar* [1940], p. 30.)

Anyone further interested in the history of these three blessings should see the detailed article by Joseph Tabory, "The Benedictions of

Self-Identity and The Changing Status of Women and of Orthodoxy,"
Kenishta, vol. 1 (2001), pp. 107-138.

*

Mitchell First thanks God every day for three things: that he is a
Jewish history scholar, that he is an attorney and that he lives in a
vibrant Jewish community.

3. The Origin of the Recital of *Shema* in the *Kedushah of Musaf*

I grew up using the Birnbaum *Siddur*. For years I stared at a line in its
commentary about a prohibition of the recital of the *Shema* in the 5th
century and an explanation of how *Shema* ended up in the *Kedushah*
of *musaf*: "In the fifth century... special governmental officials were
posted in the synagogues to prevent the congregational proclamation
of [*Shema*]. Towards the end of the service, when the spies had left,
the *Shema* was [added] in an abridged form...." Something similar
is repeated in *The Complete ArtScroll Siddur*, pp. 28 and 465. I always
wondered about the historicity of this fifth-century story. (Especially
the detail of the spies leaving early. Wouldn't they have wanted to stay
for the *kiddush*?) Eventually, I decided to research this topic.

A story about the fifth-century Persian king Yezdegerd
prohibiting the *Shema* is found in the *Shibbolei Ha-Leket*, writing in
thirteenth-century Italy. But let us look at an earlier version of this
story, that of R. Sar Shalom Gaon (9th century, Babylonia), quoted in
Seder Rav Amram Gaon.[14] Here we find a statement that *Shema* ended
up being added by rabbinic enactment to the *Kedushah* of *musaf* to
commemorate an earlier period of prohibition of the recital of *Shema*
in *shacharit*, but there is no mention of who ordered this prohibition.
(Nor is there any mention of spies leaving early!)

Eventually, I realized how the anonymous prohibition of the
Shema referred to by R. Sar Shalom Gaon was later attributed to
Yezdegerd. In the "Letter of R. Sherira Gaon" (late 10th century),
there is a reference to Yezdegerd issuing a decree prohibiting the
observance of the *Shabbat* in the year 455. At some point later,
either the *Shibbolei Ha-Leket*, or some source prior to him, decided
to combine the two separate prohibition traditions and assign the
anonymous *Shema* prohibition to Yezdegerd as well.

14. Ed. D. Goldschmidt, pp. 32-33.

Once we realize that there is no ancient tradition that the fifth-century king Yezdegerd issued a prohibition against the *Shema*, we can look anew at the question of why we are reciting *Shema* in the *Kedushah* of *musaf*.

Let us review. There is a concept of a *Kedushah* prayer. In its basic form, a verse from Isaiah chapter 6 (*kadosh, kadosh…*) and a verse from Ezekiel chapter 3 (*barukh kevod…*) are recited parallel to one another. The two verses have something fundamental in common. Both are phrases about God's glory that are recited by celestial beings.

The *Kedushah* prayer that we recite in the daily and *Shabbat* repetitions of the *Amidah*, at both *shacharit* and *minchah*, adds a theme based on a third verse, *yimlokh Hashem le-olam* (Ps. 146:10). This last verse is not integrally related to the other two verses. The *Kedushah* of *Shabbat musaf*, the one that concerns us, has a *Shema* section added, before the Ps. 146:10 section.

Now let us look at our earliest sources about the recital of *Shema* in the *Kedusuah* of *musaf*. R. Sar Shalom Gaon, in ninth-century Babylonia, explained that *Shema* was added to the *Kedushah* of *musaf* to remind us of an earlier period of prohibition of the *Shema* in *shacharit*, but he did not identify who issued the prohibition. Another ninth-century Babylonian source, Pirkoi ben Baboi, took the position that reciting *Shema* in *Kedushah* was an unjustifiable Palestinian custom that originated at a time of persecution by *malkhut Edom* in Palestine. Pirkoi did not state the time of this persecution. His reference could be to any time in the several hundred years prior to the Arab conquest of Palestine in the early 7th century C.E.

Most scholars today do not take these persecution explanations seriously, as neither of these sources is claiming to be an eyewitness to a persecution. Nor do these sources date the supposed persecution with any specificity. Moreover, with regard to Pirkoi, it is widely accepted that this is a polemical Babylonian Jewish source that is overly critical of Palestinian traditions.

How do scholars today explain the presence of *Shema* in the *Kedushah* of *musaf*? The scholar Meir Bar-Ilan (*"Kivuy Yesod Le-Hithavutah Shel Ha-Kedushah Ve-Gibushah," Daat* 25, 1990, pp. 5-20) views the *Kedushah* prayer as having evolved over time, yielding different versions. The *Kedushah* of *musaf* with the *Shema* verse just reflects a version that added a verse with a theme of *kabbalat ol malkhut shamayim.* In a similar manner, Ps. 146:10, with its own separate theme, was added to the original two verses. In Bar-Ilan's view, the *Kedushah* of *musaf* is just a collection of important biblical verses with disparate themes (something like "The Bible's Greatest Hits"!)

Other scholars note that a *Kedushah* with *kadosh, barukh kevod,* and *Shema* looks like a repetition of the earlier part of the service: the *Kedushat Yotzer* and the *Shema.* The suggestion is then made that the *Kedushah* of *musaf* originated as a brief repetition of the earlier part of the service for the benefit of latecomers.

But the most likely explanation for the *Shema* passage in the *Kedushah* of *musaf* is an entirely different one. The author of the *Kedushah* of *musaf* was expressing a parallel between the role of Israel in this world and the role of the angels in heaven. Both are engaged in the same activity, sanctifying and coronating God. But in the view of the author of the *Kedushah* of *musaf,* the angels fulfill their role daily by reciting *kadosh, kadosh, kadosh,* while Israel fulfills its role daily by reciting the *Shema.* Such an idea is expressed at *Chullin* 91b and elsewhere. (The *shirah* of Israel referred to at *Chullin* 91b is most likely the *Shema.*) This is all argued for extensively by Rabbi N. Daniel Korobkin, in his "Kedushah, Shema, and the Difference Between Israel and the Angels,"*Ḥakirah* 16 (2013), pp. 19-46. Korobkin cites earlier scholars such as Ezra Fleischer and Israel Ta-Shema. (Regarding Ta-Shema, see his *Ha-Tefillah Ha-Ashkenazit Ha-Kedumah* [2003], pp. 110-114.)

Our focusing for hundreds of years on an imaginary persecution caused us to lose sight of the idea that was being expressed! (*The Complete ArtScroll Siddur*, p. 464, does briefly suggest this explanation as well: "Israel joins the angels by proclaiming שמע ישראל, our own declaration of God's greatness."[15])

Finally, on the subject of interference by the government with our synagogue service, sometimes we do have reliable documentation of this occurring in ancient times. In a separate article, I discuss a law

---

15. *The Complete ArtScroll Siddur* (p. 464) also states that the *Kedushah* of *musaf* is based on *Pirkei De-R. Eliezer.* But the *Kedushah* of *musaf* likely preceded the material in *Pirkei De-R. Eliezer* by several centuries. The material in *Pirkei De-R. Eliezer* (fourth chapter) is merely following the format of the *Kedushah* of *musaf.*

decreed by the Roman ruler Justinian in the year 553 that interfered with the synagogue service.

*

Mitchell First is a personal injury attorney and Jewish history scholar. He would never leave shul early before the *Kedushah* of *musaf* and miss the *kiddush*.

4. *Aleinu*: A Rosh Hashanah Prayer that Migrated into the Daily Service

Every Rosh Hashanah, we are all puzzled by the flow of the *musaf Amidah*, when *Aleinu* suddenly appears. After all, *Aleinu* is a prayer recited all year long at the conclusion of the daily services. Why does it suddenly appear in the middle of the *Amidah* on Rosh Hashanah?

It turns out that the question we should be asking is the reverse. *Aleinu* was part of the Rosh Hashanah *musaf Amidah* for centuries before it began making its way into the end of the daily *shacharit* service in France, England, and Germany in the 12th and 13th centuries.

The earliest source we have that records *Aleinu* at the end of daily *shacharit* is a manuscript of *Machzor Vitry*. This is a work usually attributed to R. Simcha of Vitry (a town in northern France). The most recent scholarship dates this manuscript to the second quarter of the 12th century.[16]

We have documentation that in 1171 the martyrs of Blois (another town in northern France) chanted *Aleinu* with their last breaths as they were being burned to death. Many scholars had theorized that this is what led *Aleinu* to penetrate the hearts of the people and be incorporated into the daily *shacharit*. But now that we can document that *Aleinu* was already being recited in *shacharit* several decades earlier than this, this theory is disproven. (Of course, the events of 1171 may have caused the previous custom to recite daily *Aleinu* to become more widespread.)

---

16. See S. Stern and J. Isserles, "The Astrological and Calendar Section of the Earliest *Maḥzor Vitry* Manuscript (MS ex-Sassoon 535)," *Aleph* 15.2 (2015), pp. 199-318.

In recent years, a novel theory was proposed by the scholar Israel Ta-Shema.[17] In the 11th century, a R. Elijah of Le Mans (another town in northern France) established a special prayer service for his select circle, modeled after the *maamadot* of Mishnaic times. This special prayer service was conducted after the daily *shacharit*. *Aleinu* is included in this special service in a *siddur* from the end of 12th century. Based on this, Ta-Shema theorized that *Aleinu* first entered the daily prayer service by way of this special service, and from here made its way into the regular daily *shacharit*. But the *siddur* that Ta-Shema cites for the proposition that *Aleinu* was included in this special service is only from the end of the 12th century.[18] One can just as easily argue that *Aleinu* made its way into the special service from the daily *shacharit* service.

In my view and in the view of many others,[19] *Aleinu* was likely introduced into the daily *shacharit* as a prayer meant to express a rejection of Christianity. Probably, its introduction came as a response to the Crusades of 1096 or due to the general feeling of downtroddenness that the Jews of France felt while living as second-class citizens in a Christian land.

Interestingly, there is an instruction given in *Machzor Vitry* that the daily *Aleinu* is to be recited *be-lachash* (silently). The reason for this instruction may be that the Jews understood that the Christians would view the prayer as an anti-Christian one. (But it can also be argued that the instruction merely reflects that the prayer was viewed as a new, non-mandatory, prayer at this time.)

We have much documentation starting from the end of the 12th century and continuing for centuries that *Aleinu* was viewed by Jewish

---

17. See I. Ta-Shema, *Ha-Tefillah Ha-Ashkenazit Ha-Kedumah* (2003), pp. 139-53.

18. It is Ms. Oxford, Corpus Christi College 133, described in M. Beit-Arié, *The Only Dated Medieval Manuscript Written in England (1189 CE)* (1985), in appendix 2 of this work. Corpus Christi College 133 is not the manuscript described in the title of the book and is not a dated manuscript. But that it is from the end of the 12th century can be deduced by the notations made by its owner. He was a money lender, and on a blank page at the end of the *siddur* he recorded the names of bishops and other individuals in England who paid him and some of them can be identified and dated to the end of the 12th century.

19. See, e.g., *Encyclopaedia Judaica* 2:559 (entry for *Aleinu*, last sentence).

communities in Christian Europe as an anti-Christian prayer.[20] But this was probably already the case in the second quarter of the 12th century as well. If one looks at the text of *Aleinu*, it has the following passages: *she-lo asanu ke-goyey ha-aratzot... she-hem mishtachavim le-hevel va-rik...le-haavir gilulim min ha-aretz, ve-ha-elilim karot yikkaretun...* Jews reciting these passages in northern France in the second quarter of the 12th century would likely have recited these passages with a rejection of Christianity in mind.[21]

Some scholars have focused on the positive approach to the nations expressed in the last few lines of *Aleinu* (beginning with *ve-khol bnei vasar yikreu vi-shmekha...*). These scholars argue that it was thought appropriate to end the daily *shacharit* with a prayer that envisions the end of days when all the world will be united in divine worship. But the negative attitude towards the nations takes up more of the language of *Aleinu* than does the positive attitude. Also, the true reason for the inclusion of a prayer is usually found towards its beginning, rather than towards its end. (This principle applies to the *haftarot* as well!) As mentioned earlier, we have much documentation starting from the end of the 12th century and continuing for centuries that *Aleinu* was viewed by Jewish communities in Christian Europe as an anti-Christian prayer.

Outside of France, we have documentation of *Aleinu* in daily *shacharit* from Germany and England from a slightly later period.

---

20. See N. Wieder, *Hitgabshut Nusach Ha-Tefillah Be-Mizrach U-Be-Maarav* (1998), pp. 453-68, and Ta-Shema, p. 147, n. 20.

21. Whether *Aleinu* was originally composed, at least partially, as an anti-Christian prayer is a separate issue. It depends on when and where *Aleinu* was composed. This is still an unresolved issue, although there are statements in the Jerusalem Talmud, at *Avodah Zarah* 1:2 and *Rosh Hashanah* 1:3, that imply that *Aleinu* was composed by Rav, early 3rd century C.E., Babylonia. I have discussed this in my *Esther Unmasked*, pp. 18 and 26-27. If we work with the assumption of Rav's authorship, we should point out that although Rav gained prominence in Babylonia, prior to that he had been a student of R. Judah Ha-Nasi in Palestine. Also, Christianity was not entirely absent from Babylonia at the time of Rav. For more on the authorship of *Aleinu* (and on voluminous other issues relating to our daily liturgy), see the monumental work: *The Rhetoric of Jewish Prayer: A Historical and Literary Commentary on the Prayer Book* (forthcoming 2019), by Reuven Kimelman.

The recital of *Aleinu* in England is almost certainly an outgrowth of its recital in France.[22] Its recital in Germany may simply be an outgrowth of its recital in neighboring France, or its recital may have developed independently in Germany for its own reasons. The earliest sources for *Aleinu* in daily *shacharit* in Germany are: (1) *Siddur Chasidei Ashkenaz*,[23] a work composed by the students of R. Judah he-Chasid (d.1217) that reflects his prayer service, and (2) the writings of R. Eleazar b. Judah of Worms (d. 1230). See his *Sefer Ha-Rokeach* and his *Peirushei Siddur Ha-Tefillah*.

So far we have addressed the recital of *Aleinu* at the end of daily *shacharit*. Soon thereafter, *Aleinu* began to migrate to the end of the daily *maariv*. The earliest source we have for this practice is the *Sefer Minhagot* of R. Moses ben R. Samuel, a work written sometime after 1204 and describing the customs of Marseilles, France. We also know that R. Meir of Rothenberg (d. 1293) had the practice of reciting *Aleinu* at *maariv*. See *Kol Bo*, sec. 11. Most likely, *Aleinu* began to be recited at *maariv* because it included the statement *hu Elokeinu, ein old* and this led it to be viewed as a prayer parallel to *Shema*.[24]

---

22. The evidence for its recital in England at the end of the 12th century is Ms. Oxford, Corpus Christi College 133 (discussed above). Based on the method of binding of the *siddur* manuscript, Beit-Arié concludes (p. 28) that it was probably produced in England. It was certainly used in England, as I explained in an earlier note.

23. Ed. M. Hirschler (1972). The *Siddur Chasidei Ashkenaz* (p. 124) records a reason for the recital of *Aleinu* daily, stating that it is due to the fact that it includes both אזכרת השם and יחוד השם. While the meaning of אזכרת השם here is unclear, the reference to יחוד השם almost certainly refers to *Aleinu's* inclusion of the phrases *ein od* and *efes zulato*. Of course, the recital of *Aleinu* in daily *shacharit* in Germany may simply have been an outgrowth of its recital in daily *shacharit* in France and the explanation found in *Siddur Chasidei Ashkenaz* may just be a later rationalization consistent with the philosophy of Chasidei Ashkenaz.

24. See, e.g., the statement of R. Chaim of Tudela (early 14th century) in his *Tzeror Ha-Chayyim*, cited in Ta-Shema, pp. 140-41.

An alternative scenario has also been suggested. After *Aleinu* began to appear at the end of *shacharit*, it came to be viewed as a closing prayer. It was then felt that *maariv* needed a closing prayer, and *Aleinu* was chosen. In this scenario, the view that *Shema* and *Aleinu* were parallel prayers only arose after *Aleinu* became a closing prayer at *maariv*.

Eventually, the recital of *Aleinu* began to spread to *minchah*. A responsum of the Radbaz (Egypt, 1479-1573) records that a questioner asked him whether it was appropriate to recite *Aleinu* at *minchah*. The questioner reported that some were not reciting it at *minchah*, since there is no recital of *Shema* at *minchah*. The Radbaz's answer: precisely because there was no recital of *Shema* at *minchah*, *Aleinu* needed to be recited there![25] Based on this rationale, *Aleinu* came to be accepted as a prayer to be recited at the end of all three services, and the once widely accepted connection between *Aleinu* and *Shema* has now been largely forgotten.

Up until now, I have been addressing *Aleinu's* recital at the end of the daily services in Europe. But what was going on in Palestine and its surrounding areas? One of the most interesting finds from the Cairo Genizah is a Palestinian *siddur* that includes *Aleinu* in the middle of the daily *Pesukei De-Zimra*.[26] (Genizah texts generally date from the 10th -13th centuries.) Almost certainly, *Aleinu* was introduced into their daily *Pesukei De-Zimra* because a prayer that begins with the theme of *shevach* (*Aleinu le-shabbe'ach*) was thought of as appropriate for *Pesukei De-Zimra*, a section whose purpose is one of *shevach* and that begins and ends with blessings which focus on the theme of *shevach*.

There is perhaps earlier evidence for the entry of *Aleinu* into the daily service in Palestine. *Pirkei De-Rabbi Eliezer* originally included a statement that *Aleinu* had to be recited while standing.[27] *Pirkei De-Rabbi Eliezer* is a work from eighth-century Palestine. There would have been no reason for an instruction that *Aleinu* in the midst of the silent *Amidah* on Rosh Hashanah would have to be recited standing. Moreover, the language of the passage does not seem to be giving an instruction to the congregation on what to do during the repetition.

---

25. This responsum of the Radbaz is quoted in Ta-Shema, p. 141, n. 5.

26. See J. Mann, "Genizah Fragments of the Palestinian Order of Service," *Hebrew Union College Annual* 2 (1925), pp. 269-338 (at p. 329).

27. The statement is not found in the surviving texts of *Pirkei De-Rabbi Eliezer*, but it is quoted in the name of *Pirkei De-Rabbi Eliezer* by several Rishonim (e.g., *Sefer Ha-Makhkim, Kol Bo* and *Orchot Chayyim*). The statement in *Pirkei De-Rabbi Eliezer* is the basis for the following statement that appears in the glosses of R. Moses Isserles, *Orach Chayyim* 132: *ve-omrim achar siyum ha-tefillah "Aleinu Le-Shabbe'ach" me'ummad.* The statement appears with a citation to the *Kol Bo.*

Therefore, it is reasonable to deduce that *Aleinu* was recited in some context outside of the Rosh Hashanah *Amidah* at the time of *Pirkei De-Rabbi Eliezer*. Therefore, it is possible that what we have in *Pirkei De-Rabbi Eliezer* is an earlier reference to the practice of including *Aleinu* in *Pesukei De-Zimra*.

As I have written elsewhere (*Ḥakirah*, vol. 11, seforim.blogspot.com Sept. 3, 2013 and *Esther Unmasked*, pp. 17-29), a very strong case can be made that the original version of *Aleinu* spelled *le-tacen olam* as לתכן עולם.[28] With this spelling, the meaning is "to **establish** the world under God's sovereignty." The traditional spelling, לתקן עולם, meaning "to **perfect/improve** the world under God's sovereignty," seems to be a later erroneous spelling that arose in Europe in the time of the Rishonim. Nevertheless, the end result is fitting. As *Aleinu* evolved from being a Rosh Hashanah prayer to a daily prayer, we no longer think about establishing the world under God's sovereignty but have shifted our focus to our daily task of perfecting and improving the world under God's sovereignty.

Throughout my discussion above, I have been assuming that *Aleinu* was originally composed as a Rosh Hashanah prayer (as an introduction to the *malkhuyyot* verses). Although I and many others take this approach, there are others who believe that *Aleinu* was originally composed in another context and then borrowed into the Rosh Hashanah *Amidah*. One such scholar is Meir Bar-Ilan. See his "*Mekorah Shel Tefillat 'Aleinu le-Shabbe'ach*,'" *Daat* 43 (1999), pp. 5-24. I discuss the different approaches to the origin of *Aleinu* in *Esther Unmasked*, pp. 24-25.

*

Mitchell First is a personal injury attorney and Jewish history scholar. He knows that it is much easier to change the text than to change the world.

5. An Insight into *Kri'at Shema Al Ha-Mitah*

This prayer begins with a statement that God places חבלי שנה on our eyes. But what exactly does this term mean?

---

28. The spelling לתכן is found in R. Saadiah Gaon, Rambam, and most manuscripts from the Cairo Genizah.

The root ח-ב-ל has four different meanings in Tanakh: (1) cord, (2) take a pledge, (3) cause damage and (4) the anxiousness and/or labor pains that the expectant mother feels approaching birth. Also, from the "cord" meaning, developed a meaning of "lot, portion," because cords were used to measure portions of land. See, for example, Deut. 32:9, Josh. 17:5 and Ps. 16:6.

Let us first see how two major *siddur* commentators have dealt with the term *chevlei sheinah*. Abudarham (14th century) first suggests that it means *chalakim me-chelkei ha-sheinah*. God gives out portions from the portions of sleep. Then he suggests that it has a meaning like *chevlei leidah*, and refers to the anxiety/pains that you have when you cannot sleep.

Isaac Baer (19th century), in his *Avodat Yisrael* (1868), first suggests that it means "cords." Accordingly, the image would be of cords tying your eyes closed while you sleep. He then suggests "portions." But he states that he does not like either of these interpretations. Moreover, he points out that both the "cords" and the "portions" interpretations would require a *patach* under the ח. Yet all the *siddurim* that he knew of had a *segol*. Based on the *segol* and his uncomfortableness with the other two interpretations, he concludes that we should understand it like *chevlei leidah*, i.e., the anxiety/pains that you have when you cannot sleep.

Let us put aside the question of what the original vocalization was under the ח. (*Berakhot* 60b, where the phrase first appears, has no vocalization, so the original vocalization cannot be determined.) "Portions" of sleep is a weird idiom. Why should sleep be meted out in portions? As to the "anxiety/pains" interpretation, it does not fit the context. God is being blessed for putting *chevlei sheinah* on our eyes and תנומה (another word for sleep) on our eyelids. It seems to be a positive thing that God is doing. Another problem with both of these interpretations is the use of the word *ha-mappil* (literally: he places down upon us, from the verb נ-פ-ל). The "portions" interpretation would fit better with "*ha-mechallek*." The "anxiety/pains" interpretation would fit better with *ha-meivi*, "brings." (See the *Iyun Tefillah* commentary in the *Siddur Otzar Ha-Tefillot*.)

What about the "cords" interpretation? It is still an unusual image. Also, cords seem a bit too big for eyes.

So where does that leave us? Fortunately, there is another alternative. In the *Siddur Rav Saadiah Gaon* (10th century), the word is spelled with a כ, not a ח. (Admittedly, our earliest manuscript of this work is only from the 12th or 13th century. But that is still relatively early.) There is also at least one *Kri'at Shema Al Ha-Mitah* fragment from the Cairo Genizah with this reading. See the reference in the *Siddur Rav Saadiah Gaon*, p. 87, to a fragment published in 1925.[29]

The word כבלי means "chains." But is this any better? The root כ-ב-ל appears only two times in Tanakh, at Ps. 105:18 and 149:8. (The latter, *be-khavlei barzel*, is part of a verse that we recite daily in *Pesukei De-Zimra*.) Both times it is referring to chains used to bind and restrict someone. It is not used in a positive way.

But let us focus on where *Kri'at Shema Al Ha-Mitah* describes the חבלי or כבלי as being placed. They are placed by God on the eyes. What is so special about the eyes in connection with sleeping? The eyes are the one part of the body that are noticeably different when one sleeps, compared to when one is awake. Thus the closing and opening of the eyes serves as an effective symbol for sleeping and awakening.

There is always a presumption that the more unusual reading is the correct one (in Latin, *Lectio difficilior potior*). כבלי is a rare word. We can understand how כבלי might have evolved into the more common חבלי. The reverse scenario is much less likely.

Thus, most likely, the word was originally spelled with a כ, and the image is of God placing a small chain on our eyes and this symbolizes sleeping. There may be a symbolism of security in the chain as well.

Also, the "cord" interpretation perhaps lacks a symbolism of security and may reflect more of an image of being trapped. Also, do "cords" really fit over the eyes? "Chains" seem to be a little better fit here. Cords are perhaps more for tying than for closing and covering.

Two sources that agree that the original text was likely with a כ are: the editors of the *Siddur Rav Saadiah Gaon* (note on p. 87), and Issachar Jacobson (*Netiv Binah* [8791-4691], vol. 3, p. 254).

Two works published by ArtScroll (*The Complete ArtScroll Siddur* and *Shema Yisrael*) include the following explanation: "The expression 'bonds of sleep' figuratively depicts the whole body as

---

29. Perhaps more fragments from the Cairo Genizah with this reading have come to light since then. I have not been able to check.

being securely chained in sleep." But this explanation does not fit the text because the text of the prayer describes the חבלי as being placed only on the eyes. Nevertheless, it is interesting that the comment uses the word "chained." It seems that the author of this comment intuited that "chains" made better sense than "cord." But the author does not mention the alternative כ spelling, so I do not think that he was aware of it.

It is also noteworthy that the Talmud instructs us to recite a blessing of *mattir asurim* daily. Thus the idea of us being "bound" in some way every night is found here as well. Although admittedly the image in the case of *Kri'at Shema Al Ha-Mitah* differs since the focus is only on the eyes.

Once we realize that the correct text is probably with a כ, it would seem, based on Ps. 149:8, that the word should be vocalized as *khavlei*, not *khevlei*.

One other issue needs to be discussed. In *Kri'at Shema Al-Ha-Mitah* we recite: *ha-mappil chevlei sheinah*. But when we refer to the removal of the sleep in the morning, at the end of *Birkot Ha-Shachar*, we recite only *ha-ma'avir sheinah*. Why should there be a difference? It is interesting to note that in the standard printed Talmud at *Berakhot* 60b, חבלי שנה is recorded for both the evening and the morning blessings. There are also Rishonim like Rambam who record חבלי שנה as being recited in both the evening and morning. (See, e.g., Rambam, *Hilkhot Tefillah* 7:4, and Abudarham. See further *Siddur Otzar Ha-Tefillot*, p. 126, *Tikkun Tefillah* commentary.)

I checked the Lieberman Institute. All the Talmud manuscripts of *Berakhot* 60b that they have recorded so far have חבלי in the text of the evening blessing only. I still do not understand why there should be a difference.

Finally, it is interesting to point out that the phrase *sheinah le-einekha u-tenumah le-afappekha* is found at Prov. 6:4. This was the source for the phrase that we have been discussing. It is ironic that our spelling issue only arose because the author of the *Kri'at Shema Al Ha-Mitah* blessing decided to deviate from the verse and add an extra word. When a prayer text is based on a verse alone, we would have a clear idea how each word is spelled!

*

Mitchell First is a personal injury attorney and Jewish history scholar. He sleeps a bit better now that he recites the word with the correct spelling and vocalization (כבלי: *khavlei*). But he is still not sure if he has the correct image and understanding.

6. The Origin of Our Prayer for the Government (*Ha-Noten Teshuah*)

Every Shabbat, after the *haftarah*, our custom is to recite a prayer for the government. The prayer begins *Ha-noten teshuah la-melakhim*, "He who gives salvation to kings…." Where did this prayer come from?

Before we address this, it is important to point out that there are many sources in Judaism for the idea of praying for the government. The most widely quoted source is Jer. 29:7, where Jeremiah instructs: "Seek the peace of the city where I caused you to be exiled and pray to the Lord for it…." Even before this, at Gen. 47:7, Jacob bestows a blessing on Pharaoh. There is also R. Chaninah's statement at *Avot* 3:2 that we must pray for the welfare of the government since otherwise men would swallow each other alive. (This statement was made when the hated Romans were ruling Palestine. So even a government by the hated Romans was viewed as preferable to a lack of government!)

Also, there is an interesting legend in Jewish tradition that the Jews told Alexander the Great that he should not listen to the Cutim and their request to destroy the Temple in Jerusalem. Our Temple, the Jews explained, was a place where the Jews prayed for Alexander's kingdom. See the *baraita* to *Megillat Taanit*, day of *Har Gerizim* (21 Kislev).

Going back to the *Ha-Noten Teshuah* prayer, the earliest manuscript that includes the prayer has the name "Selim" inserted in a later hand. It is a Sephardic *siddur* manuscript. The reference could be to Selim I or to Selim II. The first was the ruler of the Ottoman Empire between 1512-20. The second was its ruler between 1566-74. So we know at least that *Ha-Noten Teshuah* had already been composed in the 16th century, and was being recited in an area that was part of the Ottoman Empire.

Earlier than that, R. David Abudarham, writing in Spain in the early 14th century, mentions a custom of blessing the king in synagogue after the Torah reading. It would seem that he was referring to a custom on Mondays and Thursdays as well as on *Shabbat*. But he does not provide any official text of the blessing. Moreover, from his brief comments, it does not seem that he was alluding to *Ha-Noten Teshuah*. Also, around this same time, the *Orchot Chayyim* of R. Aaron Ha-Kohen briefly mentions a custom in Spain of blessing the king after the reading of the *haftarah*. (See also *Kol Bo*, section 20, a work perhaps by the same author.)

Could *Ha-Noten Teshuah* have been composed in Spain prior to the 1492 expulsion? Barry Schwartz thoroughly investigated the origin of the prayer in his "*Hanoten Teshua'* The Origin of the Traditional Jewish Prayer for the Government," *Hebrew Union College Annual* 57 (1986), pp. 113-120. Based on the evidence collected by Schwartz, it seems that a pre-expulsion origin for this prayer is unlikely. On the other hand, he is able to track the later spreading of the prayer. For example, by the mid-17th century, it is found in Italy. It is also cited in the mid-17th century by Rabbi Menashe ben Israel, leader of the Amsterdam Jewish community, as part of his effort to have the Jews readmitted into England. Rabbi Menashe cited the prayer because it supported his argument that the Jews would be loyal citizens.

Was there a prayer for the king in the Ashkenazic community in the time of the Rishonim? *Entziklopedia Le-Beit Yisrael* (ed. Rafael Halperin, vol. 8, p. 116 [1994]), entry *Ha-Noten Teshuah*, includes a statement that this prayer is mentioned in a document from Worms, Germany, from the year 1096. But we do not have documents from Worms from the year 1096, so I decided to investigate this mysterious claim. It turns out that there is a manuscript that describes the rituals of Worms and includes a very short prayer for the king, but the prayer is not *Ha-Noten Teshuah*. Aryeh Frumkin,[30] in his edition of *Seder Rav Amram Gaon* (1910-12), vol. 2, p. 78, wrote that this

---

30. Frumkin is an interesting figure. He was born in Lithuania in 1845 and later became one of the founders of Petach Tikvah. He lived there as a farmer-scholar for ten years in the early, difficult stages of the settlement, braving malaria and other dangers. Eventually he had to give up living there and moved to England, where he was able to view manuscripts in the library at Oxford. He eventually was able to return to Petach Tikvah.

manuscript was written at the time of the *gezerot* of 1096 and 1146. He came to this erroneous conclusion because the manuscript included some details from these times. But scholars today realize that the manuscript, Oxford 2205, was written several centuries later. Meanwhile, Frumkin's statement assigning the above very early time period to this manuscript has been followed by many sources, including the above encyclopedia. The above encyclopedia also erroneously assumed that the prayer in the manuscript was *Ha-Noten Teshuah*, but it clearly was not, as Frumkin quotes the language of the prayer. So all we learn from this manuscript is that Worms and perhaps other parts of Ashkenaz had their own short prayer for the king, but we do not know how early this prayer arose.

Going back to *Ha-Noten Teshuah*, some claim that it is actually a subversive prayer with a hidden anti-government meaning. The prayer begins with quotes from Ps. 144:10: "He who gives salvation unto kings," and "He who rescues his servant David from the hurtful sword." But the subsequent verse in Psalms, not included in *Ha-Noten Teshuah,* is: "Rescue me and deliver me out of the hands of strangers, whose mouth speak falsehood and their right hand is a hand of lying." Perhaps the citation to 144:10 is meant to allude to the subsequent verse! Similarly, the sentence in the prayer, "*ha-noten ba-yam derekh...*" is a quote from Isa. 43:16. But just prior to that, at 43:14, the prophet describes the downfall of Babylon. Babylon may be a metaphor for governments of the Jews in exile.

I am not convinced that the author of the prayer intended these subversive hidden allusions. The material in the nearby verses can easily be just coincidence.[31] Nevertheless, perhaps we should abandon this prayer entirely and compose a new one, so as to distance ourselves from these allegations of subversiveness.

For more insights into *Ha-Noten Teshuah*, see the January 2017 article by Professor Jonathan Sarna at the Lehrhaus site (thelehrhaus. com). Sarna quotes a famous line from "Fiddler on the Roof": "A blessing for the Tsar? Of course! May God bless and keep the Tsar... far away from us!"

---

31. An interesting scenario would be if the prayer was written under government compulsion. Then perhaps the author did intend an allusion to the nearby verses as a subtle form of protest!

Additional Notes

- For material from the Cairo Genizah relevant to our topic, see S.D. Gotein, "Prayers from the Geniza for the Fatamid Caliphs..." in *Studies in Judaica, Karaitica and Islamica* (1982), pp. 52-57. (The Fatamid Caliphs ruled Egypt and its surrounding areas from the 10th to 12th centuries.)
- For a completely different interpretation of Jeremiah 29:7, see Reuben Margaliot, *Ha-Mikra Ve-Ha-Mesorah* (1964), pp. 64-66.
- *The Complete ArtScroll Siddur* does not include the text of either *Ha-Noten Teshuah* or the prayer for the State of Israel. But there is a little box on the bottom of p. 450 with the following statement: "In many congregations, a prayer for the welfare of the State is recited by the Rabbi, *chazzan* or *gabbai* at this point."
- The texts of *Ha-Noten Teshuah* and the prayer for the State of Israel were added by ArtScroll to its special "Rabbinical Council of America Edition" *siddur*. But ArtScroll had to do some strange things to the page numbers of *Yekum Purkan* so that the added material would not change all the subsequent page numbers!

*

Mitchell First is a personal injury attorney and Jewish history scholar. When he prays for the government, he also has in mind government agencies, like the New Jersey Transit Authority and the Metropolitan Transit Authority, that enable him to get to work.

7. An Insight into the
Text of *Birkat Ha-Mazon*: הקדושה or הגדושה?

As we all know, the third blessing of our text of *Birkat Ha-Mazon*, in describing God's hand, uses the phrase: *ha-meleah, ha-petuchah, ha-kedoshah, ve-harchavah*. It has been argued that *ha-kedoshah* seems out of place here. All the other words describe God giving generously. God's hand is described as full, open and wide. But *ha-kedoshah* has a different implication, and it has therefore been suggested that the original reading here was *ha-gedushah*. A hand that is *gedushah* would mean a hand that provides a large, overheaping amount. (See Mishnah *Tamid* 5:4). This would fit better in the context of the three other adjectives. The existence of the reading *ha-gedushah* was mentioned by the *Arukh Ha-Shulchan* (*Orach Chayyim*, sec. 188-6). His son, R. Barukh Epstein, the author of the *Torah Temimah*, also discussed this issue and accepted the logic of this argument. See his *Barukh She-Amar*, pp. 211-12. (Note the clever title of this work; the author's first name was Barukh!) But is there actual evidence that *ha-gedushah* was the original reading in this line in *Birkat Ha-Mazon*?

Birkat Ha-Mazon is mentioned in the Mishnah and the Talmud, but there is no text of *Birkat Ha-Mazon* in either. Only the brief titles of the sections are mentioned at *Berakhot* 48b. Our earliest source for a text of *Birkat Ha-Mazon* is the *Siddur Rav Saadiah Gaon*. R. Saadiah died in 942. (The earliest manuscript that we have of this work is from about 200 years later, but it probably largely reflects the text as composed by R. Saadiah.) Here our line is absent from the text of the third blessing that is presented. The line is also absent from the text of the third blessing in the *Seder Rav Amram Gaon*. (Rav Amram died around 875 C.E. But the manuscripts we have of this work are from many centuries later.) A text of *Birkat Ha-Mazon* is also found in the Rambam's *Mishneh Torah* (late 12th century). Here too our line is absent from the text of the third blessing presented. The line is also absent from the text of the third blessing in *Machzor Vitry* (early 12th century). It is evident that our line was not a part of *Birkat Ha-Mazon* in its earliest stages. (Our line is also not found in the texts of *Birkat Ha-Mazon* from the Cairo Genizah.)

A scholar named Moshe Chalamish did much research into our line. See his *Chikrei Kabbalah U-Tefillah* (2012), pp. 317-335. He found that since this line was not a core line of *Birkat Ha-Mazon*, many variants arose. The number of adjectives used varied from two to six. Some of the other adjectives used to describe the hand of God were: *ha-tovah, ha-ashirah, ha-nora'ah,* and *ha-seviah.* Many of the texts did not use either *ha-kedoshah* or *ha-gedushah.*

The earliest text that had either *ha-kedoshah* or *ha-gedushah* was the *Or Zarua* of R. Isaac of Vienna of the 13th century. This text read *ha-kedoshah ha-meleah ve-ha-rechavah.* So *ha-kedoshah* seems to be an earlier reading than *ha-gedushah*, based on our available evidence.

There are two possibilities as to how the reading *ha-gedushah* arose. Either the word was suggested on its own in some communities. Or alternatively, readings like that of the *Or Zarua* (*ha-kedoshah* and two others) and our present day reading (*ha-kedoshah* and three others) arose in some communities. But once they arose with *ha-kedoshah* in the context of these other words, it was noticed by some that *ha-kedoshah* seemed out of place. So in a later stage, an alteration to *ha-gedushah* was made in some areas.

*

Mitchell First is a personal injury attorney and Jewish history scholar. He was sure that *ha-gedushah* was the original reading until he read the article by Moshe Chalamish and learned that this was probably not the case. He is getting older and wiser each day.

8. When Did *Mizmor Shir Chanukkat Ha-Bayit Le-David* Enter the Daily *Shacharit*?

We are all used to reciting this prayer (=Psalm 30) in the daily *shacharit* around the time of *Barukh She-amar*. But when did Psalm 30 enter the daily *shacharit*?

If one looks at the classic Geonic sources: *Siddur Rav Saadiah Gaon* and *Seder Rav Amram Gaon*, Psalm 30 is not found in their daily *shacharit*. Nor is it found in the daily *shacharit* of the classic Ashkenazic and Sephardic sources thereafter: *Machzor Vitry*, Rambam, *Tur*, and Abudarham.

Many years ago, I began to investigate this issue. It turns out that what is written in many of the standard *siddur* commentaries (e.g., A. Berliner, I. Jacobson, E. Munk, and *The Complete ArtScroll Siddur*) is wildly speculative and far from correct.

Eventually, I found some sources that did seem to do proper research and address the issue adequately. The best discussion was in a nineteenth-century work *Tzelota De-Avraham*. Based on this, I gave a lecture with the following explanation. The daily recital of Psalm 30 is mentioned by R. Chayyim Vital (1542-1620), the principal disciple of R. Isaac Luria. The discussion is found in R. Vital's work *Etz Ha-Chayyim*. R. Vital explains how Psalm 30 (without the first line, but starting with *aromimkhah*) fits into the kabbalistic view of *Pesukei De-Zimra* in his time. For example, both the first and third sentences of the body of Psalm 30 (*aromimkhah*, and *Hashem he'elita min Sheol nafshi*) deal with the theme of "raising up." Without going into detail, the theme of "raising up" was an important one to the R. Isaac Luria and to R. Vital in general, and was appropriate to this part of the service in particular.

So I thought I was done with the issue of how Psalm 30 entered the daily *shacharit*. I believed it was first introduced into the daily *shacharit* by R. Isaac Luria. I also found many *siddurim* that included a brief note stating that the daily recital of Psalm 30 was first introduced by R. Isaac Luria.

But it turns out that I was wrong. The second part of my story begins with a Rabbi Arie Folger, now chief Rabbi of Vienna, who walked into a *shacharit* minyan in Basel, Switzerland, and was surprised that Psalm 30 was not recited. This got him interested in the issue. He researched the issue thoroughly and posted about it on his blog (rabbifolger.net) on July 31, 2009. He found the recital of Psalm 30 in daily *shacharit* in a *siddur* printed at the end of the 15th century in Lisbon, Portugal. This pre-dated the birth of R. Isaac Luria.

I later discovered that the scholar Moshe Chalamish also found some early references to the daily recital of Psalm 30 in the Sephardic world. See his *Chikrei Kabbalah U-Tefillah* (2012), p. 73. The earliest reference he found was from the 13th century.

Rabbi Folger explained that when R. Vital was writing his comments on the daily recital of Psalm 30 in *shacharit*, he was merely commenting on a *siddur* from 1524 that followed the Sephardic tradition. He was not recording a custom of R. Isaac Luria of reciting it nor was he advocating that the followers of R. Isaac Luria add Psalm 30 to their daily liturgy. He was just explaining why Psalm 30, found in the daily *shacharit* in some Sephardic traditions, would fit with the kabbalistic ideas of R. Isaac Luria.

Eventually, based on the comments of R. Vital, Psalm 30 did make it into *nusach Ha-Ari* for daily *shacharit*, but it seems to have been a slow process. Rabbi Folger notes that the *Siddur Ha-Shelah* was published in 1717 and this mainstream kabbalistic *siddur* did not yet include the recital of Psalm 30 in *shacharit*. Of course, it is possible that some kabbalists were reciting it orally from the time of R. Vital. Also, perhaps it did make it into some kabbalistic *siddurim* in R. Vital's lifetime or shortly thereafter, but we do not have evidence for this yet. But its omission as late as 1717 in the *Siddur Ha-Shelah* is significant.

After Psalm 30 made its way into the daily *shacharit* in some Sephardic traditions and later made its way into *nusach Ha-Ari*, it thereafter made its way into some Ashkenazic liturgies. Its entrance into these Ashkenazic liturgies may merely be due to printers who saw it included in the other liturgies. At present, our first source for its appearance in daily *shacharit* in an Ashkenazic *siddur* is only in the year 1788.

It never made its way into all Ashkenazic liturgies. For example, the German Jewish community never adopted it. (It is not found in Isaac Baer, *Avodat Yisrael*.) Also, the Vilna Gaon was against its inclusion.

To sum up, for some unknown reason Psalm 30 began to make its way into some Sephardic liturgies in the 13th through 15th centuries. (Perhaps the reason was based on kabbalistic ideas but these would be pre-expulsion kabbalistic ideas, ideas that preceded R. Isaac Luria.) Based on R. Vital's comments, it eventually made its way into *nusach Ha-ARI*. Later it made its way, for reasons unknown, into some Ashkenazic liturgies.

It is significant that the earliest Sephardic and kabbalistic sources that record the daily recital of Psalm 30 do not include the title line: *mizmor shir chanukkat ha-bayit le-David*. Their recital started with *aromimkhah*. Many of the conjectures offered to explain the inclusion of Psalm 30 in the daily *shacharit* had focused on the title line, and postulated some explanation related to the *beit ha-mikdash*. But the omission of the title line shows that the reason for the original inclusion of Psalm 30 in the daily liturgy, when we eventually determine it, will relate instead to the body of the psalm.

(Note: I have only been discussing the recital of Psalm 30 daily. Its recital on Hanukkah has earlier sources. Finally, the recital of Psalm 30 in the daily *shacharit* is also recorded in the Yemenite tradition. The sources that I have seen have not discussed in detail how old this Yemenite tradition is. It may be as old as the Sephardic tradition or even older.)

There is an interesting issue with regard to the text of Psalm 30. In most editions of the Tanakh today, verse 9 reads: *eilekha YHVH ekra, ve-el ADNY etchannan*. The rest of this chapter has YHVH nine times. But when we look at some editions of the *siddur*, particularly ones following *nusach Ha-Ari*, they print YHVH in both parts of verse 9, making a total of ten YHVH in the chapter. R. Vital had said that the chapter included YHVH ten times. Presumably, in his time there was such a Tanakh text, even though it apparently was not the majority one. One can even find some texts of Tanakh today that have YHVH in both parts of verse 9. For example, this is what is printed in the standard one volume *Mikraot Gedolot* in which the *Neviim* and *Ketuvim* are printed together.

A separate issue involving Psalm 30 is the relation between the title line *mizmor shir chanukkat ha-bayit le-David* and the body of the psalm.

If the title line intends to refer to a psalm composed by David at the dedication of Solomon's Temple, David was not alive at the time of this dedication. More important, the body of the psalm refers mainly to God saving an individual from troubles. It seemingly has little to do with the dedication of any Temple. Admittedly, there is an initial *aromimkha Hashem* ("I will exalt You, God"). But thereafter the psalm includes phrases like: "You raised me up," "You did not let my enemies rejoice over me," "I cried to You and You healed me," "You brought up my soul from *Sheol*," "You hid Your face and I was frightened," "what profit is there in my blood when I go down to the pit," and "you turned my mourning into dancing."

Rashi takes the simple approach that David composed the psalm to be recited in the future when the Temple was dedicated by Solomon.

But some other commentators give very creative interpretations. Ibn Ezra mentions a view that it was composed by David and intended to be sung, not at the dedication of the First Temple, but at the dedication of the Second or Third Temples. The basis for this interpretation is that the psalm alludes to numerous troubles. The suggestion is that the troubles allude to the periods of exile before either the Second or the Third Temples. More recently, Ben Ish Chai (*Rav Pe'alim, Part 3, Orach Chayyim 5*) suggested that David foresaw the troubles that Antiochus would give the Jews and that David composed the psalm to be sung by the Hasmoneans at their dedication of the Temple.

Malbim is even more creative. He thinks that the *bayit* mentioned in the title is only a symbol for the body. The psalm has nothing to do with the dedication of any Temple or building. Rather it is a psalm dedicated to the recovery of David's soul, after an illness.

With regard to his own view, Ibn Ezra looks at the caption closely and observes that it does not refer to a *bayit* for God. Rather it refers to *ha-bayit le-David*. In fact, at 2 Sam. 5:11 and 7:1-2, the verses mention that a *bayit* was built for David. Moreover, verse 7:2 tells us that David being able to live in this luxurious *bayit* was what motivated him attempt to build a Temple for God ("I dwell in a house of cedar, but the ark of God dwells within curtains"). Ibn Ezra concludes that Psalm 30 was authored by David at the dedication of his personal house. He also suggests that David must have just recovered from an illness at that time. This would explain some of the language in the psalm.

Finally, Rav Hirsch takes the position that the body of this psalm is appropriate for the dedication of a Temple. The whole purpose of a Temple is to bring to mind to Man the nearness of God on earth, and the intimate relationship between God and Man. A psalm which talks about God's detailed involvement and aid to a particular man (in this case David) is therefore most appropriate for a Temple dedication. Rav Hirsch also believes that the phrase: *ha-bayit le-David* was appropriate for a psalm to be recited at the dedication of a Temple in the time of Solomon. Solomon's Temple can indeed be called David's Temple because Solomon was the executor of arrangements made by David. It was David who prepared and left Solomon the means and material for the work. See, e.g., 1 Chron. 22:2-5.

Moving to the end of Psalm 30, we have all recited the phrase *lemaan yezamerkha khavod* hundreds of times. But what does *khavod* mean here? Soncino translates awkwardly: "So that my glory may sing praise to Thee." Rav S.R. Hirsch adopts the difficult translation: "Therefore all that is glorious shall sing to Thee." The Targum surprisingly translates *khavod* as *yekirei alma*, "the honorable ones of the world."

Alternatively, many commentaries (Radak, *Metzudat Zion*, Malbim) point out that *khavod* is sometimes an idiom in Tanakh for "soul." See, e.g., the parallelism at Gen. 49:6: *be-sodam al tavo **nafshi**, bi-kihalam* *al teichad **kevodi**.* If so, the proper translation here would be "So that **my soul** might make music to you" (*The Complete ArtScroll Siddur*) or "That **my soul** might sing praise to you" (*The Living Nach*). The soul is called *khavod* because it is the most important part of a human being. As R. Barukh Epstein explains, "without [the *neshamah*], the body is mere dust." But surprisingly, the *Daat Mikra* commentary prefers a different interpretation of *lemaan yezamerkha khavod*: "so that I will sing **a song that gives you *khavod*.**" What motivates their interpretation is a verse in the previous chapter: *u-ve-heikhalo kullo omer kavod.* I leave it up to you whether to adopt the "soul" interpretation or the one offered by the *Daat Mikra*.

On a more mundane level, in Rabbinic and Modern Hebrew the root כ-ב-ד sometimes has the meaning "to sweep" the floor. Most likely, it developed this meaning because you treat a place honorably by sweeping it.

*

Mitchell First is a personal injury attorney and Jewish history scholar. He makes sure to recite Psalm 30 daily, despite the mysterious origin of the practice (or perhaps because of it!). Please do not tell his wife that he understands the importance of sweeping the floor.

II. Jewish History

1. The Longevity of the Ancients Recorded in Genesis

We all wonder about those long lifespans recorded at the beginning of Genesis. For example, we are told that Adam lived 930 years, that Shet lived 912 years, and that Metushelach lived 969 years. How have Jewish sources understood these numbers over the centuries?

The first Jewish source to address this issue was Josephus (late 1st century). Here is his statement in *Antiquities* (I.105-06):

> Nor let the reader, comparing the life of the ancients with our own and the brevity of its years, imagine that what is recorded of them is false.... For, in the first place, they were beloved of God and the creatures of God himself; their diet too was more conducive to longevity: it was then natural that they should live so long. Again, alike for their merits and to promote the utility of their discoveries in astronomy and geometry, God would accord them a longer life....

Now I will survey the views of our Geonim and Rishonim.

R. Saadiah Gaon (10th century) discusses this issue in his introduction to Psalms. He writes that the longevity of these early generations was part of God's plan for the rapid proliferation of mankind on the earth. The longer people lived, the more children they could have. It would seem that he believed that everyone in those early generations lived a long lifespan.

R. Yehudah Ha-Levi (12th century) discusses the issue in the *Kuzari* (sec. 95). He believes that it was only the individuals listed who lived long. Each of the individuals listed was the heart and essence of his generation and was physically and spiritually perfect. The Divine Flow was transmitted from one generation to another through these exceptional individuals.

Rambam, in a famous passage in the *Guide to the Perplexed* (2:47) writes: "I say that only the persons named lived so long, whilst other people enjoyed the ordinary length of life. The men named were exceptions, either in consequence of different causes, as e.g., their food or mode of living, or by way of miracle."

Ramban (on Gen. 5:4) quotes Rambam's view and then disagrees, calling Rambam's words *divrei ruach*. Ramban writes that the individuals with long lifespans named in the Bible were not exceptional in their lifespans. Rather, the entire world had long lifespans before the Flood. But after the Flood, the world atmosphere changed and this caused the gradual reduction in lifespans.

Most of the Rishonim who discussed the issue thereafter followed the approach of either the Rambam or the Ramban. Either way, they were taking the Genesis lifespan numbers literally. (An underlying factor that motivated Rishonim to accept the Genesis lifespan numbers literally is that the count from creation is calculated based on these numbers.)

Josephus had mentioned that one of the reasons that God allowed their longevity was to promote the utility of their discoveries in astronomy and geometry. This idea of longevity to enable the acquisition of knowledge and make discoveries (and write them to be passed down) is also included in several of our Rishonim. See, e.g., Radak to Gen. 5:4, Ralbag to Genesis 5 (p. 136), and Rashbatz (R. Shimon ben Tzemach Duran) to *Avot* 5:21.

Rashbatz also mentions the idea that the early generations were close in time to Adam and Adam was not born from a *tippah seruchah* like the rest of us, but was made by God from the earth. Those early generations inherited his superior bodily constitution.

Another idea found in some of our Rishonim is that those early individuals did not chase after *taavat ha-guf*, which reduces the lifespan. See, e.g., the commentary of the Radak to Gen. 5:4.

But there were some Rishonim who were unwilling to take the Genesis lifespan numbers literally.

The earliest such source that we know of was R. Moses Ibn Tibbon (late 13th century). He suggests that the years given for people's lives were actually the years of *malkhutam ve-nimmuseihem*, i.e., the dynasties and/or customs that they established.

Another figure who took such an approach was R. Levi ben Chayyim (early 14th century). First he mentions several of the possibilities to explain the longevity, e.g., good and simple food and "marrying late" (!). But then he concludes that in his opinion the names mentioned were just *roshei avot*. In other words, the number of years given for each individual reflects the total of the years of the several generations of individuals named for that first individual.

R. Nissim of Marseilles (early 14th century) was another who did not take the numbers literally. He took the same approach as R. Moses Ibn Tibbon. The numbers did not indicate the lifespan of the specific individuals named. Rather, it included the total years of the descendants who followed his customs and lifestyle.

The most interesting approach I saw was that of R. Eleazar Ashkenazi ben Nathan ha-Bavli (14th century),[32] in his work *Tzafnat Paneach*, pp. 29-30. First, R. Eleazar refers to the view that perhaps the individual numbers were not to be taken literally, and points to other statements in the Torah that were not meant to be taken literally, e.g., (1) the Land of Israel was "flowing with milk and honey," and (2) the cities in Canaan were "fortified up to the Heaven" (Deut. 1:28). (See further *Guide to the Perplexed* 2:47.)

But then R. Eleazar suggests the following creative approach. In listing these individual numbers, the Torah was merely recording the legends about these figures, even though they were not accurate. The important thing was to provide data from which the total years from Creation to the giving of the Torah could be derived, so that the people would be able to know the length of time between these two periods. Even though the numbers for the individual lifespans were not accurate, the Torah made sure that the total that would be arrived at would be accurate. (In contrast, when it came to events from Abraham and forward, the Torah was careful to preserve a more accurate accounting.)

In modern times, many Orthodox writers have written on this topic. One is R. Aryeh Kaplan. See his *Immortality, Resurrection and the Age of the Universe: A Kabbalistic View* (1993). Another is Prof. Natan Aviezer of Bar-Ilan University. He has written much on this topic. For example, in one of his writings he explains that modern science has figured out that aging is largely caused by genes, and not by a wearing out of our bodies. He suggests that when God stated that Man would be limited to 120 years (Gen. 6:3), this was when God first introduced the gene for aging into the human gene pool.

---

32. For information on this figure, see the article by E. Lawee in *Asufah Le-Yosef*, Y. ben-Naeh et al, eds. (2013), pp. 170-86.

If you have not found any of the above answers satisfying, I have some good news. R. Saadiah Gaon writes (*Emunot Ve-Deot*, chapter 7) that in the era of the redemption the human lifespan will be approximately 500 years. Presumably, at that time we won't be bothered by those long lifespans in Genesis anymore!

(Note that Radak, commentary to Isa. 65:20, is a bit stingier. He predicts lifespans of only 300 to 500 years. See also his commentary to Ps. 92:15. But the twelfth-century Babylonian Gaon R. Samuel ben Ali predicts lifespans closer to 1000 years!)

I would like to acknowledge that most of the material above came from an article by Prof. Daniel Lasker of Ben-Gurion University, "*Arikhut Ha-Yamim Shel Ha-Kadmonim*," in *Diné Yisrael*, vol. 26-27 (2009-10), pp. 49-65.

*

Mitchell First is a personal injury attorney and Jewish history scholar. He aspires to longevity and hopes his children can tolerate him for that long.

2. Did Moses Have a Speech Impediment?

We have all heard the idea that Moses had a speech impediment, since he tells God that he is *khevad peh* and *khevad lashon* (Ex. 4:10). But what exactly do these terms mean?

To explain the first of the above expressions, Rashi uses a word from the French of his time. The word is usually translated as "stutter" or "stammer." (Rashi does not make any comment on the second expression.) But where did Rashi get his explanation from? No such view is expressed by the Tannaim or Amoraim.

James Kugel, *The Bible As It Was* (1997), p. 297, points out that there was a Hellenistic Jewish writer from the 2nd century B.C.E., Ezekiel the Tragedian, who wrote that Moses stammered. So Rashi was not the first to give the stammer interpretation.

It is possible that Rashi's source was a story that eventually made its way into *Exodus Rabbah* 1:26. There a story is recorded about a test put to the infant Moses and that Moses' mouth and tongue ended up being burned by a piece of coal and that this is what made him *khevad peh* and *khevad lashon.* But I have seen it suggested that burning to a mouth and tongue would more likely cause lisping than stuttering/stammering. More importantly, Rashi does not cite any such a story in his comments to Ex. 4:10.

Most likely, Rashi was just interpreting *khevad peh* and *khevad lashon* and offering a reasonable interpretation without any connection to the coal story.[33]

How have other commentators understood *khevad peh* and *khevad lashon*? Rashbam thought that the eighty-year old Moses was telling God that he was not familiar with the Egyptian language anymore, having left there when he was young. Ibn Ezra, in his early commentary on the verse (his shorter commentary) agreed with Rashbam. But years later, when he wrote his longer commentary on the verse, he suggested that Moses was telling God that he had difficulty with certain letters. He then suggests that God's response at 4:11-12 implied that God agreed to provide him with words without the difficult letters! A similar idea was suggested earlier by R. Chananel (quoted in R. Bachya). R. Chananel had written that Moses had difficulty with the letters that were difficult for the teeth: *zayin, shin, resh, samekh,* and *tzade,* and with the letters that were difficult for the tongue: *dalet, tet, lamed, nun,* and *tav.*

Others have focused more on Moses' oratorical and persuasive abilities. For example, S.D. Luzzatto suggested that Moses was arguing that he was not a "powerful orator who could speak at length before any audience and not cringe before anyone."[34] Luzzatto explained that this is alluded to at Num. 12:3, which refers to Moses as the most modest man on the earth. Luzzatto explained further that having spent so many years as a shepherd it was difficult for Moses to go

---

33. Strangely, Rashi only makes his comments on *khevad peh.* Perhaps he interpreted both *khevad peh* and *khevad lashon* the same way. This is supported by a comment that he makes on Isa. 6:8. I would like to thank Rabbi Ezra Frazer for the reference.

    For the alternative view, see, e.g., S. P. Gelbard, *Le-Peshuto Shel Rashi, Shemot* (1990, 2nd edition), p. 41. Gelbard writes that *khevad lashon* did not require an explanation since it can be taken literally. A "heavy tongue" implied that Moses could only speak slowly. A mouth, however, is essentially merely an opening and cannot be "heavy." This phrase required explanation.

34. Translation from D. Klein edition (2015).

before a great king and argue with him. Similarly, Umberto Cassuto explained: "the meaning is only that he did not feel within himself the distinguished talents of an orator, and in his humility, he expressed the thought with some exaggeration."[35]

Finally, to give one more example, the *Daat Mikra* commentary suggested that *khevad peh* meant that Moses "spoke slowly," and *khevad lashon* meant that his "voice was not pleasant."

We can evaluate the various suggestions by looking at God's response. At verse 12, God says: *ve-anokhi ehiyeh im pikha, ve-horeitikha asher tedabber.* The key phrase in verse 12 is the second one: "I will instruct you what to say." This phrase fits Rashbam's approach and the Luzzatto-Cassuto oratorical approach better than it fits the other approaches. But the Rashbam's approach is problematic because it does not fit well with Moses' statement. Moses refers only to a general problem of *khevad peh* and *khevad lashon.* He does not say anything about inability to speak Egyptian. Based on this analysis, it would seem that the Luzzatto-Cassuto oratorical approach has the most merit.

But after I wrote all the above, I came across a detailed article on our topic by the scholar Jeffrey Tigay.[36] He defends the "speech impediment" approach. He points to Gen. 48:10 which describes Jacob's eyes and records: *kabdu mi-zoken, lo yukhal lirot.* This suggests that כבד reflects a medical difficulty.[37] He then looks at evidence from Akkadian and Arabic. He observes that "heaviness," with respect to a body part, is a medical difficulty in these languages. His evidence from Akkadian is particularly persuasive since it is from *kabātu,* a cognate of the Hebrew כבד.[38] (He admits that the evidence from

35. Translation from I. Abrahams edition (1967).

36. J.H. Tigay, " 'Heavy of Mouth' and 'Heavy of Tongue' On Moses' Speech Difficulty," *Bulletin of the American Schools of Oriental Research* 231 (1978), pp. 57-67.

37. Tigay also discusses Ez. 3:5-6, where the phrase וכבדי לשון appears twice. Tigay suggests that here the term "has been extended from a medical affliction which causes unintelligible speech to a metaphor for speech which is unintelligible because of its foreignness."

38. H. Tawil, p. 154, also takes the view, based on Akkadian, that *khevad peh* and *khevad lashon* are idioms for a speech impediment. Tigay tried to find evidence from Sumerian as well, but here he was less successful.

these languages is not sufficient to pinpoint precisely what medical difficulty was involved.)

Most importantly, Tigay advises us to focus on Moses' entire statement at 4:10: *lo ish devarim anokhi gam mitmol gam mishilshom... ki khevad peh u-khevad lashon anokhi*. *Lo ish devarim* seems to be the complaint of lack of eloquence or ability to persuade and the like, and *ki khevad peh u-khevad lashon* seem to be adding something more specific. A speech impediment fits perfectly here. Tigay makes the reasonable assumption that כי means "because" in the above statement.

So while God's response at verse 12 supports the Luzzatto-Cassuto oratorical approach, Moses' entire statement at verse 10 supports the speech impediment approach.

But there is a response for the Luzzatto-Cassuto approach. It can interpret כי in verse 10 so that it means something like "rather."[39] Nevertheless, looked at overall, Tigay's arguments are strong ones and perhaps his approach, essentially the approach of Rashi, wins the day. It wins the day, despite the fact that it does not fit as well with God's response at 4:12.[40]

We still have a little more to discuss. At Ex. 6:12 and 6:30, Moses describes himself as *aral sefatayim*. We now have to ask whether this is a different flaw, or merely another way of referring to the flaw of Ex. 4:10. Rashi on Exodus 6:12 explains that it means that Moses' lips were blocked. Although he does not refer to his comments on Ex.

---

39. This is how the *Daat Mikra* commentary interprets כי here. It interprets it as אלא.

40. Tigay writes that is a false premise that if Moses' speech was impeded, he must request cure and God must grant it. It may have suited God's purpose, for a variety of reasons, not to cure Moses.

Tigay concludes his article as follows:

> History has known other creative geniuses and national leaders, from Demosthenes to Felix Mendelssohn and Churchill, who worked their effect on humanity despite speech impediments. The Bible viewed Moses as an agent of God whose success owed nothing to his natural endowments, but only to the persuasion worked by the words and deeds he uttered and performed under divine direction.

4:10, the simplest approach is to view Rashi as understanding *aral sefatayim* as another way of describing the stuttering/stammering problem of Exodus 4:10. Rashbam does not comment at all on 6:12. Perhaps he would view *aral sefatayim* as another idiom for inability to speak Egyptian. Ibn Ezra (shorter commentary) writes that this is just another way of referring to the articulation defect he described earlier. Luzzatto and Tigay also believe that *aral sefatayim* is just another idiomatic way of referring to the flaw described earlier, even though they disagree as to what the earlier flaw was.[41]

On the other hand, some commentators believe that what we have here is a description of a new flaw. For example, Cassuto believes that *aral sefatayim* reflects Moses' doubting his oratorical capacities in a new and more drastic form. *Daat Mikra* believes that the idiom here is that Moses' lips were closed, and the meaning is that he could not speak words that penetrated to others. Finally, R. Aryeh Kaplan translates Ex. 4:10 as: "I find it difficult to speak and find the right language." At 6:12, he translates: "I have no self-confidence when I speak."

But since most commentators are reluctant to attribute to Moses a new flaw, we can conclude that whether or not Moses had a speech impediment depends on how one interprets the flaw (or flaws) of verse 4:10.

Going back to the story about the infant Moses' mouth and tongue being burned by coal, this story eventually made its way into *Exodus Rabbah*. But this is a late midrashic compilation that was not yet available to Rashi. (*Exodus Rabbah* is cited in the 13th century by Ramban.) Can we tell if the coal story existed in the time of Rashi (d. 1105)? It turns out that a version of the story is found in the work known as *Chronicles of Moses*. This work was compiled around the 10th or 11th century. (But this work is not a part of traditional rabbinic literature.) Interestingly, James Kugel, *The Bible As It Was*, p. 297, note 6, makes a clever argument that the coal story may have already existed at the time of Josephus in the first century!

---

41. Also, with regard to Targum Onkelos, at 4:10 the translation is *yakir mamlal ve-amik lishan*, and at 6:12, it again uses *yakir mamlal*. *Yakir mamlal* means "heavy speech." Regarding, *ve-amik lishan*, this is translated as "indistinct articulation" in *Onkelos on the Torah*, I. Drazin and S. Wagner (2011).

*

Daniel Klein, in his *Shadal on Exodus* (2015), p. 74, n. 33, points out that King George VI ("Bertie," 1895-1952) had a speech therapist named Lionel Logue. To circumvent the King's stuttering problem, the therapist would study the text of the royal addresses, "spotting any words that might trip the King up, such as those that began with a hard 'k' or 'g' sound or perhaps with repeated consonants, and wherever possible, replace them with something else." This was very beneficial as the King had a debilitating stammer and pathological nervousness in front of a crowd or microphone. A book was published on this topic by Logue's grandson Mark Logue in 2010 (after the discovery of Lionel's diaries): *The King's Speech: How One Man Saved the British Monarchy.*

Klein also writes here that Luzzatto "is no doubt correct in suggesting that a search of all of Moses' recorded public statements would fail to reveal the consistent omission of any particular phonemes." (Luzzatto had made such a statement in response to Ibn Ezra's interpretation.)

One of the most important *divrei Torah* ever was given in 1882 by R. Shmuel Mohilever to Baron Edmond de Rothschild to persuade him to fund one of the early Jewish settlements in Palestine. What did R. Shmuel Mohilever say to help win the Baron over to this project (at Ekron)?

R. Mohilever posed this question. Why did God choose someone with a speech defect to lead the Jewish people? R. Mohilever wrote that only now, on his trip to the Baron, did he realize the answer. Moses was chosen not only to speak to Pharaoh but also to bring the Jews to Mount Sinai to receive the Torah. If Moses was eloquent and knew how to persuade people, the cynics would later claim that the Torah was not from God but rather from Moses who knew how to mesmerize the Jewish people into believing. Then R. Mohilever continued: Many powerful people come before you with their proposals, and with their eloquence they try to impress you and obtain your financial backing. I also come with a proposal, but I am a man of heavy tongue and have great difficulty communicating to you the great reward this proposal has for you and for our people. But therefore, if you accept this proposal and heed the request of your people to revive this desolate land, you will know that it is only because the lot of this ailing and oppressed people has touched your heart.

R. Mohilever writes that these words were able to break down the coldness of the Baron and persuade him to provide financial assistance for the project. It has traditionally been believed that this *devar Torah* changed the course of Jewish history, as Rothschild subsequently provided significant financial support for this settlement and for many of the other early Jewish settlements in Palestine. Ekron was later renamed "Mazkeret Batya," after the mother of the Baron.

The fascinating story of the settlement of Ekron, which started with ten fervently Orthodox farmers (with beards and *payot!*) from the town of Pavlovka, Russia, is told in *Rebels in the Holy Land*, by Sam Finkel (2012). Most significantly, in the revised edition (2015), p. 15, Finkel cites recently discovered evidence that Rothschild had been planning to help fund Jewish settlement in Palestine even *before* the meeting with R. Mohilever! Therefore, the meeting with R. Mohilever was not the precipitating factor that motivated Rothschild's new plan of assisting Jewish settlement in Palestine. Rather, now it seems that R. Mohilever was merely "the right man in the right place at the right time."

*

Mitchell First is a personal injury attorney and Jewish history scholar. He does not recall the Hollywood producers giving Charlton Heston any difficulties in articulation.

3. Fifty-Three Biblical Personalities Confirmed by Archaeology

One of the last kings of Judah was Yehoyachin. We know from the books of Jeremiah and Kings that he was exiled by Nevuchadnezzar eleven years before the destruction of the Temple. The exile of Yehoyachin is also mentioned in the book of Esther. (There the king's name is given in an alternate form: Yechaniah.) According to 2 Kings 24 (and the parallel in the book of Jeremiah), Yehoyachin and his servants, princes and officers (and his mother!) surrendered to Nevuchadnezzar, and Nevuchadnezzar exiled all the important people from Jerusalem at this time.

But what happened to Yehoyachin after that? We are provided with some additional information from Tanakh, thirty-seven years later. 2 Kings ends on the following positive note: "In the 37th year of the exile of Yehoyachin... Evil-Merodach king of Bavel, in the year that he began his reign, lifted up the head of Yehoyachin king of Judah out of prison. He spoke kindly to him and set his throne above the throne of the kings that were with him in Bavel. He changed his prison garments and he ate bread before him continually.... [T]here was a continual allowance given him of the king, every day a portion, all the days of his life." So for some unknown reason Evil-Merodach, the son of Nevuchadnezzar, changed the Babylonian policy towards Yehoyachin and took him out of prison (which may have meant mere house arrest) and allowed him to eat at Evil-Merodach's table for the rest of Yehoyachin's life.

From Tanakh, we did not know anything about Yehoyachin during his thirty-six years of captivity by Nevuchadnezzar. And the skeptical among us could ask: How do we even know that there was such a king as Yehoyachin?

Fortunately, archaeology came to the rescue. In the years 1899-1917, excavations were carried out in the ancient city of Babylon. In a room connected to the palace, records were found from the time of Nevuchadnezzar dealing with deliveries of oil and barley to prisoners and other foreigners. Among the records found was the following text: "To Ya'u-kinu, king of the land of Yaudu: ½ PI for Ya'u kinu, king of the land of Yahu-du, 2½ sila for the five sons of the king of the land of Yahudu...." (The "sila" was a little under 1½ pints, and the "PI" was about 6½ gallons. The reference is probably to the monthly rations of oil.) These texts all range from the tenth to the thirty-fifth year of Nevuchadnezzar. Yehoyachin is mentioned in this text and in three other texts.

So we now have mention of Yehoyachin in an archaeological source, and even some data on how he was fed while in captivity by Nevuchadnezzar!

This leads to the general question of which of the ancient kings of Israel, whether of Northern Israel or of Judah, are mentioned in archaeological sources. Fortunately, archaeology has much to contribute here. The following are the kings of Northern Israel that are mentioned in archaeological sources: Omri, Ahab, Jehu,

Joash/Jehoash, Jeroboam II, Menachem, Pekach, and Hoshea. The following are the kings of Judah that are mentioned in archaeological sources. Uzziah/Azariah, Ahaz/Yehoachaz, Hezekiah, Menasheh, and Yehoyachin. There are also references in two different inscriptions to *beit David*, implicitly referring to King David.

What about Israelite/Jewish figures mentioned in the Bible who were not kings? Which of these are mentioned in archaeological sources? We do have mention of some such figures. Examples are Hilkiah and Azariah, both of whom were high priests during the reign of Josiah.

What about foreign kings or other important foreign figures mentioned in the Bible? There is confirmation in archaeology of many of the Egyptian, Moabite, Aramean, Assyrian, Babylonian and Persian kings. This deserves an article of its own. I will merely state here that the earliest foreign biblical king confirmed in archaeology is Shishak (1 Kings 11 and 14), who reigned in Egypt from 945-924 B.C.E. In Egyptian sources his name is "Sheshonq" or "Shoshenq."

The scholar Lawrence Mykytiuk of Purdue University has dedicated many years to identifying all biblical figures mentioned in archaeology. In March-April 2014, he published an article in *Biblical Archaeology Review*: "Archaeology Confirms 50 Real People in the Bible." You can access his list and evidence at www.biblicalarchaeology.org/50. His list is continually updated. The last time I went to this site, 53 biblical figures were listed!

Providing a list of biblical figures mentioned in archaeology is not an exact science. Some archaeological inscriptions may be forgeries. Other times, the archaeological source refers to someone with the same name as a biblical figure but the match may merely be a coincidence. Mykytiuk tried to be conservative with his list. He excluded inscriptions that were probably forgeries and included only identifications that he believed to be firm. He made a separate list of seven other identifications that are possible and reasonable, but not firm yet. For example, there is a seal from ancient Lachish that reads "Belonging to Gedalyahu, the overseer of the palace." This may belong to the well-known Gedalyah ben Achikam mentioned in Tanakh who was appointed governor by the Babylonians and later assassinated. "Overseer of the palace" may have been his prior position. But since scholars are not certain of the identification with

Gedalyah ben Achikam, Mykytiuk omitted Gedalyah ben Achikam from his main list and included him only in his separate list.

The most interesting material on his short list is an inscription that refers several times to a figure named "Bilam" son of "Beor." This inscription was found at Deir Alla in Jordan, a site slightly east of the Jordan River, in the general area where the biblical Bilam ben Beor would have lived. It dates to around 700 B.C.E. But since the biblical Bilam ben Beor would have lived several hundred years earlier than this, it is only conjectural to identify the reference with the biblical figure.

Mykytiuk did not include very conjectural identifications. A famous one not that he did not include is the possible identification of "Amrafel," king of Shinar (see Genesis 14), with "Hammurabi." (His name may even have been pronounced "Hammurapi.") The names "Amrafel" and "Hammurabi/Hammurapi" are very close (M-R-F vs. M-R-B/M-R-P). Hammurabi lived in the 18th century B.C.E. The precise century of Amrafel (who lived at the time of Abraham) is still hard to pinpoint. (The fact that we can calculate from the lifespans specified in Genesis that Abraham was born in the year 1948 does not help. It is too hard to go into this complex topic here. As a first step, you should read my book *Jewish History in Conflict* [1997].)

None of the names on Mykytiuk's firm list of 53 are earlier than the 10th century B.C.E (and none are women). I am hoping that one day we can dig up some earlier figures. For example, I am hoping we can find a reference to Kushan-Rishatayim, king of Aram Naharayim (Judges, chapter 3). Scholars have suggested that the Tanakh did not record his name properly but adjusted it so it would have the meaning "doubly wicked."[42] I am waiting for his real name to be discovered to see if this suggestion is true!

Finally, Mykytiuk limited himself to confirmations based on archaeology. He did not include confirmations based on literary sources. The earliest and primary example of a literary source that can confirm biblical figures is the *Histories* of Herotodus (middle of the 5th century B.C.E.) Herodotus writes much about the biblical kings Cyrus, Darius, and Xerxes (=Achashverosh). He also mentions the next king, Artaxerxes (=Artachshasta.) Moreover, in several passages, Herodotus refers to Amestris, the wife of Xerxes. The suffix

---

42. I would like to thank Rachel Friedman for mentioning this idea to me.

"-is" at the end of this name is almost certainly a Greek addition. Therefore, we can deduce that her Persian name would have been based around the consonants M, S, T, and R. As I have argued in my *Esther Unmasked*, this is very likely a reference to Esther. I also discussed there that a later historian, Ctesias (c. 400 B.C.E.), perhaps refers to Mordechai.

*

Mitchell First is a personal injury attorney and Jewish history scholar. By the time you are reading this article, I am sure that the number of confirmed biblical figures will be higher than 53!

P.S.: A few weeks after I wrote the above sentence, it was announced that an ancient seal impression belonging to someone named ישעיה was discovered in 2009 in the Ophel excavations in Jerusalem. (The name may be ישעיהו. There is enough space for there to have been a *vav* at the end originally. The seal was damaged on its left side.) The seal impression includes the letters נבי on the next line. It may (or may not!) have belonged to the biblical prophet Isaiah. For details, see the March-June 2018 issue of *Biblical Archaeology Review*.

4. Nevuchad<u>n</u>ezzar or Nevuchad<u>r</u>ezzar?

During the reading of the *haftarot* of *Parashat Va'era* and *Parashat Bo*, we are all jarred when this king's name is read with that middle *resh*. What is going on here?

Let us look at the name as it appears in the various biblical books. In 2 Kings, 1 and 2 Chronicles, Esther, Daniel, Ezra, and Nechemiah, the name always has the middle *nun*. In Ezekiel, all four references to the king have the middle *resh*. Jeremiah has both versions of the name, but there is consistency within each chapter. Chapters 27, 28, and 29 have the name with a middle *nun*, while the balance of the chapters have the name with a middle *resh*.

What are we to make of all of this?

It turns out that in Babylonian sources, his name always has the middle "r" sound. His true name was "Nabu-kudurri-uṣur." The meaning is: "Nabu, protect my son." (Nabu was one of their gods and was the son of Marduk.) The book of Ezekiel, with its setting in Babylonia, did a good job of recording the name.

So why does the Tanakh have the name with a middle *nun* in many places? No one knows, but I will make a few observations.

1. When names transfer from one language to another, the result is almost never an exact match. Aside from the fact that the letters and sounds often differ from language to language, people are used to the word structures and patterns in their own language. Moreover, they typically do not understand the meaning of the name in the other language. Different ways of recording the name is the norm, not the exception.

2. In this particular case, it is possible that the initial *nun* led to the *resh* being transformed into a *nun*. There is a linguistic term for this: sound assimilation at a distance.

3. There is a relationship between the sounds for L, M, N, and R in many languages, and there are many examples of interchange of these letters. For example, another *nun/resh* switch in Tanakh is found in the case of Achan. Even though the Tanakh usually spells his name *ayin-caf-nun*, there is one place, 1 Chron. 2:7, where his name is spelled *ayin-caf-resh*. (See the commentary of the Malbim there.)

4. Some scholars believe that the name "Nevuchadnezzar" was intended as an insult. While the original Babylonian name (with the "r" sound) meant "Nabu, protect my son," the version with the "n" sound would mean "Nabu, protect my jackass."[43] Perhaps the version with the "n" sound originated in Babylonia by enemies of the king, or by an Israelite who knew the language of the Babylonians.[44]

---

43. See H. Tawil, p. 461.
44. On a homiletical level, I would like to add that the arisal of the variant with the middle *nun* enabled the following story, 2500 years later. In the years just prior to World War I, the imperial Russian government was trying to suppress all revolutionary activity. At that time, a book with the title "Nebuchadnezzar" was published. The government noticed that when you pronounced the title of the book, it sounded like you were saying "No God and no Czar!" ("*N'ye Bog a n'ye Tsar!*") The government banned the book! See C. Berlitz, *Native Tongues* (2005 edition), p. 255. I would like to thank Dr. Zal Suldan for this reference.

Something similar in Tanakh may have occurred in the case of "Kushan Rishatayim," king of Aram (Judges 3). Is the Tanakh recording his name accurately? Perhaps the name was tweaked so that it would have the meaning "doubly wicked."

A remaining issue is why the book of Jeremiah records both versions of the name. The most likely explanation is that chapters 27 through 29 reached the compiler of the book from a different source.[45] Chapters 27 through 29 have other variant spellings as well. For example, in these chapters "Yirmiyahu" is sometimes spelled without the last *vav*. None of the other chapters have this variant spelling.

The topic of Nevuchadnezzar leads me to one of my favorite Hebrew roots: ג-ל-ה. This root has two different meanings: "uncover/reveal" and "go away/emigrate." An issue is whether these two ג-ל-ה meanings have a common origin.

Most scholars believe that the two roots are related. See, e.g., the entry for this root in *Theological Dictionary of the Old Testament*, vol. 2. But exactly what the relation is and which meaning came first is still subject to debate. Phoenician has a root G-L-H which means "uncover." This suggests that the "uncover" meaning came first. But Ugaritic has a root G-L-Y which is a verb of motion. This suggests that the "go away/emigrate" meaning came first. (There is still a dispute as to the precise meaning of the root G-L-Y in Ugaritic. It may mean "leave" or it may mean "arrive/enter." But it does not mean "uncover/reveal.")

If the "uncover/reveal" meaning came first, then "emigration" can be understood as an uncovering of the land. If the "go away/emigrate" meaning came first, then the connection is that when people "go away/emigrate," the land becomes "uncovered/ revealed."

There is another way to look at the relationship between the two ג-ל-ה meanings, focusing on the people and not the land. Did you ever pick up a rock and discover ants underneath? The instant they are revealed, they are on the move! By analogy, when enemies come and are ג-ל-ה another people, they are first "uncovering them" by forcing them out of their homes and hiding places. This causes the victims to

---

45. See *Encyclopaedia Judaica* 9:1355 and S.R. Driver, *An Introduction to the Literature of the Old Testament* (1956), p. 272.

be on the move. This approach is mentioned by Solomon Mandelkern in his concordance.

I will close with one of my favorite instances of name transformations. For reasons I have elaborated on in *Esther Unmasked* (2015), the Greeks referred to Achashverosh as "Xerxes." Xerxes' son had a Persian name that sounded like Artachshathra, which is recorded in Tanakh as ארתחשסתא (or ארתחששתא). But how did the Greeks refer to him? They called him "Artaxerxes." They recorded the first part of his name correctly, "Arta," but then oversimplified the second part of the name into "xerxes." To the Greeks, since he was the son of Xerxes, that is how they heard and recorded the latter part of his name!

*

Mitchell First is a personal injury attorney and Jewish history scholar. His name is often misspelled by others as Furst. This is not that intriguing and would not warrant an article.

5. Archaeology Sheds Light on King Darius

I spent many years studying the period from 539-332 BC.E. This is the period when the Jews were subject to the rule of the kings of ancient Persia. I focused on this period because here there is much material outside of Tanakh that can shed light on the figures in Tanakh. In this article, I am going to discuss one of the ancient Persian kings: Darius I. He reigned from 522-486 B.C.E. I will summarize the extraordinary amount of material that we have about him in archaeological and other sources. This is the king in whose reign the Second Temple was built.

As further background, I have to point out that the Talmud assumes that the kings Koresh (Cyrus), Achashverosh, and Daryavesh (Darius) reigned in that order. (See *Megillah* 11b, based on *Seder Olam*, chapter 28.) But the accepted view today of the order of these kings is different: Koresh, Cambyses, followed by a usurper for seven months, then Daryavesh (=Darius I), and then Achashverosh (=Xerxes). The *Daat Mikra* commentary (published by Mossad Harav Kook) follows the accepted (=non-talmudic) view. I will be following this accepted view as well.[46] So when I write about the Daryavesh/Darius in whose reign the Second Temple was built, I am taking the position that he is the *father* of Achashverosh. (This is the opposite of what most of you reading this were taught as youths.)

If you look at Tanakh, there is only one story involving our Daryavesh/Darius. The story runs through Ezra chapters 4-6. The work on rebuilding the Temple had started in the reign of Koresh. But because of complaints made against the work by the opponents of the returnees, the work ceased. Due to the encouragement of the prophets Haggai and Zechariah, the returnees renewed their rebuilding work in the reign of Daryavesh. This was almost 20 years after the initial permission by Cyrus. Accordingly, the Persian governor asked the returnees who had given them permission to engage in this work. They responded that Cyrus had given the permission and that Darius should search for this decree. Darius had a search made and in the palace at Achmata (the modern day Hamadan), Cyrus' decree was found. Accordingly, Darius allowed the Jews to continue their work. He also ordered funds and supplies given to them, so that they would offer their sacrifices and pray for the life of the king and his sons. The Temple work was allowed to continue and it was finished in his sixth year (=516 B.C.E.).

That is the limited role of the Persian King Daryavesh=Darius I in Tanakh: one story in the book of Ezra, in which he orders a search for a prior decree and is willing to go along with it.

But what happens when we look for material about Daryavesh=Darius I outside of Tanakh? It turns out that we have many inscriptions that he ordered, found in the remains of the three ancient Persian palaces: Shushan, Hamadan, and Persepolis. We also learn from these inscriptions that it was he who authorized the building of the palace at Shushan. More importantly, Herodotus (middle of the 5th century B.C.E.) writes extensively about his reign and military adventures. For example, we learn that he led a failed invasion of Greece. (The famous Battle at the Bay of Marathon took place in this invasion.) But the most important thing that Darius is known for is his trilingual inscription at Behistun.

---

46. Both of my previous books, *Jewish History in Conflict* (1997) and *Esther Unmasked* (2015) have discussed this topic at length.

Darius was not the son of Cambyses. Rather, he was the son of a satrap named Hystaspes. (Hystaspes was a distant cousin of Cambyses.) So how exactly did Darius become king? Herodotus tells the following story. After reigning seven years, Cambyses died while out of the country. He had no children. He had previously ordered his brother Smerdis to be killed, but this was not known to the populace. While Cambyses was away, someone who looked like Cambyses' brother Smerdis (and was also named Smerdis!) was able to instigate the populace to rebel against Cambyses and he usurped the throne, pretending to be Cambyses' brother Smerdis. He ruled for seven months. But eventually a few individuals figured out, with the help of one of Cambyses' wives, that this Smerdis was an impostor. (This wife was able to inspect his ears one night while he was sleeping. She had been told that the true Smerdis would have ears, while the impostor Smerdis had previously been punished by having his ears cut off. Her inspection revealed no ears!) Then Darius and six others decided to join together in a conspiracy to overthrow the impostor. After the conspiracy was successful and the impostor was killed, the conspirators agreed to make Darius the king. (I have just tremendously oversimplified a very long story told by Herodotus.)

But is there any truth to this story? How credible is Herodotus?

In the 17th and 18th centuries, European scholars began to travel to Persia (modern day Iran). They found the remnants of Persian palaces in Shushan, Persepolis, and Hamadan, with many surviving inscriptions. There was also a very lengthy inscription at a site called Behistun (in Western Iran). This was a text with an accompanying relief, inscribed high above the ground on a rockface, overlooking a main road. At first, no one could decipher any of these inscriptions. Eventually, several scholars made contributions towards deciphering this language (=Old Persian cuneiform). The most important work was done by Henry Rawlinson. Rawlinson was an officer in the British army serving in the area, and he became obsessed with trying to decipher the Behistun inscription. First he risked his life climbing the rockface and copying it. (This was with the help of a Kurdish boy, also named Smerdis. Just kidding! The boy's name remains unknown.) Then Rawlinson dedicated many years in the 1830's and 1840's to deciphering this inscription.

So what was this inscription that Rawlinson ended up deciphering? It turns out that it was the story of how Darius became king, this time told by Darius himself! Lo and behold it largely agreed with the material in Herodotus. Of course, there were some contradictions, but the basic story matched. For example, Herodotus had written that Darius became king with the help of six conspirators. Darius too wrote about six individuals who assisted him and five out of the six names given by Darius matched the names given by Herodotus!

What about the relief that accompanied the inscription? It turns out that it centered around an image of Darius, stepping on top of the impostor.[47]

So we see that the Behistun inscription ordered by Darius is a key source in ancient Persian history and a key source in evaluating the credibility of our main ancient narrative historical source, Herodotus.

But the Behistun inscription is important for an entirely different reason. This inscription was a trilingual one. It told the same story in Old Persian, Akkadian, and Elamite. After the Old Persian portion was deciphered, scholars were able to decipher the Akkadian and Elamite versions. Akkadian was the language of ancient Assyria and Babylonia. The decipherment of Akkadian opened up a new field of archaeology, as the cuneiform inscriptions of ancient Assyria and Babylonia could now be read! So our king Darius, with a minor role in Tanakh, is one of the most important kings in ancient history. It was his Behistun inscription that opened the door to the study of the cuneiform inscriptions of ancient Assyria and Babylonia![48]

*

Mitchell First is a personal injury attorney and Jewish history scholar. He hopes that the U.S. and Iran can make peace one day so that he can lead an expedition to Behistun.

---

47. There are many other figures in the relief as well. A picture of the Behistun inscription is found at Y. Landy, *Purim and the Persian Empire* (2010), p. 14. There are many pictures of it online.
48. Allied troops used the Behistun inscription for target practice during World War II! It is now a UNESCO World Heritage site.

6. The Most Important Dead Sea Text:
A Lost Paragraph from the Book of Samuel!

Among the ancient texts found in the Dead Sea region are both biblical and non-biblical texts. In this column, I am going to focus on the biblical texts.

Texts of a large percentage of Tanakh have been discovered, and material continues to come to light periodically. (But to date nothing at all has been discovered from the book of Esther.)

The Dead Sea texts date from the 3rd century B.C.E. to the 1st century C.E. This makes them older by many centuries than the earliest manuscripts of biblical texts that we had previously possessed. For example, the Aleppo Codex dates from the 10th century C.E. (and is missing most of the Pentateuch). The Leningrad Codex, which has a complete text of the Bible, dates to the early 11th century.

What happens when we examine these Dead Sea texts? There are differences from the Masoretic Text but they are generally very minor. Most of the differences involve different spellings of the same word. Sometimes there is a different word altogether. For example, at Deuteronomy 32:8, our Masoretic text has *Bnei Yisrael*, while the Dead Sea text has *Bnei Elohim*. Very rarely, there are a few additional words. (One such example is at Deut. 32:43.) Sometimes the letters are the same, but the division of the letters into words differs.

Another interesting variant is in the first chapter of Lamentations. The Masoretic Text of Lamentations has an unusual inconsistency. The *pe* verse precedes the *ayin* verse in the acrostics of chapters 2, 3 and 4, while the acrostic in chapter 1 is in the traditional *ayin* preceding *pe* order. But in the Dead Sea text of Lamentations chapter 1, the *pe* verse precedes the *ayin* verse here too as well. In other words, verses 1:16-17 are in the reverse order from the Masoretic Text, giving a consistent *pe* preceding *ayin* order throughout chapters 1 through 4. (Much more needs to be explained here regarding this *pe* preceding *ayin* order, but this is not the place. For the full discussion, see my *Esther Unmasked* [2015], pp. 207-230.)

There is one glaring exception to our principle of minor differences between the Dead Sea and Masoretic Texts. At the beginning of 1 Samuel 11, the Dead Sea text has *a few extra sentences* and it is very likely that they were there originally and got lost!

Here is our present text of 1 Sam. 11:1-3:

Nachash the Ammonite went up, and encamped against Yavesh Gilead. The men of Yavesh Gilead said to Nachash: 'Make a covenant with us and we will serve you.' Nachash the Ammonite said to them: On this condition will I make a covenant with you, that all your right eyes be put out; and I will make this a reproach upon all Israel. The elders of Yavesh said to him: Give us seven days respite that we may send messengers throughout the borders of Israel. Then if there will be none to deliver us, we will come out to you.

Now let us read the story with the added material from the (slightly fragmentary) Dead Sea text:

[Na]chash, king of the people of Ammon, sorely oppressed the people of Gad and the people of Reuven, and he gouged out a[ll] their right eyes and no [redeem]er was given to [I]srael. There was not one left among the people of Israel bey[ond the Jordan who]se right eye was no[t put o]ut by Nacha[sh king] of the people of [A]mmon; and seven thousand men [were saved from the hand of] the people of Ammon and entered [Y]avesh Gilead. About a month later, Nachash the Ammonite went up....[continue with the paragraph above].[49]

In the Masoretic Text, Nachash besieges the Israelites of Yavesh Gilead for no reason. Like the area of Ammon, the city of Yavesh Gilead was on the east side of the Jordan River. But it was far north of Ammon and it was not in the area that we would expect Nachash to be fighting for.

With the added material from the Dead Sea text, we now understand why Nachash besieged Yavesh Gilead. He began his attack on his main territorial enemy, the tribes of Gad and Reuven, and they became subservient to him. It was only after seven thousand

---

49. Translation adapted from *Understanding the Dead Sea Scrolls*, ed. H. Shanks (1993), p. 161, and F. M. Cross, *Discoveries in the Judaean Desert XVII* (2005), pp. 65-66.

members of the tribes of Gad and Reuven fled north to Yavesh Gilead that Nachash decided to attack Yavesh Gilead.[50]

Probably the missing paragraph was lost because a scribe was copying the word "Nachash," and then took his eyes off and went back to the word "Nachash" on a later line. This caused him to omit everything in between. This is a common type of scribal error. (It even has a fancy name: "homeoteleuton.") This scribe's defective text was then copied by others.

Note also that in the Masoretic Text, Nachash is introduced merely as "Nachash the Ammonite." In contrast, in the Dead Sea text, he is introduced with a full title: "Nachash, king of the people of Ammon." This also supports the idea that the Dead Sea text is preserving the original material. In Tanakh, kings are typically (although not always) introduced with a full title.

It is also evident that Josephus (1st century C.E.) had the additional material. See Josephus, *Antiquities* VI.68-69.

There are many other minor differences between the Masoretic Text of Samuel and the Dead Sea text. One example is the height of Goliath. In our text (1 Sam. 17:4), Goliath is described as having a height of six *amot*. In contrast, in the Dead Sea text, his height is given as four *amot*. Also, at 1 Sam. 15:27, a tear is made in the garment of Samuel. (It is a very important tear, symbolizing the tearing away of Saul's kingship.) Our text is ambiguous as to whether Samuel or Saul made the tear. In the Dead Sea text, the tear is explicitly attributed to Saul.

Finally, I will mention three other interesting Dead Sea scroll variants:

- The Dead Sea Isaiah scroll has *kadosh, kadosh* at verse 6:3, instead of our *kadosh, kadosh, kadosh*.[51] I was very surprised when I first came across this. Then I investigated further and found that many times, when the Masoretic Text has a doubling of words, the Dead Sea texts have the word only one time. There must have been some ancient symbol on their words that indicated when a

---

50. Admittedly, there are words missing from the Dead Sea text regarding the 7000 men and words have been supplied by Cross to fill the gap, based on reasonable conjecture.
51. This scroll can be viewed online.

word, written once, was meant to count twice. Probably such a symbol was once found on one of the two *kadosh* words (either in the Dead Sea Isaiah scroll that survived or in earlier Dead Sea Isaiah texts no longer extant).

- At the beginning of Psalm 145, the Dead Sea text has "*tefillah le-David,*" instead of our "*tehillah le-David.*"
- The Dead Sea text of Psalm 145 includes a verse that begins with *nun* ("*ne'eman Elokim be-devarav, ve-chasid be-khol maasav*") See J.A. Sanders, *The Dead Sea Psalms Scroll* (1967), p. 66. As is well-known, the Masoretic Text of Psalm 145 has no *nun* verse. Most likely, the verse in the Dead Sea text was a later addition. The name used for God, *Elokim*, is not the name as the one used in the rest of the psalm, and *chasid be-khol maasav* is suspicious because it is already found elsewhere in the psalm. See further the *Daat Mikra* edition of Psalms, p. 579, note 23, and *Esther Unmasked*, p. 220.

*

Mitchell First is a personal injury attorney and Jewish history scholar. When copying material from another source, he is always careful to make sure he makes no omissions.

7. A Decree by the Roman Emperor
Justinian Interfering with the Synagogue Service

In a different article, I discussed the origin of reciting *Shema* in the *Kedushah* of *musaf*. I wrote that various sources from the Geonic period had suggested that there was a decree by the government forbidding the recital of the *Shema* in its regular place and that this led to the insertion of the *Shema* into the *Kedusuah*. Like most modern scholars, I concluded that there was no such decree and that the recital of the *Shema* in the *Kedushah* could be explained in a different manner.

Here I will discuss a situation where there is reliable documentation of an ancient governmental decree affecting the synagogue service. A book by Amnon Linder, *The Jews in Roman Imperial Legislation* (1987), collects laws enacted by the second through sixth-century Roman rulers relating to the Jews. The book includes an interesting law passed by Justinian in the year 553. The background is that there was a dispute among the Jews in a certain area in the Roman empire as to what language should be used in reading or translating the Torah in the synagogue and they asked the Roman government to get involved and decide the issue. The decree of Justinian records:

> We have learned from their petitions, which they have addressed to us, that while some maintain the Hebrew language only and want to use it in reading the Holy Books, others consider it right to admit Greek as well, and they have already been quarreling among themselves about this for a long time. Having studied this matter we decided that the better case is that of those who want to use also Greek in reading the Holy Books, and generally in any language that is the more suited and the better known to the hearers in such locality.

The decree continues that when a Greek translation is used, it must be the Septuagint version, because it is more accurate than all the others. Also, the Septuagint is preferable because of the miracle that was described in the Letter of Aristeas: the translators translated separately, but nevertheless came out with the same version. The decree then reluctantly grants additional permission to use the Greek translation of Aquilas, even though it "differs not a little from the Septuagint."

But then the decree continues: "What they call *deuterosis* [= Mishnah], on the other hand, we prohibit entirely.... It is an invention of men in their chatter, exclusively of earthly origin and having in it nothing of the divine."

Scholars have been puzzled by this decree prohibiting the *deuterosis*. Most are in agreement that *deuterosis* is a reference to the Mishnah. But what is a decree forbidding the Mishnah doing in a decree whose context is the synagogue service? Moreover, the decree seems to prohibit the Mishnah in all contexts, not just the context of the synagogue.

One scholar thinks that *deuterosis*, in this particular case, includes all the oral law, including Talmud and Midrash. The interpretations of the Bible used in the synagogue drew on the entire resources of rabbinic thought, and the intent was to prohibit these types of interpretations in the synagogue. Another scholar thinks that this particular decree reflected an effort by Justinian to close down all the Jewish *batei midrashot*. It just happened to get recorded in a decree that was mainly about the synagogue service.

The interpretation that I found most reasonable was expressed by Albert I. Baumgarten in his article "Justinian and the Jews," in the *Rabbi Joseph H. Lookstein Memorial Volume* (1980), pp. 37-44. Baumgarten believes that Justinian, a Christian, enacted this law because the Mishnah represented the Jewish claim to have the true understanding of the Bible. Justinian was here making a symbolic statement against the Mishnah and the Jewish interpretation of the Bible, even though he knew that his prohibition could not be enforced. The general context of the decree was an attempt to control biblical interpretation and limit interpretations to acceptable ones. To Justinian, the Mishnah represented unacceptable Jewish biblical interpretation.

As a postscript, it is interesting how this whole scenario developed. The Jews asked the Romans to intervene in a synagogue dispute about a narrow issue. The Romans exploited the opportunity and issued a broad prohibition on the study of the entire Mishnah!

*

Mitchell First is an attorney and Jewish history scholar. When he reads the Torah in Greek translation, he does not use the Septuagint or the translation of Aquilas. Rather, he prefers the Greek translations of Symmachus and Theodotion.[52]

8. The Fast Days of *Megillat Taanit Batra*

We are all familiar with the four biblical fast days in Tishrei, Tammuz, Av, and Tevet. We are also familiar with the post-talmudic fast of 13 Adar. (I have written much about this last one. See my 2010 article in *AJS Review*, vol. 34.)

But if one looks at R. Yosef Caro's *Shulchan Arukh* (16th century), *Orach Chayyim* 580, one sees an additional list of fast days. R. Yosef Caro wrote that it is ראוי (=worthy) to fast on them. (Admittedly,

---

52. I hope that this joke is not too obscure!

he does not say it is obligatory.). The list begins: "1 Nissan, death of Aaron's sons; 10 Nissan, death of Miriam and end of her well; 26 Nissan, death of Joshua; 10 Iyyar, death of Eli and his sons and the capture of the ark...." It goes on with various other fast day dates through the rest of the year. The total number of dates listed here is twenty-one.

Before he wrote his *Shulchan Arukh*, R. Yosef Caro wrote a commentary called *Beit Yosef*. There he wrote (sec. 580): "I never saw or heard about anyone who fasted on these days." Nevertheless, when he later composed his *Shulchan Arukh*, he chose to codify them! (It has been suggested that his codification of these fast days may have been due to his well-documented ascetic and kabbalistic tendencies.)

So what is going on here? These fast days were not observed in biblical times and they are not found in the Mishnah or either Talmud. Where did these fast days come from?

It has been known for centuries that this list of fast days (with many variants) has been found in sources that long preceded the *Shulchan Arukh*. For example, a list like this is in the *Halakhot Gedolot* (9th century, Babylonia). A list like this is also found in other well-known sources such as *Seder Rav Amram Gaon* and *Machzor Vitry*. It is found in various other Rishonim as well.

But since the discovery of the Cairo Genizah at the end of the 19th century, several earlier sources have come to light. This enabled much progress to be made on the issue of the origin of these fast days.

Before I discuss this further, I have to address the name for these lists of fast days that appear starting with the *Halakhot Gedolot*. The convention now is to call these lists *Megillat Taanit Batra*. This is an artificial name, first suggested in 1908. Other scholars had used other names such as *Perek Ha-Tzomot*.

(Of course, *Megillat Taanit Batra* should not be confused with the much older *Megillat Taanit*, an ancient list of happy days on which one was *not allowed* to fast. Nevertheless, our list of fast days was sometimes appended to manuscripts and printed editions of *Megillat Taanit*!)

Now that the material from the Cairo Genizah has come to light, we see that we have evidence of the existence of these fast days long before the *Halakhot Gedolot* in 9th century Babylonia. It turns out that these fast days originated in Palestine hundreds of years earlier. For example, a *piyyut* from R. Eleazar Kallir includes many of the fast days. Moreover, on several occasions in this *piyyut*, Kallir does not even give the date of the fast day, only specifying the month and the event. This suggests that the fast days he included were well-known and may have been observed for generations by his time. The most recent scholarship estimates Kallir's lifespan as 570-640 CE.

One scholar who has investigated this whole topic is Shulamit Elizur. She is a professor at Hebrew University who is an expert on *piyyut*. She published a book in 2007: *Lammah Tzamnu? Megillat Taanit Batra U-Reshimot Tzomot Ha-Krovot Lah*. Here she collected all the various sources and compared them to see how the list of fast days evolved over the centuries. Based on all the evidence, she concluded that the original custom to fast on such days began in Palestine in the 5th or 6th century. Over the centuries, additional days were added, and many variants arose.

That these fast days originated in Amoraic Palestine is not surprising. There seems to have been an affinity for fasting there. There is documentation that it was the practice among some Jews in Palestine in the Tannaitic and Amoraic periods to fast regularly on Monday and Thursday.[53]

So we can now estimate that our list of fast days originated in Palestine in the 5th or 6th century. But what we do not know is whether these fast days were observed by a large segment of Palestinian Jews or perhaps by only by a small segment. Elizur suggests the latter.[54]

Thereafter, the list of fast days spread to Babylonia and Europe, but this does not mean that the fast days were actually observed there. Perhaps they were observed, but only by very few.[55] But R. Yosef Caro nevertheless chose to include them in the *Shulchan Arukh*.

Elizur conjectures that the earliest list included fasts for only the following events: the death of Joshua, the death of Eli, the death of Samuel, the killing of the sons of Zedekiah, the translation of the Torah into Greek, the war between the rest of the tribes and the tribe of Benjamin (Judges 19-20), a certain violent physical dispute that broke

---

53. See Elizur, p.160.
54. See Elizur, pp. 25 and 230-32.
55. See Elizur, pp. 227-42.

out between the students of Shammai and Hillel, and the killing of the two Jewish brothers Pappus and Lulianus in the 2nd century C.E.[56]

One of the most interesting dates in the list at *Shulchan Arukh, Orach Chayyim* 580, is 9 Tevet. R. Yosef Caro wrote that "we do not know what bad event happened on it." He wrote this because *Halakhot Gedolot*, in the 9th century, wrote: *lo katvu rabboteinu al mah hu*, "the Sages did not write what event this fast was meant to commemorate." Thereafter, in the 19th century, several Jewish scholars suggested that the fast commemorated the birthday of Jesus and for this reason the basis for the fast was purposely not specified.

This suggestion and another suggestion related to Christianity motivated Dr. Shnayer Leiman to write a comprehensive article about this topic. See Sid Z. Leiman "The Scroll of Fasts: The Ninth of Tebeth," *Jewish Quarterly Review*, 74/2 (1983), pp. 174-95. (It can be accessed at his site leimanlibrary.com.) He investigated the issue thoroughly and concluded that we still do not know what event this fast day was meant to commemorate.

Moreover, as stated by both Leiman and Elizur, the reason no explanation was given may simply have been that whoever decided to include the fast of 9 Tevet on the list may not have had the origin information himself. We do not have to read in *lo katvu...*, a desire for secrecy. As Elizur suggests for various reasons, it is possible that the origin of the fast of 9 Tevet may have been the death of Ezra. Whoever wrote the line "*lo katvu*" may have known that the date should be included in the list of fast days, but may have not known the reason for the fast, so he recorded the date of the fast and then added *lo katvu....*

*

Mitchell First is a personal injury attorney and Jewish history scholar. He would much rather write a joyful column about *Megillat Taanit*, the list of holidays where fasting is prohibited.

---

56. Regarding this last event, see *Encyclopaedia Judaica* 13:69 and the issues raised at Elizur, pp. 202-04.

9. Abraham Ibn Ezra: His Unique
Life and Some Lessons We Can Learn

The life of Abraham Ibn Ezra can be divided into two periods. The first was a stable one. According to the most recent scholarship, he was born in either 1091 or 1092. He lived in the Muslim portion of Spain, and received a traditional Spanish Jewish education, studying Torah as well as philosophy, mathematics, astronomy, astrology and poetry.

In 1140, the second period of his life began, the life of a poor wandering scholar. For reasons that we can only guess at, Ibn Ezra left Spain in 1140. Thereafter, he lived the rest of his life in Ashkenazic lands. (Things got worse for Jews in Muslim Spain a few years after Ibn Ezra left, due to the invasion of the Almohades, a fanatical Islamic sect.)

Ibn Ezra went first to Italy, living variously in Rome, Lucca, Mantua, and Verona. After Italy, he went to Provence. Then he lived in northern France. (Here, he was able to befriend the Tosafist R. Jacob Tam.) After northern France, he lived in London for a few years, and then went back to Provence in 1161. We do not know where he lived when he died in 1167. (There are four conjectures as to where he was buried: London, Spain, Rome, and Israel.)

It was in the second part of his life that he wrote his biblical commentaries and works on Hebrew grammar. He supported himself, just barely, with commissions from patrons. He wrote a poem about how difficult it was to live this way: "When I come to the patron's house early in the morning, they say 'he has already ridden away' (*kevar rakhav*). When I come in the evening, they say: 'he has already gone to sleep' (*kevar shakhav*).... Woe to the poor man born in misfortune (*bli kokhav*)!"

He also wrote in a poem about his bad luck and poverty: "If my business were in candles, the sun would not set until I died... If I dealt in shrouds, no one would die as long as I lived."

Four of his children probably died in infancy. His wife also may have died early in his life. His other son Yitzchak also died in his father's lifetime. (Yitzchak spent most of his life in the Near East. It seems that he converted to Islam while living in Baghdad, but it was probably only a conversion for the sake of appearances.)

When Ibn Ezra arrived in Italy in 1140, he entered a Jewish world vastly different from the one in which he had been raised. The Jews of Italy were Ashkenazic and had no familiarity with the Arabic language. Being among these Italian Jews prompted Ibn Ezra to translate the grammatical works of R. Yehudah ibn Hayyuj (10th century) from Arabic to Hebrew. Hayyuj's works had inaugurated a new era in the understanding of Biblical Hebrew among the Arabic-speaking Jews of Spain and Ibn Ezra's translation of them into Hebrew greatly benefitted Ashkenazic Jewry. (It was Hayyuj who developed the idea that Hebrew was a language with three-letter roots.) Ibn Ezra was also motivated to write his own works on Hebrew grammar for the benefit of Ashkenazic Jewry.

Ibn Ezra is reported to have composed over 100 different works. (But most of his works are lost.) He even composed some works in Latin, with the assistance of a Christian scholar. His magnum opus was his commentary on the Torah. He may have written commentaries on all the books of the *Neviim* and *Ketuvim*. The only ones that have survived are: Isaiah, Twelve Prophets, Psalms, Job, Daniel, and Five Megillot. (The standard printed commentaries labeled as "Ibn Ezra" to Proverbs, Ezra, and Nechemiah were not authored by him.)

According to the most recent scholarship, his basic Torah commentary on the five books was written over the years 1142-45. (He had already started some of his *Nakh* commentaries in 1140.) We are also in possession of a second, longer commentary to Exodus. It was the longer Exodus commentary that was printed in the *Mikraot Gedolot*. We do not know what motivated him to write a second commentary on Exodus. One theory is that it was a revision in response to Rashbam's commentary, which he had not yet read in the years 1142-45. In the longer version, Ibn Ezra frequently mentions Rashbam's commentary, although never by name, referring to it simply as *yesh omrim*. (Rashbam lived in France, c. 1080-1160.) Ibn Ezra also attempted a longer commentary on Genesis, but he only completed about one quarter of it. We also have fragments of a third Genesis commentary by him.

Ibn Ezra's introduction to the Torah also deserves mention. He explained that although previous Torah commentaries had been written, none had explicated the simple, literal meaning. He found the commentaries written by the Geonim too long and unsatisfactory.

The Karaite commentaries ignored rabbinic traditions. The Christian commentaries were too allegorical. The Jewish commentaries written in Christian lands took the *midrashim* too literally and were lacking a proper understanding of Hebrew grammar. Therefore, a new commentary in the way of *peshat* was necessary, founded on the pillars of rationalism and knowledge of Hebrew and its grammar.

There are a few lessons for us all in the life of Ibn Ezra:

- One's main accomplishment may not occur until late in life. Ibn Ezra did not even start working on his Torah commentary until 1142, when he was age 50 or 51.

- An individual has no idea of the lasting impact he may have. Ibn Ezra had a very difficult life, due to his emigration from his homeland, his subsequent poverty and wanderings, and the tragedies in his family. He would certainly be shocked with regard to his long-lasting influence. It is 900 years later and he is not only still being read, he is still being studied extensively! (This is aside from the fact that we still sing some of the *zemirot* he composed: *Ki Eshmerah Shabbat* and *Tzamah Nafshi*. I would be happy if my three books were still being read 50 years from now!)

- Most important, God works things out for us in unusual ways. If not for the troubles he was having in Muslim Spain, Ibn Ezra would have remained there. His works would have been composed in Arabic, and would have probably been lost. Even if they would have survived, they would have had little influence on Ashkenazic Jewry at the time and over the centuries thereafter. It is only because he ended up in Ashkenazic lands that he composed his commentaries in Hebrew and they had the tremendous influence that they did. (Ibn Ezra is difficult enough today with all his cryptic remarks! Imagine if we would have to be reading him in translation!) Also, it was his poverty that forced him to continually travel and seek out patrons and write new commentaries, meanwhile benefitting from the exposure to diverse scholars and cultures. Finally, it was an oath taken during a health crisis that forced him to finally start his Torah commentary and not delay it any further. In sum, it was only his travails and troubles that enabled him to bring the intellectual traditions of Spain to non-Arabic speaking Ashkenazic Jewry, and have the lasting influence that he did.

Postscript: There is a widely quoted ethical will from Rambam to his son with the following language: "I exhort you not to pay attention or distract your mind by concentrating on commentaries, treatises and books other than those of Ibn Ezra, which alone are meaningful and profitable...." But it seems that this was not written by Rambam. See Y. Shilat, *Iggerot Ha-Rambam* vol. 2 (3ʳᵈ edition, 1995), p. 698. Shilat argues convincingly that this was just a literary forgery from a later period, the period of the polemic against the Rambam's writings, and that it was written by a proponent of the Rambam and Ibn Ezra. Shilat points out that Rambam only refers to Ibn Ezra one time, very briefly, in all of his known writings! (The reference is not to anything Ibn Ezra wrote. Ibn Ezra's writings may never have even reached Rambam in Egypt. Rambam died in 1204.)

Acknowledgements: Much of what I wrote above is taken from the excellent summary of Ibn Ezra's life and works in Rabbi Yonatan Kolatch, *Masters of the Word*, vol. II (2007). Another very useful source is the article by Nahum Sarna, "Abraham Ibn Ezra as an Exegete," in *Rabbi Abraham Ibn Ezra: Studies in the Writings of a Twelfth-Century Jewish Polymath* (1993), pp. 1-27. Finally, two important recent articles are S. Sela and G. Freudenthal, "Abraham Ibn Ezra's Scholarly Writings: A Chronological Listing," *Aleph* 6 (2006), pp. 13-55, and I. Kislev, "The Relationship between the Torah Commentaries Composed by R. Abraham Ibn Ezra in France and the Significance of this Relationship for the Biographical Chronology of the Commentator," *Journal of Jewish Studies* LX, no. 2 (2009), pp. 282-97.[57]

*

Mitchell First is a personal injury attorney and Jewish history scholar. He has authored three books but no *zemirot*. For his favorite Ibn Ezra comment, see the last four words of the commentary on *rakkot* at Gen. 29:17.

---

57. I would like to thank Rabbi Ezra Frazer for referring me to these two articles.

10. The Story of the *Pentateuch* of Rabbi Dr. J. H. Hertz

The Pentateuch and Haftorahs of Rabbi Dr. J.H. Hertz is one of the most important works of the Jewish religion in the 20th century. To quote one scholar, it "almost single-handedly [gave] shape to the way in which English-speaking Jewish laymen the world over have understood their Judaism over the course of the past two generations." I recently came across a book which told the story of this work. The book is: *A Vindication of Judaism: The Polemics of the Hertz Pentateuch,* by Harvey Meirovich (1998). I would like to share some of what I learned from this book.

First, a bit of biography. Joseph Herman Hertz was born in 1872 in Slovakia. He was brought to the U.S. in 1884 and grew up in New York City on the Lower East Side. He attended City College and Columbia University. He received his rabbinic ordination from the Jewish Theological Seminary in 1894, as part of their first graduating class of eight students. After serving congregations in Syracuse (1894-98), Johannesburg (1898-1911), and New York City (1912), he was appointed chief rabbi of England in 1913. He held that position until his death in 1946.

R. Hertz began work on his commentary in 1920. But it was not until 1929 that the first volume came out. The last volume, Deuteronomy, came out in 1936. He did not produce this monumental commentary on his own. He had four Anglo-Jewish collaborators: Joshua Abelson, Abraham Cohen, Gerald Friedlander, and Samuel Frampton. Periodically, these men submitted their initial drafts of the sections assigned to them. Then R. Hertz recast their material into his own style.

What was the background to this work? In England in 1901, one year before his move to New York, Solomon Schechter wrote: "[T]he new century does not open under very favourable auspices for Judaism…. [O]ur Scriptures are the constant object of attack, our history is questioned, and its morality is declared to be an inferior sort…. [T]he younger generation… if not directly hostile, are by dint of mere ignorance sadly indifferent to everything Jewish, and incapable of taking the place of their parents in the Synagogue…."

Schechter argued that an English commentary on the Five Books (and the rest of the Bible as well), written under Jewish auspices, was needed to respond to these challenges.

There were already English commentaries on the Five Books before that of R. Hertz, but since they were almost always written by non-Jews, they would typically have an anti-Jewish bias. R. Hertz once remarked about such commentaries: "It is as if a version of Shakespeare were made into Spanish by a Spaniard who had but an imperfect acquaintance with English... and who was filled with hatred and contempt for the British character and the entire British people."

In his preface, R. Hertz mentions the few and limited English commentaries written by Jews before him: a commentary published in 1844 by De Sola, Lindenthal, and Raphall, of which Genesis alone appeared, and commentaries by Marcus Kalisch on Genesis, Exodus, and Leviticus, which appeared over the years 1855-72. He also mentions some glosses in English on the Five Books published David Levi and Isaac Delgado in 1796.

Schechter repeated his plea for a Jewish commentary again after his move to New York in 1902 (when he came to head the Jewish Theological Seminary). The commentary of R. Hertz was a response to the need expressed in Schechter's plea.

Meirovich explains further that traditional Judaism at the time of R. Hertz was threatened by the late nineteenth-century biblical criticism of Julius Wellhausen and by its reconstruction of history. This reconstruction characterized Jewish law as anachronistic compared with Christianity's emphasis on faith and morality. Also, R. Hertz was troubled by the mounting self-confidence of Liberal/Reform Judaism. The work of R. Hertz should be read as a reaction to these challenges.

In his preface, R. Hertz makes the following remark: "[T]he criticism of the Pentateuch associated with the name of Wellhausen is a perversion of history and a desecration of religion." Using archaeology and philology, R. Hertz crafted a sophisticated work that attempted to underscore the Divinity and unity of the Torah, and the integrity of Judaism and its moral superiority to Christianity.

Aside from the need for a commentary on the Five Books to defend and promote traditional Judaism, there was the more practical need for a commentary that could be used in the synagogue. Before the commentary of R. Hertz, if an English-speaking Jew wanted to follow the Torah reading in synagogue with one work in his hand that included a Hebrew text of the entire *chumash*, an English translation, and any kind of English commentary, there was no such work! As we walk into our synagogues with hundreds of ArtScroll and Hertz *chumashim*, this is hard for us to imagine!

While R. Hertz' work was completed before the Holocaust, it became even more useful thereafter, as the destruction of European Jewry shifted the center of gravity in Jewish life to the English-speaking world. As one scholar wrote: "Hertz had forged in advance for the Jews of England and America a tool to sustain their fortitude and faith."[58]

The two most interesting discussions in the Meirovich book are the story of the complaint of the collaborators, and the story of how the work did not sell well initially, despite the tremendous amount of work that went into it.

With regard to the collaborators, on July 8,1929, after Genesis came out, three of his four collaborators (the other one was already deceased) wrote a letter of complaint about how their names were not included on the title page, even though R. Hertz did acknowledge their assistance in the introduction. They wrote: "On the title page of the Commentary the names of your collaborators do not appear. In all similar works, proper tribute is paid in this way to those who have collaborated, as for instance in Kittel's 'Biblia Hebraica.' Accordingly, we feel strongly that following the words: 'Edited by the Chief Rabbi' some such phrase as 'With the collaboration of...' should certainly follow. We do not consider that our point is covered by the bare reference in the Introduction. We submit that in the subsequent volumes, and also when a new edition of Genesis appears, we should be favored in the way indicated."

R. Hertz wrote back: "[N]othing is further from my nature than to deprive others of the honour which is justly their due.... Your complaint, moreover, is unjustified. The English usage in regard to any collective enterprise of a literary nature is that only the editor's name appears. (The example of Kittel's Bible is not an analogous case)…. Such is the rule when the contribution of each man is reprinted as

58. See Meirovich, p. x. (foreword).

it is, without any recasting on the part of the editor. How much the more should it apply in a case where the contributions have been recast and often altogether rewritten by the editor!"

Genesis sold very poorly initially, causing R. Hertz extreme disappointment. He even considered canceling the publication of the remaining volumes! But people were hesitant to buy the single volumes in view of the anticipated publication of the entire five books in one work. In 1936, the Soncino Press approached him, as they understood that tremendous sales would result by combining the five volumes into one. Also, a large donation by a friend of R. Hertz enabled the work to be sold at a much lower price. The Soncino Press edition also changed the text used for the English translation at the top. Instead of the revised King James Version, the more readable 1917 Jewish Publication Society translation was chosen. With the Soncino Press edition, sales took off and the work became the mainstay of English-speaking synagogues of every denomination for decades.

P.S. The Soncino Press published its own *chumash* in 1947: *The Soncino Chumash: The Five Books of Moses with Haphtaroth*. The following remarks in its introduction are of interest: "[The] plan of the Commentary is different [=compared to the Prophets and Writings commentaries.] It does not supply exegetical notes which combine modern scholarship and traditional Jewish lore, because an edition of the Pentateuch and Haphtaroth on these lines was edited by the late Chief Rabbi, Dr. J. H. Hertz." They subtitled their work: "Hebrew Text and English Translation with an Exposition based on the Classical Jewish Commentaries."

*

Mitchell First is a personal injury attorney and Jewish history scholar. He still uses the Hertz Pentateuch in synagogue every *Shabbat*. He thinks that the most memorable line in this work is in the index on p. 1054: "No references are given to standard expositors of the Text (Rashi, Ibn Ezra, Dillmann, etc.)." He still has never come across a comment by Dillmann!

III. Hebrew Language

A. Particular Hebrew Words and Phrases:

1. What is the Origin of the Word ברית (Covenant)?

The word *brit* is a fundamental word in Tanakh. But where does this word come from? Nouns do not just appear out of nowhere in Hebrew. Rather, they are typically derived from a three-letter verb. Of course, there is no verb ברת in Hebrew. But perhaps we can look at roots like ברה or ברר and find the origin of the word there.

There is a verb ברה in Hebrew that means "to eat." (See, e.g., 2 Sam. 12:17.) Based on this, it has been suggested that the word *brit* has its origin in the festive meal that may have accompanied covenantal ceremonies. However, ברה is not the normal verb for eating in Tanakh. Rather, it is typically used for someone who is not well and who is being brought food for recuperation. Therefore, it would not seem to be the appropriate word for a festive covenantal meal. (Moreover, we have no evidence that covenantal agreements were originally accompanied by the eating of food. Even in the paradigmatic *brit* ceremony of Genesis 15, animals are sacrificed but there is no mention of eating them.)

An alternative suggestion is based on the biblical root ברר. This root sometimes means "purify," and other times means "choose." (These two meanings are related.). A *brit* is an agreement with someone you choose. But more fundamentally, a *brit* is a pledge to someone else. The idea of "choosing" is not so related to the fundamental nature of a *brit*. (One commentary who suggests this "choosing" meaning as a possible origin for the word *brit* is Ibn Ezra. See his commentary to Gen. 6:18.)

Another approach looks at the *brit bein ha-betarim* as a model for the meaning of *brit*. There, animals were cut in half and God (in some form) walked between them. Based on this, the suggestion can be made that perhaps *brit* means "separation." Ibn Ezra (on Gen. 6:18) mentions this as a possibility. Rav S.R. Hirsch (on Gen. 6:18) adopts this approach, suggesting a relation between ברת and פרד (separate). S.D. Luzzatto (on Gen. 15:10) adopts this approach, suggesting that

ברת is merely a metathesis of בתר (separate, divide). The root בתר is used three times in Genesis 15. The idea of "separation" can also be implied in the root ברר, since things that are chosen are separated.

But a *brit* seems more likely to be a word of unity than a word of separation. So intuitively it is hard to accept "separation" as its original meaning.[59] The commentators who adopt this approach are probably overly influenced by the *brit bein ha-betarim* story (and by something similar at Jer. 34:18-19). They are also likely influenced by the expression *koret brit*.

So far I have suggested explanations based on the concepts of "eating," "choosing," and "separating." But none have the "ring of truth" (pun intended, as you will see). Therefore many scholars adopt a very different approach. There is a word found in the Mishnah in *Shabbat* (chapter 6) and in the Tosefta to *Kelim* (chapter 5 of its middle section): *beiri* or *burit*. Marcus Jastrow (p. 166) defines it with words like: "ring," "hoop," and "thing cut in circular form." It turns out that this is a later version of a word found in Akkadian in the biblical period. The Akkadian word is *birītu* and it means "clasp, fetter," i.e., it is something that *binds* things together. (Akkadian is the language of ancient Assyria and Babylonia. It is a Semitic language that is related to Hebrew.)

Since a *brit* is in its essence something that binds people together, this approach based on Akkadian would be a very sensible approach to understanding the origin of the word. This approach is advocated in the *brit* essay in *Theological Dictionary of the Old Testament*. It is also the approach taken long ago in the classic work *Brown-Driver-Briggs*. After finding this approach in these two sources, I found that it was already adopted by Jastrow! In his *brit* (covenant) entry, p. 194, Jastrow gives the fundamental meaning of the word *brit* as "circle, ring, chain," and he refers you to his earlier *beirit* entry on p. 166. There he refers to the Akkadian word.

The most common expression for entering into a *brit* in Tanakh is *koret brit*. Can the term *koret brit* help us understand the original meaning of the word *brit*?

---

59. R. Hirsch does make an interesting attempt to justify the "separation" idea. He writes that *brit* "is an arrangement which is to be carried out, quite *independently* of all external circumstances, even in opposition to them. It literally corresponds to the conception of the 'absolute,' something separated, cut off... something absolutely unconditional."

The "separation" understanding of the word *brit* fits with the phrase *koret brit,* even though it is a bit tautological ("cutting a separation"). But what about the "ring" interpretation? Jastrow's entry for *brit* includes the following conjectural statement: " '*koret brit,*' to cut a ring out; to make a covenant." I believe that Jastrow is suggesting that the way a "ring" was created involved cutting. That is how the term *koret brit* could have arisen with *brit* meaning "ring."

Looking at our word from a different angle, how does one annul a *brit*? The word typically used is *hefer* which comes from the root פרר (=break). So the common words used with *brit,* namely *koret* and *hefer,* both go well with understanding *brit* as a "ring" that unites two parties.

Finally, *Theological Dictionary of the Old Testament* points out that the Akkadian and Hittite terms for "treaty" (terms not related to *brit*) both have the meaning "bond."

For all of the above reasons, I believe that the "ring" meaning of *brit* was the original meaning.

(I am not ruling out other possible interpretations of *koret brit.* One possible interpretation is that it refers to a ceremony of cutting the animals that may have often accompanied a *brit.* But this does not mean that the word *brit* itself had a meaning of "cutting." Another interpretation is that *koret* (cut) is figurative for "decide, decree." In Hebrew and Aramaic, we have both a "cut" and "decide/decree" meaning in roots like ח-ת-ך, ח-ר-ץ , ג-ז-ר and פ-ס-ק.

Regarding the ceremony of cutting of animals that may have often accompanied a *brit* (see Genesis 15 and Jer. 34:18-20), perhaps the ceremony symbolized the uniting of the parties through common blood. This is suggested by Rabbi Dr. J.H. Hertz.[60] Or perhaps this cutting ceremony makes palpable the punishment befalling the one who violates the pact. This is what Rashi suggests at Jer. 34:18. But no one really knows.

As long as we are on the subject of *brit,* I will briefly discuss the term for the "United States" in modern Hebrew: *artzot ha-brit.* When and

---

60. J. H. Hertz, *The Pentateuch and Haftorahs* (2nd edition, 1975), comm. to Gen. 15:10.

why was this term adopted? *Artzot* (or *medinot*) *me'uchadot* would have been more appropriate. The editor of the site balashon.com did some preliminary research on these issues.[61] Although he could not determine precisely when the term *artzot ha-brit* was first used in Hebrew to refer to the U.S., he found that this term was already used to refer to the U.S. in 1857. But more interestingly, he found that in 1859, the term was used to refer to Germany (=the German confederation). It is possible that it was used to refer to Germany before it was used to refer to the U.S.!

*

Mitchell First is a personal injury attorney and Jewish history scholar. Shortly, he is going to go to a post-circumcision meal. There he will **slice** a bagel in two, **choose** some friends to sit next to, and simultaneously sit **jointly** with many others. All of this will be symbolic of the various possible original meanings of the word *brit*.

2. A Column About Nothing:
What is the Origin of the Word הפקר?

The title of this column alludes to a famous TV show. (For the handful of you who do not understand it, it is not worth explaining.) In any event, my intent here is to write a serious column about the root of the word *hefker* (ownerless property). The word *hefker* is not found in Tanakh.

I got interested in this topic when someone pointed out to me that in the edition of Mishnah *Peah* that this person had been using, the word *hefker* was spelled two different ways at Mishnah 6:1: once as הבקר and then as הפקר. Why would there be such an inconsistency, I was asked, and what was the root of this word?[62]

Since the prevalent spelling today is הפקר, our first thought should be that the root is פ-ק-ר. But there is no root פ-ק-ר in Biblical Hebrew.

The first source I typically go to for questions like this is Ernest Klein, *A Comprehensive Etymological Dictionary of the Hebrew Language for Readers of English* (1987). This source is very useful

---

61. See his post of April 23, 2010.
62. The questioner in this story was Mollie Fisch. I thank Mollie for getting me interested in this word.

because it covers words from all periods of Jewish history, not just words from Tanakh. This source had an entry for פ-ק-ר and it related *hefker* to this root in two possible ways. First it suggested that the root פ-ק-ר was a metathesis from the well-known root פ-ר-ק, which meant things like "break" and "throw off the yoke." Then it suggested that the root פ-ק-ר was derived from the philosophy of the ancient Greek thinker Epicurus (3ʳᵈ century B.C.E). Neither of these ideas sounded like good explanations for the word *hefker*, so I began to research further. (But the Epicurus explanation is almost certainly the explanation for the Mishnaic term *apikoros*.)

My research led me to Ramban on Lev. 19:20. Here Ramban states that the Mishnah consistently spells *hefker* as הבקר, and that the spelling הפקר is a later variant that arose in Babylonia.

Of course, today we do not have Mishnah manuscripts from the time of R. Judah Ha-Nasi (200 C.E.) or anything close to that. The earliest Mishnah manuscript extant today is the Codex Kaufmann. It dates to the 10ᵗʰ or 11ʰ century. But it does spell the word הבקר. I suspect that Ramban is correct that this was the original Hebrew spelling in the Mishnah. Over time, the הפקר spelling in the Babylonian Talmud must have influenced the copyists and printers of the Mishnah and this led to some הפקר spellings in Mishnah manuscripts and printed editions.

It is still possible that *hefker* has a relation to Epicurus or *apikoros* (one who abandons his religion), but the הבקר spelling opens up new possibilities. For example we can now connect *hefker* to the fact that *bakar* often graze on abandoned, ownerless land. But scholars today usually take a different approach to understanding the origin of the word *hefker* with its ב spelling, as I will now explain.

A verse at Lev. 19:20 refers to a case of a man who has relations with a female slave who is already designated (נחרפת) to another man. The term נחרפת is very unclear and many facts of the case are unclear as well. In any event, in discussing the conclusion, the verse uses the phrase: בקרת תהיה, "it shall be a *bikkoret*." Rashi and many others have understood the term has implying an investigation. But when you see the phrase in context, it seems to be more of an explanation or legal conclusion, and not just a call for an investigation. Therefore, Ramban took the position that the meaning here was related to the meaning of הבקר and that the meaning was that the female slave was to be treated as if she was free of marital commitments (so that the usual death penalty for adultery would not apply).

In our time, scholars continue to adopt the general approach of the Ramban and view the meaning of הבקר as tied to the meaning of בקרת תהיה. But they often disagree with Ramban on the details of the interpretation. For example, a detailed article on this root was published by Shamma Friedman.[63] Based on Akkadian, he believes that the biblical root ב-ק-ר can mean "freedom" (שחרור), and movement from one *reshut* to another, and he understands בקרת תהיה as freedom from a death punishment, and הבקר as movement from one *reshut* to another.

(Note that the Talmud (*Keritot* 11a) understood בקרת תהיה as implying a punishment of lashes. But the two reasons offered there to justify this interpretation are not plain sense ones.)

A general lesson we see from all of the above is that when you see an obvious problem, i.e., two different spellings of the same word found very near one another, it cries out for investigation (*bikkoret*!) And then you can learn much from the answer and get a completely new perspective. Something similar happened to me many years ago. I was bothered by a severe inconsistency within the book of Lamentations. In the acrostics in chapters 2, 3 and 4, the *pe* verse preceded the *ayin* verse (an unusual phenomenon in itself). But there was a further problem that the acrostic in the first book was in the regular order of *ayin* preceding *pe*. I suspected that Lamentations was too small a book to have two different acrostic patterns. After many sleepless nights, I finally did the research and discovered that in the Dead Sea text of Lamentations 1, the *pe* verse preceded the *ayin* verse. Now at least there was consistency within the book of Lamentations (assuming the Dead Sea text reflected the original text). This discovery, along with some other archaeological discoveries made in the 1970's, made me realize that *pe* preceding *ayin* was in fact the original order in ancient Israel. I ended up publishing several articles on this topic.[64]

---

63. S. Friedman, "*Ha-Milon Ha-Mechkari Le-Lashon Ha-Ivrit Shel Ha-Tannaim: Erekh Hevker/Hefker: Bikoret,*" *Sidra* 12 (1996), pp. 113-127.
64. One in the July-Aug. 2012 issue of *Biblical Archaeology Review*, and the

Does our different spelling of *hefker* have any consequences for *halakhah*? Today most of us include the word הפקר in our recital of *bitul chametz*.[65] Since we are typically more strict when it comes to Pesach observance, perhaps someone will eventually suggest that we recite both the words הפקר and הבקר!

Anyone interested further in the meaning of *hefker* can go to balashon. com and find a discussion of "*apikoros* and *hefker*" (in the post dated March 2, 2016). There the article by Friedman can be accessed along with some other sources.

*

Mitchell First is a personal injury attorney and Jewish history scholar. He hopes you learned something from this column about nothing!

3. Males and Memory: The Meanings of the Root ז-כ-ר

As we all know, the letters ז-כ-ר generate two different words in Hebrew: male and remember. Is there a connection or is this merely a coincidence? In my youth, there were always jokes about of husbands forgetting their wives shopping instructions.[66] Surely those wives will deny any connection! But we have to initially presume that there is a connection, and see if we can uncover it.

Solomon Mandelkern, in his concordance, makes the suggestion that it is only through males that the family's name and memory are perpetuated.

Alternatively, Rav S.R. Hirsch writes (on Ex. 23:17): "the special function of [males] … is זוכר, to form the chain of tradition of the human race, by which the achievements of each age are handed down from generation to generation."[67]

---

other in *Journal for the Study of the Old Testament*, vol. 38 (2014). Thereafter, I published my longest article on this topic in my book *Esther Unmasked* (2015).

65. This was not always the case. Whether *bittul chametz* is related to a *hefker* process is a dispute. See, e.g., M. Kasher, *Haggadah Shelemah* (1967, 3rd ed.), p. 54.

66. Now with cellphones and texting, that is all a dim memory.

67. With this in mind, M. Clark, in his *Etymological Dictionary of Biblical Hebrew* (1999), defines ז-כ-ר as "male; bearer of tradition."

How does my favorite source, *Theological Dictionary of the Old Testament,* deal with the two meanings of ז-כ-ר? To give you some background, this is a multi-volume work with essays on many of the important words of Tanakh.[68] Each essay is composed by a different author. In the article on ז-כ-ר with the meaning "remember," the author writes that זכר with the "male" meaning "does not belong to the same root, although many attempts have been made to find a common background." In the article on ז-כ-ר with the meaning "male," a different author writes that a connection with the root ז-כ-ר, "remember," has often been conjectured, "but this remains obscure and unsupported." So we struck out two times in this work!

Nevertheless, I am going to mention one "memorable" suggestion.[69]

I first have to admit that I have been misleading you a bit when I describe one branch of the root ז-כ-ר as meaning "remember." In the other Semitic languages, this branch of ז-כ-ר also has meanings like "mention" and "name." Moreover, this branch of ז-כ-ר is not used exclusively with reference to past events. It can be used with reference to future events as well.[70] A broader and more accurate summary of this branch of ז-כ-ר is "an active cognitive occupation with a person or situation."[71] I am going to loosely paraphrase this as "having something on your mind."

Looking at the other branch of ז-כ-ר, we have to realize that it may not have originally meant "male." Rather, a widespread view is that it originally meant the male sexual organ.[72] Evidence for this is that in Arabic, their root *dhakar* means both "male" and the male sexual organ. The next reasonable conjecture, given the primary function of the male sexual organ, is that ז-כ-ר was originally a verb that meant

---

68. As seen from its title, it generally limits itself to "theological" words, i.e., words that have religious significance. It is not interested in mundane words.

69. One suggestion that should *not* be remembered is that ז-כ-ר originally meant "to be called to worship" and the word later became a reference to males because only males were competent to worship.

70. See, e.g., Isa. 47:7 and Lam. 1:9. See also Job 40:32, where it also has a broader meaning than "remember."

71. *Theological Dictionary of the Old Testament*, vol. 4, first of the two זכר essays, p. 66.

72. See, e.g., E. Klein, p. 198 and *Theological Dictionary of the Old Testament*, vol. 4, second of the two זכר essays, p. 83.

something like "pierce."[73] (There is a similar sounding Hebrew root in Tanakh, ד-ק-ר, that means "pierce."[74])

Accordingly, the two concepts that we are trying to relate are not "males" and "memory," but "pierce" and "having something on your mind." The connection is that when you have something on your mind, this is because it has pierced itself into your mind. Perhaps this was the way that "having something your mind" was looked at in the ancient Near East. One scholar who cites this suggestion with approval is Ernest Klein.[75]

I am not convinced that this suggestion is correct but I am not ready to rule it out either.

Whether you agree or not, I hope that you remember this penetrating article!

*

Mitchell First is a personal injury attorney and Jewish history scholar. He may forget to tell you but he has a very good memory.

4. חבלי מות Have Encircled Me (Psalms 116:3)

We all know the term חבלי משיח. Although this term is not found in Tanakh and is a later expression, the word חבלי is found in Tanakh. It has the meaning of the anxiousness and/or labor pains that the expectant mother feels approaching birth. So חבלי משיח means the period of anxiousness or pains before the coming of the *mashiach*.

Psalm 116:3 (*Hallel*) refers to חבלי מות (with a *segol* under the ח).What is the meaning of this phrase? If חבלי here meant the same as it did in the term חבלי משיח, this would be a strange metaphor: a combination of a pre-birth image with a death image. Is this what חבלי means here?

In order to solve this problem we have to analyze the root ח-ב-ל. Aside from the meaning we just discussed, it has three other meanings

---

73. As we all should realize, the word נקבה derives from the root נ-ק-ב. Giving the root ז-כ-ר a meaning that was fundamentally sexual would be consistent with this.

74. See, e.g., Num. 25:8 (*va-yidkor et shneihem.*) In Aramaic, the word for memory has the root ד-כ-ר.

75. See E. Klein, p. 198.

in Tanakh: (1) cord, (2) to take a pledge, and (3) to cause damage.[76] (A reason that roots with the Hebrew letter ח often have multiple meanings is that the Hebrew letter ח is a merger of two different earlier ח letters.[77] The distinction between these two earlier letters is preserved in some of the other Semitic languages, such as Akkadian, Ugaritic and Arabic.)

Going back to our original question, the sentence that interests us (Ps. 116:3) reads *afafuni ḥevlei*[78] *mavet, u-metzarei Sheol metzauni....* The word *afafuni* means "encircled," and the last three words mean "the confines of *Sheol* have found me." All of this suggests that *ḥevlei mavet* is utilizing the "cord" meaning of the root ח-ב-ל.

Our phrase *afafunei ḥevlei mavet* is also found at Ps. 18:5. There, in the next verse we find *ḥevlei Sheol sevavuni* (encircled me), and a reference to *mokshei mavet* (snares of death). These phrases also suggest that *ḥevlei mavet* is utilizing the "cord" meaning of the root ח-ב-ל.

One of the main functions of cords in biblical times was to trap and kill animals by tying them to a stake. That is the image that *ḥevlei mavet* of Ps. 18:5 and 116:3 is trying to conjure. The image is one of imminent mortal danger, of one already entwined in the bonds of death.

The Rishonim usually interpret *ḥevlei mavet* (Ps. 18:5 and 116:3) in one of two ways. Some give a "pains of death" meaning, based on the "birth anxiousness/pain" meaning of the root ח-ב-ל.[79] Others point to 1 Sam. 10:5 and 10:10 (*ḥevel neviim*), where the word seems to mean a "group/band" (probably deriving from a "cord/tied together" meaning), and interpret *ḥevlei mavet* to mean a group of enemies who are trying to kill.

But the *Daat Mikra* commentary realizes that all the contextual clues point to *ḥevlei mavet* meaning "cords of death" and that the image is one of the trapped animal. However, the *Daat Mikra* commentary is hesitant to give this as the primary interpretation,

76. This meaning of ח-ב-ל is the origin of the Hebrew word חבל (*chaval*), which M. Jastrow (p. 420) translated as "woe!"
77. See E.Y. Kutscher, *A History of the Hebrew Language* (2d. ed., 1984), pp. 17-18.
78. In the rest of this book, I represented the Hebrew letter ח with "ch." In this article, I made an exception and decided that it was best to use "ḥ."
79. Also, *The Complete ArtScroll Siddur*, p. 637, has "pains of death."

because usually the expression "cords of" is vocalized as *ḥavlei* (with a *pataḥ*), not *hevlei* (with a *segol*) as it is here. (This may also be why the Rishonim avoid the "cords of death" interpretation.) Therefore, the *Daat Mikra* commentary concludes that the literal meaning of *ḥevlei mavet* must be "pains of death," but that the underlying image of "cords of death" and a trapped animal is surely intended as well. (Their main discussion is on verse 18:5.)

My own review of the word חבלי in Tanakh revealed that even with a *segol*, the meaning is sometimes "cords of." See *ḥevlei Sheol sevavuni* at Ps. 18:6 and 2 Sam. 22:6. See also probably *ḥevlei reshaim* at Ps. 119:61. (See the *Daat Mikra* commentary.) So there is no bar to adopting the "cords of death" meaning as the primary meaning of *ḥevlei mavet*. Of course, even if the primary meaning is "cords of death," perhaps the other ח-ב-ל meanings of "anxiousness, pain," or "damage," were intended to be alluded to as well.[80]

Can we connect the "cords" meaning of the root ח-ב-ל with the "anxiousness/pain of pregnancy" meaning? Solomon Mandelkern, in his concordance, suggests that the pregnant woman is writhing and twisting as if she was tied. But this sounds farfetched.

Now I would like to tie up (!) a few loose ends: (1) The root ח-ב-ל means "sailor" at Jonah 1:6 and four times at Ezek. 27. This is surely because tying a rope was an integral part of ancient sailing. (2) Every day shortly after *Barukh She-Amar*, we recite the following phrase from 1 Chron. 16: *lekha eten Eretz Cenaan, ḥevel naḥalatkhem.* Here, חבל has the sense of a surveyed and allotted tract of land. Why? Because it was surveyed and measured with a cord!

(For further reading on the root ח-ב-ל, see the several essays on this root in *Theological Dictionary of the Old Testament*, vol. 4.)

*

Mitchell First is a personal injury attorney and Jewish history scholar. Analyzing this root ח-ב-ל has caused him a lot of anxiousness and at times left him fit to be tied.

---

80. For a classic example of a double meaning in Tanakh, see Gen. 18:23: *ha-af tispeh tzaddik im rasha?* (=will you **also** destroy the righteous with the wicked?). *Af* certainly has a double meaning here, meaning primarily "also" but clearly intending the additional meaning "anger."

5. What is the Origin of the Word חלום (Dream)?

I had always wondered what view of dreams was reflected in Biblical
Hebrew. My initial thought was that ח-ל-ם might have derived from
ח-ל-ה (sick). As I investigated, I learned that the issue is really the
opposite. Two times in Tanakh (at Isa. 38:16 and Job 39:4) there are
words that seem to be from the root ח-ל-ם and that mean something
like "healthy" or "strong." Therefore the issue that scholars discuss
instead is whether there a connection between "dream" and "healthy,
strong"?

One suggestion made is that from an initial "healthy/strong/
youth" meaning evolved the meaning "sexual dreams," and from
this, the meaning evolved into "dreams" in general. This suggestion
is based on the fact that in Arabic there is a root similar to ח-ל-ם that
has the meanings "dream" and "come of age" (=become mature). I
find the above interpretation to be farfetched.

Marcus Jastrow, in his dictionary (p. 471), also seems to relate
the two ח-ל-ם roots "dream" and "healthy, strong." His fundamental
definition of ח-ל-ם is "to sleep well." This too seems farfetched.

I also have to point out that the words with the letters ח-ל-ם at Isa.
38:16 and Job 39:4 may instead derive from the word חיל (= strength),
so perhaps there was no root ח-ל-ם in Hebrew that meant "healthy" or
"strong." (A response to this is that Syriac does have this root with the
meaning "powerful.")

Another scholar claims that we should relate ח-ל-ם, "dream," to
the root א-ל-ם. One of the meanings of this root is "bind." Accordingly,
he suggests that dreams reflect "the entanglement of ideas during
sleep when they are free of the rule of the intellect." But obviously we
would prefer to understand the root ח-ל-ם without having to make a
substitution of א for ח.

Rav S.R. Hirsch is another figure who tries to understand the
ancient biblical view of dreams. In his commentary to Gen. 20:3,
he sets forth an entire biblical philosophy of dreams that he believes
is implicit in the root ח-ל-ם. But there is a problem with his analysis.
There is an unusual word at Job 6:6: חלמות. The Targum understands
this as meaning "the yoke of an egg." Rav Hirsch's theory is based
on assuming that this word חלמות is related to dreams and that its
translation is "yolk of an egg." (Rav Hirsch writes: "Every חלום is a

חלמות, a return of the psyche, the mind, to the embryonic state.") But today most scholars believe that this word חלמות has nothing to do with dreams and also is not the "yoke of an egg." Rather, it is a plant that has liquid flow from it. (Rav Hirsch does use the word "healing" in his discussion. He believes that dreams have an aspect of healing to them, consistent with the other ה-ל-ם meaning.)

Now I would like to offer my own speculative suggestion for the etymology of חלום. The word חלון (window) derives from the root ח-ל-ל/opening. Perhaps חלום comes from this root as well and even the ancients understood that a dream is an "opening" into the mind! (Of course, all such suggestions have to be evaluated in light of the form of the word in all the Semitic languages. Typically, suggestions that sound like they have potential based on Hebrew alone fail when the form of the word in all the Semitic languages is taken into account.)

Theological Dictionary of the Old Testament concludes that the etymology of the root ח-ל-ם/dream "has not been completely explained." This is a tremendous understatement! They should have written "the search for its origin still remains a dream!" But as you can see, I did learn many interesting things along the way.

I also learned that the vowel חולם may be called this because it is a "strong" vowel. (So says Ibn Ezra.)

In my ח-ל-ם/dream research, I also came across a very interesting interpretation of a phrase that we are all familiar with. Psalm 126:1 use the phrase היינו כחלמים to describe the Jewish reaction to the return to Zion with the permission of the Persian kings. We are used to understanding these words to mean "we were like dreamers," i.e., the turn of events was so surprising that it was unreal. Interestingly, the Targum offers a different interpretation: "we were like sick people who were healed." Professors Shmuel and Zeev Safrai, in their classic work *Haggadat Chazal* (1998), p. 232, take the position that this is most likely the correct interpretation! They also mention a text of this verse in the Dead Sea Scrolls that has the following spelling: כחלומים.[81] They claim that this spelling certainly fits their interpretation. But I would not rely on the spelling in the Dead Sea text (very possibly an error) to understand the meaning of our traditional text. Also, the post-talmudic Masoretes certainly knew of the Targum's interpretation. If they thought it was correct, they would have likely

81. See J. A. Sanders, *The Dead Sea Psalms Scroll* (1967), p. 40.

chosen a different vocalization for our word. Finally, since ח-ל-ם with a meaning like "healthy/strong" is rare in Tanakh, only appearing two times, it is unlikely that this alternative (but creative!) interpretation of Ps. 126:1 is the correct one.

As part of my research for this column, I was also investigating another sleep-related root: ל-י-ן (alternatively, ל-ו-ן). We are all familiar with this root. It means to "spend the night" and it is the root of the word מלון =lodging place. I discovered that according to many scholars the root of this word is ל-י-ל, "evening" and that the second *lamed* evolved into a *nun*. For some further examples of *lamed/nun* switches, see Rashi to Isa. 21:15. Such switches are common.

This is also an appropriate time to mention a fascinating work from the early 13th century, authored by one of the French Tosafists, R. Jacob of Marvège. R. Jacob would seek answers from heaven about *halakhah* (by means of seclusion, prayer, and uttering divine names), and his questions were replied to in a dream! R. Jacob then compiled the answers he received and published them as *She'elot U-Teshuvot Min Ha-Shamayim*. I wish there was someone around now who could use this method and finally determine for me the origin of the word חלום!

(For other Rishonim who relied on dreams for *pesak*, see the introduction in Reuven Margaliot's edition of R. Jacob's work [1957, third ed.], and Ephraim Kanarfogel, *Peering Through the Lattices* [2000], pp. 164 and 238.)

I would like to close on a homiletical note. R. Mayer Twersky in "A Glimpse of the Rav," *Tradition* 30:4 (1996), p. 108, observes that the root ח-ל-ם has two meanings: "dream" and "healthy, strong." He then elaborates on this in the context of R. Joseph Soloveitchik and the strong dream that he had for fostering Torah growth in America. R. Twersky writes:

> The ideal dream is not an idle, but rather a guiding vision. It does not represent a flight from reality, but rather a blueprint for improving it. As the righteous Yosef of old, the Rav was not an idle dreamer. He combined vision with conviction [and] prophecy with persistence.

*

Mitchell First is a personal injury attorney and Jewish history scholar. He will not be able to sleep and dream properly until the origin of the word חלום is finally determined.

6. The root חלץ and the Meaning of
החליצנו in the *Birkat Ha-Mazon* of *Shabbat*

In order to understand the word החליצנו in the *Birkat Ha-Mazon* of *Shabbat*, we must first survey the root ח-ל-ץ.

We are all familiar with this root from the procedure of *chalitzah* (=shoe removal). The root also appears many other times in Tanakh. For example, *le-maan yeichaltzun yedidekha* appears at Ps. 60:7 and 108:7, and is incorporated into the prayer *Elokai Netzor. Ki chilatzta nafshi mi-mavet* appears at Ps. 116:8. Also, the root ח-ל-ץ appears many times in Tanakh in a military context, e.g., *chalutzei tzava*.

Most likely, the root initially meant something like "remove" or "pull out." It then expanded into a more general meaning of "rescued," "released," or "saved." This meaning of "rescued, released, saved" is its meaning in the verses in Psalms cited above and in many of its other occurrences in Tanakh.

With regard to ח-ל-ץ in the military context, most scholars see this as evidence of ח-ל-ץ also having a connotation of "strength." But I am going to adopt the alternative scholarly view set forth by the scholar Hayim Tawil (see below). Tawil suggests that the military meaning is merely a reflection of the original "remove/pull out" meaning. The military men were "pulled out" from the main part of the nation. See, for example, Num. 31:3: *heichaltzu mei-itkhem anashim la-tzava*. Thus, we see that the meaning of "remove, pull out, rescue, release, save" can explain almost all of the occurrences of the verb ח-ל-ץ in Tanakh.

The only difficulty is the phrase ועצמתיך יחליץ at Isa. 58:11. We see from the context that this is meant as a blessing. (This phrase in Isaiah is the source for the monthly request for *chillutz atzamot* in *Birkat Ha-Chodesh*.[82]) What could the blessing be in the "pulling out"

---

82. This phrase likely made its way into *Birkat Ha-Chodesh* because the Talmud cites the phrase ועצמתיך יחליץ as a very important blessing. See *Yevamot* 102b and *Bava Batra* 9b.

or "removing" of ones bones? Most scholars see this verse as further evidence of a "strength" meaning in the root ח-ל-ץ. They think the meaning here is "he will strengthen your bones."[83]

But the *Daat Mikra* commentary to Isaiah, in a footnote, suggests an alternative approach to verse 58:11. The meaning can be that one's bones will be made "loose/released." This is a blessing. A symptom of bad health is bones being stuck to one's flesh or stuck together. See Ps. 102:6 and Job 19:20. This happens, for example, to one who is starved due to a famine.

There is also a detailed article, authored by the scholar Hayim Tawil with his son Arye, that interprets verse 58:11 like the above *Daat Mikra* footnote and suggests that the verse was an allusion by Isaiah to chiropractic practice in biblical times![84] (Arye Tawil is a chiropractor. Perhaps the unstated purpose of the Tawil article was to remind people monthly, during *Birkat Ha-Chodesh*, that they should visit their chiropractor!) Based on the *Daat Mikra* footnote and the Tawil article, it is a very reasonable approach to conclude that the root ח-ל-ץ does not mean "strengthen" at Isa. 58:11 or anywhere in Tanakh. (But admittedly most scholars prior to Tawil did not adopt this approach.)

Let us now return to our original question: the meaning of *hachalitzeinu* in the *Birkat Ha-Mazon* of *Shabbat*. (All can agree that the *ha-* at the beginning means: "cause us to.") R. Barukh Epstein takes the position that *hachalitzeinu* means "cause us to be strong," so that we can keep the commandments. See his *Barukh She-Amar*, p. 212. He bases his view on the supposed "strength" meaning at Isa. 58:11. Alternatively, *Leviticus Rabbah* 34:15 takes the position that *hachalitzeinu* in the *Birkat Ha-Mazon* of *Shabbat* means "cause us to rest" (giving it a meaning like: נ-ו-ח). But this source is a puzzling one. Its evidence for the "cause us to rest" meaning seems to be only that

---

83. The meaning of *ve-atzmotekha yachalitz* at Isa. 58:11 is addressed in the Talmud, at *Yevamot* 102b. The Talmud offers the interpretation זרוזי of the bones. The precise meaning of this statement is unclear. The *ArtScroll Talmud* translates זרוזי as "strengthening" and "readying or strengthening." M. Jastrow (p. 412) had translated it as "quickening."

How does *The Complete ArtScroll Siddur* translate *chillutz atzamot* in *Birkat Ha-Chodesh*? They use the vague term "physical health." See p. 453.

84. "Was Chiropractic Known In Biblical Times?," *Nachalah*, vol. 2 (2000), pp. 1-14.

hachalitzeinu is recited on *Shabbat*. Moreover, from Mishnah *Eruvin* 3:9 we see that *hachalitzeinu* was seen as a request that could be made on Rosh Hashanah and Rosh Chodesh. This implies that there is no connection between *hachalitzeinu* and resting; the latter is not a main theme of Rosh Hashanah or Rosh Chodesh.

It seems to me that the *hachalitzeinu* that we recite in the *Birkat Ha-Mazon* of *Shabbat* (and that was included in Mishnah *Eruvin* 3:9 in the Rosh Hashanah and Rosh Chodesh contexts) means something like: "cause us to be released [from our troubles]." Supporting this is the later phrase in the same paragraph: *she-lo tehei tzarah ve-yagon va-anachah be-yom menuchateinu.*

The *Complete ArtScroll Siddur* (p. 189) makes the poor choice of translating *hachalitzeinu* as "give us rest," following the strange interpretation found at *Leviticus Rabbah* 34:15. But the commentary points out that the word *hachalitzeinu* has multiple connotations and gives examples such as "save us [from troubles that have engulfed us]." Fortunately, ArtScroll's *Tehillim* volume (in their Tanakh series), commentary to Ps. 60:7, mentions *hachalitzeinu* of the *Birkat Ha-Mazon* of *Shabbat* and translates it as "release us" from our weekday worries, just as I am advocating.[85]

*

Mitchell First is a personal injury attorney and Jewish history scholar. He has not yet started a monthly chiropractic regimen.

---

85. Admittedly I have not dealt with the noun *challatzayim*. This noun appears 10 times in Tanakh (in various forms) with the meaning "loins." H. Tawil does not deal with it either. I suspect that Tawil believes that ח-ל-ץ was not the original root for "loins" in Semitic languages. For example, in Aramaic the word for loins has the root ח-ר-ץ. The corresponding Akkadian, Arabic, and Syriac words also do not exactly match the root ח-ל-ץ. See *Theological Dictionary of the Old Testament*, vol. 4, p. 441.

If one wants to give an explanation for חלצים based on the verb ח-ל-ץ, the explanation may be that the loins were viewed as the source of the power to produce offspring. See, for example, Gen. 35:11: *u-melakhim mei-chalatzekha yeitzeiu.* (See similarly 1 Kings 8:19 and 2 Chron. 6:9.) Thus, the loins were viewed as the area in the body where the male seed was stored and then "sent out." See the commentary of S.D. Luzzatto to Gen. 35:11.

7. What is the Origin of the Words חתן and כלה?

The biblical word *chatan* means both "son-in–law" and "bridegroom." The simplest assumption is that the "son-in–law" meaning came first. There is also a related word, *choten*, which means "father- in-law." It has been suggested that this word means "one who has a son-in law."[86]

There is much speculation as to where the word *chatan* came from. Possibly *chatan* originally meant something like "connected." Ernest Klein mentions this as a possibility based on the Arabic word *chatana* which means "joined, connected."[87]

An alternative theory points to an Arabic word *chatana* which means "circumcised."[88] This suggests that there may have been an ancient custom to circumcise young men before their marriage! (An original "circumcision" meaning for ח-ת-ן might also shed some light on the strange story at Ex. 4:24-26, where Tzipporah circumcises her infant and twice makes a comment about *chatan damim*.)

What about the reflexive form התחתן? I would like to suggest that this did not originally mean "make oneself into a son-in-law" or "make oneself into a groom." Rather, if we take the (admittedly speculative) approach that ח-ת-ן originally meant something like "connect," then התחתן could have meant "to put oneself in a relationship of connection."

The reason I like this suggestion is that it helps explain some difficulties. At 1 Kings 3:1, the text records: ***va-yitchatten Shelomoh et Paroh** melekh mitzrayim, va-yikkach et bat Paroh....*" Let us look at those first four words. At first glance, they cry out for textual emendation! To obviate the male-male difficulty, a standard Jewish translation translated: "Solomon became allied to Pharaoh king of Egypt by marriage." But perhaps we can translate more simply: "Solomon put himself in a relationship of connection with Pharaoh." An even better support is 2 Chron. 18:1, which uses *va-yitchatten* in the context of the males Yehoshafat and Achav, without a subsequent immediate reference to a marriage. The verse reads: *va-yehi le-Yehoshafat osher ve-khavod la-rov, **va-yitchatten le-Achav**.*

---

86. *Theological Dictionary of the Old Testament*, vol. 5, p. 274.
87. E. Klein, p. 237.
88. *Theological Dictionary of the Old Testament*, vol. 5, p. 273. E. Klein, p. 237.

(Admittedly, there was a marriage between the son of Yehoshafat and the daughter of Achav, but that is not mentioned until 2 Chron. 21:6.)

With regard to the word *chatunah*, it appears one time in Tanakh, at Song of Songs 3:11 (*be-yom chatunato*). A *chatunah* is called this because it is the day you become a son-in-law.

An interesting issue related to the word *chatan* is its use on Simchat Torah: *Chatan Torah, Chatan Bereshit,* and *Chatan Maftir.* A scholar who did extensive work on the history of Simchat Torah was Abraham Yaari. See his *Toldot Chag Simchat Torah* (1964). There he asked why the word *chatan* is used in connection with these reading rituals.[89] (The earliest source we have that uses the term *chatan* in the context of these rituals is *Machzor Vitry*, 12th century France, which uses it in connection with the one who reads the last eight verses of the Torah and with the one who reads from *Bereshit.* Similar is *Siddur Rashi*, sec. 308.) Yaari mentions a few explanations that do not satisfy him, and then theorizes that the word was probably originally *chatam.* *Chatam* means "completion." This would be an apt description of the one who completed the reading of the Torah. The term then spread to the other readers as well.

Yaari even finds some sources, the earliest from the 16th century, that use the phrase *chatam Torah* to describe the Simchat Torah readers. He argues that these sources reflect a preservation of the original term (as opposed to being a later evolution from *chatan*). He suggests that *chatam* evolved into *chatan*, since the completion of the reading of the Torah was a *simchah yeteirah*, just like the *simchah* of a *chatan* and *kallah*.

Daniel Sperber, in his *Minhagei Yisrael*, vol. 1 (1990), pp. 135-37, discussed this issue further. Sperber pointed out that there are many examples in the talmudic period and thereafter of words with a final *mem* that came to be spelled with a final *nun* in Palestine. Some examples are the words אדם (man) which evolved in Palestine into אדן, and כרם (vineyard) which evolved in Palestine into כרן. Sperber suggests that similarly an alternative חתן spelling arose for חתם. This חתן word was then misunderstood as "bridegroom," instead of what it really was: a variant spelling of חתם ("completion").

---

89. See pp. 65-67.

Moving now to the word *kallah*, we are also unsure as to its origin. As in the case of *chatan*, we are faced with two meanings, "bride" and "daughter-in-law," and we are not sure which was primary.

Some point to an Akkadian verb K-L-L that meant "to conceal the face or head." This could have developed into a word for "bride," due to the bridal veil. Others point to an Akkadian verb K-L-L that meant "to crown." (There was also a similar sounding noun in Akkadian for "crown.") Perhaps Hebrew long ago had such verbs. (The Akkadian verb and noun for "crown" seems to be the source for the post-Biblical Hebrew word for crown: *kelil*, and its Aramaic equivalent: *kelila*.) Marcus Jastrow is one source that believes that *kallah* =bride derives from "crown."[90]

Alternatively, some speculate that *kallah* meant "bride" based on the Hebrew root כ-ל-ה, which meant something like "closed." The *kallah* is one who is closed off to the world, except to her husband.

My favorite approach is the one taken by Rav S.R. Hirsch. He theorizes that *kallah* comes from the Hebrew root כ-ל-ה: "complete." (We all know this root from the beginning of *kiddush* on Friday night: ויכלו.) The bride/daughter-in-law is the one who completes the family of her father- in-law," i.e., the family unit of father, mother, and son is not complete until the arrival of this new member. See the commentary of Rav Hirsch to Gen. 11:31 and 19:12. (One can also suggest that the bride is what the husband needs to become "complete." But this does not sound like a plain sense interpretation.)

I am surprised that this interpretation of Rav Hirsch is not mentioned in the entry for כלה in *Theological Dictionary of the Old Testament*. Surely some scholar must have suggested such an interpretation. But the author of the entry does make the observation that he does not think that the word *kallah* derived from any verbal root. This would explain the omission.

The word כלולתיך at Jer. 2:2 is also of interest. One can speculate from this word that the root of *kallah* may be כ-ל-ל. But based on a review of the parallels to the word *kallah* in the other Semitic languages, this seems unlikely.

*

Mitchell First is a personal injury attorney and Jewish history scholar. He recalls the words of a wise comedian: "Marry the right woman,

---

90. M. Jastrow, p. 639.

you are **complete**. Marry the wrong one, you are **finished**. And if the right one catches you with the wrong one, you are **completely finished**!"

8. What is the Meaning of the Word יובל?

At Lev. 25:10, we are told: "[This year] shall be a *yovel* to you. You will each return to your land…." What is the meaning of this word *yovel*?

Rashi notes that at Lev. 25:9 there is a statement that the shofar is blown to proclaim the *yovel* year. He concludes that the year is called *yovel* based on this shofar blowing, i.e., in Rashi's view, *yovel* means something like "year when the ram's horn is blown."

What is the basis for Rashi's explanation? The word *yovel* and words based on it (e.g., *ha-hovel, ba-yovel*, etc.) appear 27 times in Tanakh. Of course, 21 of these times the reference is to the *yovel* year without any explanation. But in Joshua 6, we have four references to *shofarot yovlim* or *shofarot ha-yovlim*. There, it is clear that the word means "ram." It is also clear that the word means "ram" at Josh. 6:5 and Ex. 19:13.

So there is a basis for Rashi's explanation. But Ramban asks the obvious question on Rashi. Based on *mishnayot* in the third chapter of *Rosh Hashanah*, we see that the shofar blown to declare the year of the *yovel* does not have to be specifically from a ram. The preferred animal for this shofar blowing is a *yael* (= goat). So why would the year be called "the year when the ram is blown"? Moreover, the *yovel* year would much more likely have a name related to its fundamental aspect as a year of *deror* (=freedom).

Therefore, Ramban takes a completely different approach to the word *yovel*. He cites verses such as *yoviluha raglekha mei-rachok la-gur*, "whose legs carried her off from afar to live," (Isa. 23:7) and *yuval shai*, "a gift is brought" (Isa. 18:7), and he shows that the root י-ב-ל often has something to do with an object being brought. He believes that הבאה (= being brought) is the fundamental meaning of the root י-ב-ל. He concludes that this better accords with the plain sense of: "[This year] shall be a *yovel* to you. You will each return to your land…" (Lev. 25:10).

Rav S.R. Hirsch agrees with Ramban. At Lev. 25:10, he translates
yovel as "homebringer"![91]

Modern scholars are largely in agreement with Ramban and
Rav Hirsch about this root. They view י-ב-ל as fundamentally a word
meaning "movement" or "flow," but they agree that it also has the
related meaning of "being brought."

Other notable verses with the root י-ב-ל are *mi yovileini ir matzor*,
"who will lead me into the fortified city?" (Ps. 60:11), *ka-seh la-tevach
yuval*, "as a lamb is led to the slaughter" (Isa. 53:7), and *u-ve-shalom
tuvalun*, "and you will be led out with peace" (Isa. 55:12). Also, the
root י-ב-ל is connected to water in several verses. See, e.g., Isa. 30:25
and 44:4, Jer. 17:8 and Ps. 1:3.

I am explaining all of this because it helps us better understand
the word מבול. This word is commonly translated as "flood" (see,
e.g., ArtScroll's Stone *Chumash* and *The Pentateuch and Haftorahs* of
Dr. J.H. Hertz) But in order to truly understand the meaning of a
word, we must determine its three-letter root. There is no root מ-ב-ל
in Biblical Hebrew, so we have to look harder for the root. Also, an
initial *mem* is usually not part of the root; it is what is added at the
beginning to turn the word into a noun. So we have to figure out what
third root letter was there originally and dropped out.

Some see the root as ב-ל-ל, with the meaning: "mixture/
intermingling/confusion." (See, e.g., Ibn Ezra.) Others believe that
the root is נ-ב-ל, which has the meaning of "fall, decay, destroy."
(See, e.g., Ibn Ezra, Seforno, Radak and S.D. Luzzatto.) But now we
realize there is a third possibility: the root is י-ב-ל, with its meaning
of "movement, flow." This is probably the correct approach. It is the
approach adopted in the *Daat Mikra* commentary to Gen. 6:17. It is
also adopted by Moses David Cassuto in his commentary to Genesis,
and by many other modern scholars.[92] I discussed this all at length in
an Oct. 11, 2014, article at seforim.blogspot.com ("The Root of the
Word *Mabul*: A Flood of Possibilities."). I have included this article as
an appendix to this book.

Interestingly, Rashi conducts practically the same analysis of the
word מבול that I did. In his explanation of the word at Gen. 6:17, he

---

91. I am referring to the edition produced by Rav Hirsch's grandson Isaac
Levy (2nd edition). Admittedly, this is a translation from the original German.
92. See, e.g., H. Tawil, p. 196.

writes: "*she-**billah** et ha-kol, she-**bilbel** et ha-kol, she-**hovil** et ha-kol min ha-gavohah la-namukh*...." בלה means "destroy and wear down," similar to נבל. בלבל means "mix," the equivalent of בלל. הוביל means "move" and is from the root יבל. But Rashi seems to believe that the word מבול was purposely chosen to convey all three connotations.

Going back to our original word *yovel*, is there a connection between the "movement/bringing" meaning and the "ram" meaning? Rav S.R. Hirsch (on Lev. 25:10) makes the following suggestion: "[T]he ram is the leader of the flock, the one who 'brings' them to their pasturage... who goes in front, and the flock following him, 'brings them home.'" This approach is also adopted by Ernest Klein.[93] I am mentioning this approach because it is interesting but I am not convinced.

What about the word *yevulah* in the second paragraph of the *Shema*? It turns out that

י-ב-ל also has the related meaning of "carry," e.g., *yovilu shai*, "carry presents" (Ps. 76:12). In the *Shema*, the word *yevulah* is used to mean the produce of the land. Most likely, it has this meaning because produce must be carried in or brought in from the land. (See Ramban to Lev. 25:10.) Alternatively, *yevulah* means "produce" because produce "flows" from the land.

Finally, why is the *yovel* year called the "jubilee" year in English? The first English translation of the Bible, the King James Version published in 1611, used the word "jubile." (This was the spelling of our word "jubilee" at that time.) But why did they use this celebratory word? The answer is that those who were responsible for this English translation should have just transliterated from the Latin and wrote "jobel." Instead, they got a bit creative and used the word "jubile" which they knew had a positive, celebratory meaning. In this way, they created a connection between the fiftieth year and a jubilant celebration, even though such a connection is absent from Tanakh. (I admit that the fiftieth year is a year of *deror* [=freedom]. But this is not the same as a year of joy.)

*

Mitchell First is a personal injury attorney and Jewish history scholar. He is jubilantly looking forward to the next jubilee year, but unfortunately, we seem to have lost the *yovel* count long ago.

93. E. Klein, p. 256.

9. What is the Meaning of the Word כסף?

At Genesis 31:30, Lavan says to Jacob: *nikhsof nikhsafta le-veit avikha*, "you **longed for** your father's house." The two words *nikhsof* and *nikhsafta* are both from the root כסף. כסף is the word for "money."

What is going on here? Is the Hebrew language, the language of the Jewish people, a language in which "money" and "longing for" have the same root? Are the anti-Semitic stereotypes about Jews true?

Fortunately, while we do long for money to pay yeshiva tuition, the etymology of the word כסף is not going to provide any evidence for the anti-Semites. Most likely, the verb כ-ס-ף originally meant "to become pale with longing." The noun כסף did not originally mean "money." Rather, it meant "silver." Why did silver get this name? Because of its whiteness, it became known as the "pale metal." So the common aspect between "silver" and "longing" is the "paleness" aspect, and not that we long for silver.

In Aramaic, we can still find the root כסף meaning "to grow pale."[94] It also has the related meanings in Aramaic of "to be frightened" and "to be put to shame." In Tanakh, we can find the "shame" meaning one time, at Zephaniah 2:1. (In the rest of Tanakh, the root means either "silver/money" or "long for.")

For the above explanation relaheting "silver" and "longing," I followed Ernest Klein.[95] Klein's work, *A Comprehensive Etymological Dictionary of the Hebrew Language for Readers of English* (1987), was one of the most useful books that I ever purchased! It answers almost all of the Hebrew word questions that you (and your children) will ever have! It is not limited to the biblical period like a typical concordance. Rather, it covers the Hebrew language in all its eras.

Rav S. R. Hirsch takes a different approach to כסף. In his commentary to Gen. 31:30, he writes that the verb כסף is "to long

---

94. See, e.g., M. Jastrow, p. 655.
95. E. Klein, p. 282. The explanation was suggested long before this in *Brown-Driver-Briggs*. *Theological Dictionary of the Old Testament* and Koehler-Baumgartner both mention the view that the noun כסף originally meant "white metal." But they both also mention an alternative view that the noun כסף comes from a verb in Akkadian and Arabic that means "break off." The basis for this view is that originally a piece of silver was probably broken off from a larger bar to make a purchase.

for something." He then suggests that the meaning of "silver, money" arose because כסף is that with which one attains ones longings.

There is a widely used etymology book, *Etymological Dictionary of Biblical Hebrew,* by Matityahu Clark (1999). This work is work based on the commentaries of Rav Hirsch, but sometimes goes beyond them. This work implies that "silver" is called כסף because it is a "desired asset." But why should only silver be a "desired asset," why not gold? And why are not all precious metals called כסף? Therefore, the best approach is the one taken by Klein.

The book by Clark, while very useful, must be used with much caution. It includes both reasonable definitions and very speculative ones without distinguishing between them. The innocent reader has no idea which definitions have solid support and which are based on farfetched speculation.

*

Mitchell First is a personal injury attorney and Jewish history scholar. Since he is a personal injury attorney, people assume that he loves money. As a Jewish history scholar, his face is often pale from exhaustion after reading texts in small print.

10. ל-ח-ם and מלחמה : Is There A Connection?

This question has been bothering me (and hopefully you as well) since childhood. Is the noun לחם (bread) related to the verb ל-ח-ם (fight) and its related noun מלחמה? Undisputedly, all these words have the root ל-ח-ם.

English includes the term "food fight." Was Biblical Hebrew modeled on some ancient kindergarten where children fought over morsels of bread?

Interestingly, the English word "companionship" is derived from an original meaning of "sharing of bread." Therefore, in English, "bread" ends up with a friendly connotation, not a military one!

Going back to our original question, is it possible that bread is the fundamental meaning of the letters ל-ח-ם, and the other meanings arose because wars in ancient times were primarily fought over bread, or more broadly, over economic/sustenance issues? This is what I thought for decades, until I began to research this topic.[96]

It turns out that Rav S.R. Hirsch took an approach opposite to my initial assumption. In his view, the verb ל-ח-ם meant "to struggle," and bread is called by this term to reflect that man has to struggle for his daily bread. As Rav Hirsch observes, a man first has to struggle to wrest his daily bread from nature, and then has to struggle with his fellow man to keep it! See his commentary to "with the sweat of your countenance, you shall eat bread" (Gen. 3:19).

After doing further research, I discovered a very interesting suggestion that is adopted by some scholars.[97] Looking at the verb, it seems that the original meaning of the verb ל-ח-ם was "to be pressed together" and the "fight" meaning is just an expansion of this original meaning. Looking at the noun, it seems that the original meaning of the Semitic noun ל-ח-ם was not "bread," but "solid food." For example, in Arabic, their word for *lechem* (*lahm*) means "meat."[98] All the meanings of ל-ח-ם can be united if we take one further step and view "solid food" as something that is "pressed together."[99]

Of course, one does not have to accept this approach. (Like bread and meat, it needs time to be digested!) In fact, it seems that most scholars today do not accept it and remain unwilling to connect ל-ח-ם (solid food) and ל-ח-ם/מלחמה (pressed together, fight, war).[100] The

---

96. I also saw a source that suggested that מלחמה originated with the meaning: "a group raid for spoils." Radak (*Sefer Ha-Shorashim*) suggested that מלחמה reflects "*ma'akhal ha-cherev*," i.e., the sword eating its meal (=destroying all). Also, a friend suggested a humorous answer to me: part of the process of making the bread was "beating" the dough!

97. See *Theological Dictionary of the Old Testament*, vol. 7, pp. 521-22.

98. In the South Arabic dialect of a certain island, *lehem* means "fish."

99. The author of the *Theological Dictionary of the Old Testament* entry explains further: "Flesh and bread share the characteristic of being a soft, adhesive mass."

100. For example, a connection is not suggested in either Koehler-Baumgartner, E. Klein, or *Brown-Driver-Briggs*.

In my article on חבלי מות, I mentioned that roots with the Hebrew letter ח often have multiple meanings because the Hebrew letter ח is a merger of two different earlier ח letters. Arabic is one of the languages in which the two different earlier ח letters are preserved. In our case (*lahm*), the relevant Arabic cognates are using the same ח letter.

idea that "solid food" was viewed fundamentally as something that was "pressed together" is a bit of a stretch.

Note also that the noun בשׂר (meat) does not seem to have any connection with the verb בשׂר ("herald, announce"). (Although Rav Hirsch makes an attempt to connect them: your body is the herald of your spirit to the world. See his commentary to Gen. 2:21.)

In sum, where there is a common three-letter root, there is usually, or at least often, a connection. But there is not always a connection, so we do not have to postulate connections if the roots seem unconnected. But admittedly Rav Hirsch would disagree and believes that there must always be a connection.

*

Mitchell First is an attorney and Jewish history scholar. He would much rather eat bread than be pressed together or fight a war. He is getting hungry for some shwarma now. I wonder why.

11. What is Origin of the Word מדבר (Desert)?

It is very easy to intuit that the root of the word מדבר is ד-ב-ר, since a typical way that Hebrew forms its nouns is by taking a three-letter verbal root and adding an initial *mem*. But our next question is much harder: what meaning of ד-ב-ר generated the noun *midbar*?

Of course, we all know the verb ד-ב-ר, "to speak." Could a *midbar* fundamentally be a place where people went to speak (to themselves!)? Creative but unlikely. We also know the letters ד-ב-ר as one of the ten plagues. Could a *midbar* fundamentally be a place of plague, disease, and pestilence? Again, creative but unlikely.

I am going to present what I think is the most reasonable explanation. (But admittedly not everyone agrees with this.) In Akkadian and Arabic, there is a root ד-ב-ר which means something like "to push from behind and drive away."[101] With this in mind, when you look through Tanakh, you see that this was probably the meaning of the root at *va-tedabber et kol zera ha-mamlakhah*, "she drove away

---

101. See, e.g., H. Tawil, p. 71, and E. Klein, p. 113.

all the royal seed" (2 Chron. 22:10),[102] and perhaps elsewhere as well.[103] (Based on this meaning, a later meaning also developed: to subdue/ rule over: *va-yadber ammim tachtai* (Ps. 18:48) and *yadber ammim tachteinu* (Ps. 47:4).)

When a shepherd was out with his animals, what he was doing was pushing them from behind and leading them in this manner. The explanation I am now offering is that a *midbar* was called this because it was fundamentally a place where one went to push and lead one's animals.[104]

Radak, in his *Sefer Ha-Shorashim* (root ד-ב-ר), also understands *midbar* as a place where one leads animals. Although he does not mention anything about the Arabic root ד-ב-ר (and Akkadian had not yet been discovered!), he does explain (citing Targum Onkelos) that in Aramaic, the root ד-ב-ר is the equivalent of the Hebrew נ-ה-ג (lead). He concludes that a *midbar* is called this because this is where a shepherd is *noheg* his animals.

Even though we are used to thinking of a *midbar* as a dry area, it could have been any wide and open area that was used for pasturing animals. As S.D. Luzzatto writes in his commentary to Ex. 3:1: "Perhaps because the term *midbar* was used for places of pasturage with no houses or trees but only wide, open space, the term was retained for dry desert places which are likewise wide and open without houses or trees."[105]

We now have a reasonable explanation of the origin of the word *midbar*. We also see that the letters ד-ב-ר have at least three entirely different meanings in Tanakh: speaking, pushing, and pestilence. This is a strong proof against those who claim that words composed of the same three letters in Hebrew must **always** be connected. There

102. There is a parallel to the above verse at 2 Kings 11:1. There, a different verb is used, א-ב-ד (destroy).
103. See Isa.32:7 and Ps. 127:5. On the latter, see the *Daat Mikra* commentary, n. 7.
104. One scholar who adopts this approach to the word *midbar* is E. Klein, at p. 317.This approach is also adopted by Koehler-Baumgartner, at pp. 209-210 and 546-547, but without sufficient explanation. Biblical verses that refer to צאן being led in the *midbar* are Ex. 3:1 and Ps. 78:52.
105. Translation from the edition of D. Klein.

is usually, or at least often, a connection, but there is not always a connection. (It was suggested to me that when one speaks, one is pushing the words out of one's mouth, but this is farfetched.)

Finally, an interesting issue is whether the word for "bee," *devorah*, has some relation to the "speak" meaning of ד-ב-ר. I have seen it suggested that the root ד-ב-ר originally meant "to buzz or to hum" before it meant "to speak," and that this is the relation to the word *devorah*![106]

*

Mitchell First is a personal injury attorney and Jewish history scholar. His favorite meaning of ד-ב-ר is speaking. This is much better than pushing animals or being affected by a plague.

12. What is the Meaning of the Word משתאה (Genesis 24:21)?

Genesis 24:21 begins: והאיש משתאה לה .... The איש is Eliezer and the לה refers to Rebecca. So what exactly is Eliezer doing? We will learn a lot about Biblical Hebrew by attempting to decipher this word.

The first step is to realize that משתאה should be understood as if it was written מת -. מתשאה is a standard *hitpael* prefix, but sometimes the ת of the *hitapel* and the first letter of the root have ended up in switched positions (for reasons related to ease of pronunciation). This is what happened here. Therefore, we have to reverse the order of the second and third letters to properly decipher the word, and pretend we are looking at the word מתשאה.

As to the meaning of the *hitpael* stem, many of us are taught in our youth that the *hitpael* stem means "to do something to yourself." But it has other functions as well.[107] For example, sometimes it means "to do something continually." (An example is התהלך means "to walk continually.")

We have now gotten over the preliminaries in our attempt to decipher מתשאה. We see that our word has the root ש-א-ה and is in the *hitpael* stem, and that the *hitpael* can serve a few different functions.

---

106. See, e.g., E. Klein, p. 113, and Koehler-Baumgartner, p. 210.
107. I have discussed the different functions of the *hitpael* in the article in the appendix: "The Meaning of התפלל."

Do you know this root שׁ-א-ה? Of course you do, since you know the word שׁואה. This word was chosen to describe the destruction of European Jewry because the root שׁ-א-ה appears in Tanakh with meanings like "crash into ruins" and "desolation." (Probably it originally meant "loud noise" (see Zech. 4:7). Then it encompassed the meaning "crash into ruins" because of the associated loud noise. Finally, it developed into "desolation," since this is the fate of ruins.)

The reason we are not so familiar with the biblical root שׁ-א-ה is that all the occurrences of this root are found in *Nakh*. The only time this root appears in the *Chumash* is here at Gen. 24:21, and it is hard to fit the "loud noise," "crash into ruins," or "desolation" meanings into this verse.

R. Saadiah Gaon viewed the root of מִשְׁתָּאֵה as שׁ-ת-ה. The phrase would then mean that Eliezer was waiting for or accepting a drink from Rebecca. But this approach does not account for the *aleph*, so most authorities reject his approach. Rather, as I stated above, the widespread understanding of the structure of the word is that the word is in the *hitpael* and that the root of the word is שׁ-א-ה.

Rashi provides a lengthy attempt at explaining our word. He takes the position that the root of the word is שׁ-א-ה with its meaning of "ruin, desolation." How does that fit into the context? Rashi notes that there is another root שׁ-מ-ם which meant "ruin, desolation," and that root developed a secondary meaning of "confused, silent and deep in thought" (e.g., Job 18:20, Jer. 2:12, and Dan. 4:16). Rashi believes that the same thing happened in the case of our root שׁ-א-ה.

"Ruin and desolation" evolving into "confusion/silence/ astonishment"? Initially, I disliked this approach. But then my dentist Richard Gertler reminded me of the modern English expression: "blew my brains away." So we see that in English a term of "ruin" can be a metaphor for "astonishment." (Due to their familiarity with teeth and tongues, my experience is that dentists have very good linguistic abilities!)

Rashi's view is followed by many, such as Rashbam and Ibn Ezra. Rav S.R. Hirsch writes something similar. He takes the position that the fundamental meaning of שׁ-א-ה is "bleak, dull, desert," and from that we get "unclearness of mind."

If you are not satisfied with Rashi's approach (and I am not completely satisfied), the best alternative is to understand the *aleph* of

מׁשׁתאה as if it were an *ayin*. The biblical root שׁ-ע-ה means "to look" (see, e.g., Gen. 4:4 and Isa. 31:1). Many scholars advocate this approach.[108] This approach is also mentioned in the *Daat Mikra*.

Although we do not ordinarily want to understand words by postulating switches of *aleph* and *ayin*, such switches are not uncommon. For example, twelve times in Tanakh the root ג-א-ל appears with a negative meaning and clearly does not mean "redemption." Biblical Hebrew has a root ג-ע-ל that means "loathe, reject." A widespread view today understands all those twelve ג-א-ל occurrences with a negative meaning as if they were spelled ג-ע-ל. For some examples, see Malachi 1:7 and 1:12. *Aleph* and *ayin* must have originally been very close in pronunciation. Also, spelling in ancient times was probably much more fluid than it is today.

If we understand the *aleph* of מׁשׁתאה as if it were an *ayin*, and if we adopt the meaning "look," we have a simple understanding of the role of the *hitpael* as well. Then מׁשׁתאה would mean "continually looking" towards her. This fits the context well.

We all know that שׁ-ע-ה is also a measure of time. But this meaning is only found in the Aramaic portions of the book of Daniel. It is nowhere else in Tanakh. It originally meant "a short period." Most likely it has no relation to שׁ-ע-ה =look. Solomon Mandelkern, in his concordance, attempts to connect the two שׁ-ע-ה meanings, but most scholars do not accept his suggestion.

Earlier, we mentioned the root שׁ-ת-ה, "to drink." The root שׁ-ק-ה is another verb that means "to drink." But there is an important difference. When you yourself drink, the root is שׁ-ת-ה. But when you give a drink to someone else, the root is שׁ-ק-ה. Why should there be this difference? There are other examples of verbs which have similar meanings with *tav* and *kof*. An example is פ-ת-ה and פ-ק-ה. Both mean "open." One day, when I understand this exchange of ת and ק better, I will write about it. I even recall that my dentist Dr. Gertler had some insight on this one as well!

*

Mitchell First is a personal injury attorney and Jewish history scholar. He has to stop writing now. He is having too many ruinous and astonishing thoughts and is also getting thirsty.

---

108. See, e.g., E. Klein, p. 633.

13. What is the Origin of the Word נביא?

In English, the word נביא is usually translated as "prophet." "Prophet" has a connotation of someone who is able to predict the future.[109] But what is the root of the Hebrew word? Is ability to predict the future implied in the Hebrew?[110]

Rashi (on Ex. 7:1) connects נביא with the word ניב, relying on the phrase *niv sefataim* (Isa. 57:19). The word ניב in this verse in Isaiah means something like the "outgrowth of" or "something that flows from." From his further comments, we see that Rashi views a נביא as one who expresses words of reproach to the people. Rashbam (on Gen. 20:7) also connects נביא with ניב. He adds that a נביא is someone who is *ragil* with God and speaks God's words, and that God loves his words and answers his prayers.

But Ibn Ezra argues strongly that the root is נ-ב-א. Despite the eminence of Rashi and Rashbam, it is hard to disagree with Ibn Ezra here. The *alephs* are always present in the word, so it seems very likely that the *aleph* is a root letter here. With regard to the meaning of the root נ-ב-א, Ibn Ezra tries to infer its meaning from the context at Amos 3:7. There it is stated that God will not do anything unless he is *galah sodo el avadav ha-neviim*. Therefore, Ibn Ezra concludes, a נביא is fundamentally someone to whom God reveals his secrets.

Rav S. R. Hirsch (on Gen. 20:7) also accepts נ-ב-א as the root. He tries to deduce its meaning by extrapolating from a similar root: נ-ב-ע. The latter means "to flow" or "to be the source of." Rav Hirsch concludes that a נביא is not one who foretells the future. Rather, he is "the source from which the word of God issues, the organ through which the spirit of God speaks to men."

Most scholars today view the root as נ-ב-א. But based on Akkadian and several other Semitic languages, they view the fundamental

---

109. The English word is derived from a similar sounding Greek word. Did the Greek word have the connotation of "foreteller"? According to the *Encyclopaedia Judaica* (13:1153), the Greek word meant merely "one who speaks on behalf of."

110. I admit that I had always erroneously thought this, since the letters בא were part of the word.

meaning of this root as "to call." Then the issue becomes whether the נביא was "one who was calling out to the people," or "one who was called (=appointed)." According to *Theological Dictionary of the Old Testament*,[111] the earlier scholars preferred the former view, but now the prevailing view is the latter.[112]

In most instances in Tanakh, a נביא is someone who was called by God to communicate a Divine message to the people. One place where this is not the case is at Ex. 7:1. Here God tells Moses that "Aaron your brother will be נביאך." We see from here that not just God can have a נביא. A human can have one as well.

Scholars also suggest that, most likely, the Hebrew verb נ-ב-א was derived from the noun.[113] (Usually, the process is the reverse.) The meaning of the verb in Hebrew was "to act as a נביא."

We see from all the above that it is obviously a mistake to rely on English translations. We must ignore the common translation "prophet" and whatever that may imply. We first have to determine the Hebrew root. But sometimes, like here, that is only half the battle. Figuring out what the root means can be another battle. For example, here Ibn Ezra tried to learn it from a context (Amos 3:7). Rav Hirsch tried to learn it from a different but similar root. Scholars try to learn it from related Semitic languages.

*

Mitchell First is an attorney and Jewish history scholar. He has not (yet) been called upon by God to deliver any lexical discourses.

14. What is the Meaning of the Word עולם?

The word עולם appears over 400 times in Tanakh (in various forms). Even though we are used to it meaning "world," this was not its

---

111. Vol. 9, p. 133.

112. Koehler-Baumgartner, p. 662, also concludes that the latter is more probable. See also, H. Tawil, p. 231 and *Encyclopaedia Judaica* 13:1152. On the other hand, E. Klein (p. 402) only mentions the first view: "one who calls/proclaims to the people."

113. See, e.g., Koehler-Baumgartner, p. 659 and *Theological Dictionary of the Old Testament*, vol. 9, p. 130.

original meaning. Rather, almost every time the word appears in Tanakh, it is being used with a time-oriented meaning: e.g., "a remote period in the past," "a remote period in the future," or "in perpetuity."

Some examples of the last are: *chok olam, chukkat olam*, and *brit olam*. For an example of "a remote period in the past," this is how we end every *Amidah*, quoting the verse *kiyemei olam u-khe-shanim kadmoniot*, "as in the days of the remote past and as in ancient years" (Malachi 3:4). But most of the time in Tanakh, the reference is to "a remote period in the future."

Many sources that discuss the word *olam* write that it does not mean "world" anywhere in Tanakh except perhaps at Eccl. 3:11. Its meaning in this verse is still unresolved. See, e.g., Ibn Ezra and *Daat Mikra* to this verse. But *olam* probably means "world" in the phrase *va-yishava be-chei ha-olam* (Dan. 12:7).[114] The *ha-* prefix is what points to the "world" meaning here. (It also means "world" at Ben Sira 3:18 and perhaps elsewhere in that book.)

The consensus of scholars today is that the book of Daniel dates to the middle of the 2nd century B.C.E. As to Ecclesiastes, the consensus of scholars today, based on the language of the book, is that it is one of the latest biblical books. See, e.g., *Encyclopaedia Judaica* 2:349.

Based on all of the above, it seems that *olam* did not take on its meaning of "world" until somewhere in the middle or late Second Temple period.[115]

(The phrase that we are all familiar with from our blessings, *melekh ha-olam* [=king of the world], never appears in Tanakh, although *melekh olam* appears at Jer. 10:10 and Ps. 10:16. The term *ha-olam* appears in Tanakh but is rare.)

---

114. This verse is also the source for a phrase that is common in our liturgy: חי העולמים.

115. There are scholars who would disagree with the above analysis and who believe that *olam* means "world" in passages earlier than Daniel and Ecclesiastes. They point in particular to Gen. 21:33, and Isa. 40:28. Other *olam* passages with a possible "world" meaning have been suggested as well. Nevertheless, I am adopting a widespread position when I take the position that *olam* did not take on its meaning of "world" until somewhere in the middle or late Second Temple period.

For an excellent article on the evolution of the word *olam*, see K.A. Fudeman and M.I. Gruber, "'Eternal King/King of the World' From the Bronze Age to Modern Times: A Study in Lexical Semantics," *Revue des Études Juives* 166 (2007), pp. 209-242.

Why is the evolution of the meaning of the word *olam* important? It helps us date our prayers. For example, the second paragraph of *Aleinu* uses the phrase לתקן עולם and *olam* is used here to mean "world." This indicates clearly that the second paragraph of *Aleinu* was not composed by Joshua or in the First Temple period. There are also strong reasons to think that both paragraphs of *Aleinu* were composed at the same time. (They go well together, and both paragraphs quote or paraphrase from Isaiah 45.) Thus, our knowledge of the evolution of the term of *olam* enables us to conclude that both paragraphs of *Aleinu* were not composed by Joshua or in the First Temple period. (Note also that *ha-kadosh barukh hu*, found in the first paragraph, was not an appellation for God in biblical times. This is another ground for rejecting the early time period for the first paragraph. There are other phrases in both paragraphs of *Aleinu* that do not seem to have existed in the biblical period.) (Regarding the word לתקן, almost certainly the original reading in this line in *Aleinu* was לתכן, meaning "establish.")

The belief that *Aleinu* was composed by Joshua did not arise until the time of the Rishonim.[116] From statements in the Jerusalem Talmud (*Avodah Zarah* 1:2 and *Rosh Hashanah* 1:3), it can be deduced that there is a good chance that *Aleinu* was composed by Rav in the 3rd century C.E. (I have discussed all of these *Aleinu*-related issues extensively in my book, *Esther Unmasked*, pp. 17-29.)

Going back to the meaning of *olam* in Tanakh, there is one more verse that must be mentioned, Ps. 89:3. This verse begins: *ki amarti olam chesed yibaneh*.... There are statements of our Sages interpreting *olam* here as "world." See, e.g., *Sanhedrin* 58b. But in the plain sense of this verse, *olam* means "forever." See, e.g., the *Daat Mikra* commentary to the verse, and the commentaries of Ibn Ezra and Radak. Also noteworthy is that in the prior verse, 89:2, *olam* also means "forever."

How *olam* evolved from its initial "time-oriented" meaning to its later additional meaning of "world" is not yet completely understood.[117]

---

116. Please disregard the reference to R. Hai Gaon in the *The Complete ArtScroll Siddur*, p. 158. See *Esther Unmasked*, p. 18, n.4.

117. But the fact that there was such an evolution at all is interesting because (at least on a homiletical level), it anticipates the findings of modern science that there is a relation between time and physical space. I would like to thank Joel Chudow for this insight.

Various suggestions have been made. Of course, the "time-oriented" meaning of *olam* did not disappear; the word was still often used in Rabbinic Hebrew in this manner.[118]

With regard to the etymology of the word *olam*, some scholars conjecture that it is related to the Hebrew root ע-ל-ם and its meaning "to hide." In this view, the biblical, time-oriented meaning of *olam* reflects the hidden (= unknown) past and future. See, e.g., S.D. Luzzatto on Ex. 15:18. See also Ernest Klein, who mentions this view and an alternative view that relates it to an Akkadian word *ullanu* (=remote time).[119] On the other hand, the entry in *Theological Dictionary of the Old Testament* observes that the etymology of the word *olam* "has been and remains disputed or at best uncertain... no real progress has been made." In other words, the etymology of the word is still "hidden"!

Now that we know that *olam* has two different meanings, which meaning is being used in the first two words of the poem *Adon Olam*? (The author of this poem is unknown, as is the time period it was authored.) *The Complete ArtScroll Siddur* translates the first two words as "Master of the Universe." The *Encyclopaedia Judaica* is similar: "Lord of the World." (As to the distinction between "world" and "universe," that is a separate issue.) But many others translate *Adon Olam* as something like "Eternal Lord." See, e.g., *The Encyclopedia of Jewish Prayer*, and the Birnbaum Siddur. Which translation is correct?[120]

---

118. A very interesting issue is the meaning of the phrases *olam ha-zeh* and *olam ha-ba* in Rabbinic Hebrew. Which of the two meanings of *olam* is being used in these phrases? Today the terms are commonly translated as "this world" and "the world to come." But a strong case can be made that a more appropriate translation would be: "pre-eschatological **era**" and "post-eschatological **era**." See the article cited in the previous note, pp. 210 and 217. This is a very significant change!

The blessing recited after one is called to the Torah must also be commented upon. Like many blessings, the blessing initially includes the phrase *melekh ha-olam*. But a few words later, the blessing includes the phrase *ve-chayei olam*. The result is two different meanings of *olam* in this short blessing.

119. E. Klein, p. 466.

120. Some sources have suggested that the difference in meaning has a ramification in the vocalization. If *olam* means "world," the *aleph* of *adon* should be vocalized with a *chataf patach*. If *olam* means "eternal," the *aleph* of *adon* should be vocalized with a *kametz*.

The first line of the poem reads: *adon olam asher malakh be-terem kol yetzir nivra* = אדון עולם who reigned before any form was created. In this context, the simplest meaning of *adon olam* is "eternal Lord." Also, two lines later we have: "after all has ceased to be, the awesome one will reign alone." So again the author is describing an eternal Lord.

But it has been pointed out that there is a statement in the Talmud (*Berkahot* 7b) that, from the time God created העולם, Abraham was the first person to call God "אדון." Perhaps the author of *Adon Olam* had this passage in mind when he wrote the poem, in which case the עולם in the poem would mean "world." On the other hand, the poem uses the word עולם and not העולם. This is some evidence that the author of the poem did not have this passage in mind.

The best solution to how to translate *Adon Olam* in the poem is to realize that our question is unfair. Perhaps the author had both meanings of *olam* in mind, and we cannot express this double meaning when we limit ourselves to a two-word translation. My own conclusion based on the context is that, on the simplest level, the words mean "eternal Lord." Nevertheless, it is likely that the author had the "world" meaning in mind as well, as a secondary meaning (even if he did not have the passage at *Berakhot* 7b in mind.) Poems often use wordplay. The fact that both meanings can be read into it is some evidence that the author was using wordplay and had both meanings in mind.[121]

It is interesting that the phrase *adon olam* also appears in *Yigdal* and there all will admit that *olam* is being used with the meaning "world."

I will conclude with the following liturgical tidbit. We use the phrase *ha-yom harat olam* on Rosh Hashanah to mean "the day the *world* was conceived." But the phrase *harat olam* originates at Jer. 20:17. There it means "pregnant *forever*"!

P.S.: There is another root ע-ל-ם in Tanakh with meanings like "young woman" and "young man." It is possible that it is related to the ע-ל-ם root that I discussed in this article. But more likely it is

---

121. For another discussion of this issue, see the posts by the scholar Marc Shapiro of Sept. 4, 2007 and Nov. 15, 2011 at seforim.blogspot.com. Shapiro first argued for the "eternal" meaning and then changed his mind in the second post and adopted the "world" meaning.

not. For a discussion of the etymology of this other ע-ל-ם root, see *Theological Dictionary of the Old Testament*, vol. 11, pp. 154-159.

*

Mitchell First is a personal injury attorney and Jewish history scholar. He hopes to continue writing scholarly articles *ad olam*.

15. What is the Meaning of עַל־מוּת (Psalms 48:15)?

At the end of *shacharit* every Monday, we recite Psalm 48 as the *shir shel yom*. This psalm ends (48:15): "This is God, our God forever and ever; He will lead us עַל־מוּת."

I am now going to present many of the interpretations of the עַל־מוּת of this verse. Note that in the Tanakh and in our *siddurim*, the five letters are printed as two separate words. This is the Masoretic tradition. But many of the interpretations are willing to interpret the five letters as if they were one word. Note also that our difficult phrase עַל־מוּת also appears at Ps. 9:1.

First, I will mention a few interpretations of Psalms 48:15 that interpret the five letters as two separate words:

- He will lead us until we die. (The import is that God will lead us in this honorable manner until we die — Radak.)
- He will inspire us to overcome our fear of death. (Something like this is one of the suggestions in the *Daat Mikra*.)
- He will lead us beyond mortality, i.e., He will make us immortal as a nation (Rav S.R. Hirsch).

Of course, the first of the two words is עַל, not אַל. This makes the first of these interpretations difficult. עַל has a connotation of "above," not "until" or "towards." The second of these interpretations is difficult because it does not fit the context. The third of these interpretations is creative but does not seem like a plain sense interpretation.

A different approach interprets the five letters as if they were one word. Those who adopt this approach observe that עלמות can be seen as related to the word עלם which means "youth."

Accordingly the following interpretations are offered:

- He will lead us slowly, like we are children (Rashi).
- He will lead us so our nation will have eternal youth, i.e., immortality (Rav S. R. Hirsch).
- He will lead us as He led us when our nation was young (Targum, Radak, one view cited in Ibn Ezra).
- He will lead us with strength, i.e., "youth" symbolizes "strength." (This is one of the suggestions made in the *Daat Mikra*.)
- He will lead us in a way that maintains our youthful strength all of our days (Meiri).

Alternatively, Ibn Ezra mentions the possibility that עלמות is related to the root ע-ל-ם with the meaning "hidden." The meaning of the verse could be: "God leads us [in a good way] in a manner that is hidden [from humans]."

The main problem with all of these "youth" and "hidden" interpretations is that the text does not read בעלמות or כעלמות.

An entirely different approach sees עלמות as related to עולם. Then the verse could be translated: "He will lead us eternally." This would fit nicely as a continuation of the earlier part of the verse: "This is God, our God forever and ever." Rashi mentions that this approach was advocated by Menachem ben Saruk. Long before this, this approach was taken by the Septuagint. Many of our commentators adopt this approach. Of course, our text does not read עולם or לעולם.

Perhaps עלמות was originally עלמית (*olamit*)? This means "eternally." However, there is no word עלמית (*olamit*) in Tanakh. This is a word that appears in the Mishnah and Tosefta. It is unlikely that there was such a word at the time of Psalm 48.

Another approach to על־מות can be to interpret על as אל. The Even-Shoshan concordance lists over 3000 instances of the word על, and for more than 20 of them, it suggests that it has the meaning אל. (Our traditional commentators also sometimes interpret על as אל.) Then the statement could be interpreted as, "He will lead us to death [=until our deaths]." The implication would be that he will lead us for our entire lives. But such a statement sounds too negative. There were surely more pleasant ways that this point could have been made.

Now I will mention a completely different approach that is suggested by many scholars, and also included as a possibility in the *Daat Mikra*. They notice that Psalm 9 has על־מות in its first verse, and

Psalm 46 has עלמות (*alamot*) in its first verse. Both of these verses are introductory verses that begin with למנצח. This suggests that these unusual words may be musical instructions, and that על־מות should read as עלמות (*alamot*). That *alamot* is related to music is also evident from 1 Chron. 15:20. Accordingly, perhaps our על־מות/עלמות is also a term of musical instruction, and should be read as *alamot*.

The musical instructions in the book of Psalms are usually found in the first verse, but sometimes they are found mid-chapter (see, e.g., 9:17 and 47:8). Are they ever found at the end of a chapter? The book of Habakkuk ends with a musical instruction as its last phrase (3:19). In the book of Psalms, the word *selah* appears as the last word of chapters 3, 9, 24 and 46. Although the meaning of the word *selah* has been much debated over the ages (see *Encyclopaedia Judaica* 13:1321-22), the prevailing view now is that it was some kind of musical instruction for the singers or musicians.[122]

If our על־מות is a musical instruction at the end of the chapter and should be read as *alamot*, then the substance of verse 48:15 ends with הוא ינהגנו. (Some scholars are more creative and suggest that our musical instruction belongs in the first verse of chapter 49, similar to its location in chapter 46.)

With regard to the meaning of the musical instruction, there is a word *alamot* found at Ps. 68:26 and Song of Songs 1:3 and 6:8. There it means "young women." The suggestion is then made that our *alamot* is a musical instrument with a high-pitched tone.

To sum up, interpreting על־מות as originally reading עלמות (*alamot*) and as reflecting a musical instruction placed at the end of the psalm is a very simple approach, and seems to be the likeliest explanation. (But admittedly this approach disagrees with the Masoretic Text that there are two separate words here.)

With regard to the other interpretations, interpreting the phrase as two words: "He will lead us beyond mortality," or "He will lead us until death" (with על functioning as אל) are also simple interpretations consistent with the text. But I find the first too creative and the second too simplistic.

---

122. See *Daat Mikra* to Hab. 3:3 and Ps. 3:3. See also Radak, *Sefer Ha-Shorashim*, p. 240. The root of *selah* is probably סלל/raise.

Our verse is interpreted in the Talmud Yerushalmi, at *Megillah* 2:4, and in a parallel passage at *Leviticus Rabbah* 11:9. (The latter passage is the clearer one.) The passage is a homiletical one, and four interpretations are offered. I am not going to mention the two most homiletical ones. But one of the interpretations offered is ,בזריזות בעלמות (with youth/vigor, and alacrity). Another interpretation offered is: בשני עולמות, this world and the world to come.

So after all this, how does *The Complete ArtScroll Siddur* (pp. 164-65) translate our phrase? In their main translation, they ignore the Masoretic tradition that these are two separate words and translate: "He will guide us like children." In their commentary, they mention the views of the Targum, Rashi, and Meiri, all of whom translate the two words as if they were one. But then they conclude: "According to the Masoretic tradition that these are two words, they mean that God will continue to guide us *beyond death*, i.e., in the World to Come." Interestingly, the talmudic interpretation that they seem to be alluding to (see the previous paragraph) arrived at the "World to Come" interpretation by interpreting the two words as one word!

*

Mitchell First is a personal injury attorney and Jewish history scholar. He hopes that he will eventually be vigorously led, with the accompaniment of the music of *alamot*, to *olam ha-ba*. In the interim, he can be reached at MFirstAtty@aol.com.

16. What is the Origin of the Words ערב and בקר?

Erev (evening) and *boker* (morning) are words that are well-known to us. How did these words develop these meanings"?

The root ע-ר-ב has several meanings, one of them is "mix." See, e.g., Ps. 106:35: *va-yitarvu va-goyim*. The "mix" meaning very likely lies behind the term *erev rav* (the mixed multitude that lacked a common identity and left Egypt with the Israelites). The "mix" meaning may also underlie the use of the root ע-ר-ב in connection with weaving, as weaving combines both vertical and horizontal directions. Also, the "mix" meaning likely underlies the name of the plague of *arov*, assuming that it was a mixture of wild animals or of very small harmful creatures.[123]

I had always thought that the "mix" meaning was the explanation for *erev*/evening as well. Indeed, two such explanations are often presented in traditional Jewish sources. One is that *erev* is the time when there is a mixing/confusion of objects to the human eye due to the lack of light. (This is in contrast to *boker*, where items can be inspected and distinguished.) The other is that *erev* is the time when the conditions of light and dark begin to mix. For these suggestions, see, e.g., the concordance of Solomon Mandelkern, p. 912, and the commentaries of Ibn Ezra, Radak, S.D. Luzzatto, and Rav SR. Hirsch to Gen. 1:5.

I was therefore surprised to learn that modern scholars take a different approach. In Akkadian (a Semitic language that was the language of Assyria and Babylonia), there is a root ע-ר-ב that means "to enter." Most modern scholars believe that *erev* is called this because it is the time when the sun has set and early man viewed it as having entered into its resting location.[124]

This "set/enter" meaning also explains the related word *maarav* (=west). The *maarav* is the place where the sun sets. (This is in contrast to *mizrach*, the place where the sun begins to shine, derived from the root ז-ר-ח.) The "set/enter" meaning of the verb ע-ר-ב is perhaps seen in the Tanakh at Prov. 7:9 and Judg. 19:9. (It may be implicit in the ע-ר-ב of "weaving" as well.)

On the subject of ע-ר-ב, these letters have many other meanings in Tanakh.[125] For example, an *aravah* is a desolate, wilderness area.

---

123. But I have written an article in this book describing an alternative approach to the plague.

The "mix" meaning also underlies the word עירוב (in Rabbinic Hebrew), since this term typically relates to the "mixing/joining" of areas.

124. See, e.g., *Theological Dictionary of the Old Testament*, vol. 11, p. 335, and H. Tawil, p. 283.

125. A reason that roots with the Hebrew letter ע often have multiple meanings is that the Hebrew letter ע is a merger of two different earlier (=Proto-Semitic) ע letters The distinction between these two earlier ע letters is preserved in Arabic. They are distinguished in Arabic by means of a diacritical point. The Hebrew letter ח is also a merger of two different earlier (=Proto-Semitic) ח letters, distinguished in Arabic by means of a diacritical point. See E. Y. Kutscher, *A History of the Hebrew Language* (2d. ed., 1984), pp. 17-18.

Also, an *aravah* is a willow, and an *orev* is a raven. I have seen the speculation that *orev* for raven derives from it being a bird of the *aravah*/wilderness, or from it being a dark bird (=from the "evening/dark" meaning of *erev*). Alternatively, the name may derive from the sound that the bird makes. Finally, an unusual use of ע-ר-ב is found at Ps. 68:5 where God is described as a *rokhev ba-aravot*. I have dealt with this in a separate article.

The verb ע-ר-ב also means to be a surety/guarantor (see, e.g., Gen. 43:9: *anokhi e'ervenu*). There are also related nouns, *eiravon* and *arubah*, which mean "pledge." It has been suggested that these meanings come from the "enter" meaning and are related to entering under the authority of another.[126]

To conclude this section on a positive note, there is also another meaning of ע-ר-ב in Tanakh. The last sentence of the *Amidah* is: *ve-arvah... minchat Yehudah vi-Yerushalayim*. This phrase comes from Malachi 3:4. The root ע-ר-ב here means "pleasant, sweet."[127] The root ע-ר-ב has this meaning elsewhere in Tanakh as well.

Hopefully, I have not mixed you up too much, as now it is time to deal with *boker*.

The verb ב-ק-ר only appears a few times in Tanakh. It generally has a meaning of "inspect" or "investigate." As mentioned earlier, a common view in our commentaries (e.g., Ibn Ezra and Radak) is that *boker* is the time when items can be inspected (unlike *erev*, when they are mixed and hard to distinguish.)

However, two other approaches to the origin of *boker* deserve mention. One is the approach of S.D. Luzzatto (on Gen. 1:5) who notes that ב-ק-ע means "split" or "break." Luzzatto then suggests that *boker* is simply a contraction of *baka or* (=the light broke through). To support his position, he cites Isa. 58:8: *az yibbaka ka-shachar orekha*.

---

126. See E. Klein, p. 483.

In Ezekiel 27, ע-ר-ב is used as a verb meaning "to exchange/trade" and there is also a noun "מערב" that means "merchandise." These are usually considered as related to the "surety" meaning. See E. Klein, p. 483, and Koehler-Baumgartner, p. 877.

127. It has been suggested that this originated from the "ע-ר-ב /mix" meaning and originally meant "mixed well." See E. Klein, p. 484. But this suggestion is not found in either Koehler-Baumgartner or *Theological Dictionary of the Old Testament*. I suspect that this suggestion is no longer accepted.

The other approach to *boker* is one supported by many modern scholars. This approach observes that in Arabic, *baqara* means "to split" or "to open." The suggestion is that this was the original meaning of the verb ב-ק-ר in Hebrew as well. "Inspect/investigate" was just a later expansion, since this is what you do after you split something open (e.g., a sacrificial animal). See *Theological Dictionary of the Old Testament*, vol. 2, p. 219. If the original meaning of ב-ק-ר was "split," then *boker* can be the time when the light first breaks through. (A parallel is our English word "daybreak.") Moreover, under the assumption that the original meaning of ב-ק-ר was "split" or "open," we can suggest why *bakar* were called by this name. It may be because these animals plow, thereby making openings in the ground.[128]

Finally, I will make a point about another time-related word, *shachar*/the morning light (שחר). We all know that *shachor*, with the same three root letters, means "black"! To explain this anomaly, some have suggested that *shachar* really means "the blackness just before the dawn." Others have suggested that *shachor*/black derives originally from a different root, *chet-resh-resh*, which means "burn." But both of these suggestions are farfetched. Most likely, it is just coincidence that ש-ח-ר has two opposite meanings.

*

Mitchell First is a personal injury attorney and Jewish history scholar. He does his best writing in the very early morning before *boker* and *shacharit*.

17. John Lennon and the Plague of ערב (*Arov*)

When I started the research for this article, I intended to survey the various traditional understandings of the plague. But along the way, I discovered a little-known and intriguing alternative understanding.

Most of us assume that this plague consisted of an attack by various wild animals. This is essentially the approach taken by Rashi. But a midrash records two different Amoraic understandings of this

---

128. See, e.g., E. Klein, p. 81.

plague. According to R. Yehudah, the plague consisted of *chayot me'uravevot* (=a mixture of wild animals). According to R. Nehemiah, the plague consisted of *minei tzirin ve-yitushin* (=various species of hornets and mosquitoes/gnats). See *Exodus Rabbah* 11:3. Both of these Sages are interpreting the word *arov* as mixture. Just that in the view of R. Yehudah, it is a mixture of large animals, and in the view of R. Nehemiah, it is a mixture of much smaller ones. In the view of both, the precise animals are not identified in the name of the plague.[129]

The reason for the disagreement about the identity of the specific animals involved is that the description of the plague at Ex. 8:17-27 does not give enough clues. The text does state that the *arov* will fill the houses of the Egyptians and be on their land, and *va-tishachet ha-aretz mi-pnei he-arov*. The text also records that after the plague was removed, "not one remained." But these statements are vague as to the precise nature of the *arov*.

Descriptions of many of the plagues are also found in Psalms 78 and 105. With regard to the plague of *arov*, there is a reference to it at 105:31, but it is not helpful. However, at 78:45 the reference to the plague does provide some information. We are told: *yeshallach ba-hem arov va-yokhlem*. The last word ("and it will eat them") at first glance seems to support the view of R. Yehudah that large animals were involved.

Do we have earlier sources for the meaning of *arov* prior to the Amoraim? Our earliest source is the translation of the Torah into Greek, composed in Egypt in the 3rd century B.C.E. Here the translation is *kunomuia*, literally: "dog-fly," a particularly unyielding type of fly. Perhaps this translation was based on an older tradition as to the nature of *arov*. But there is another possibility. The authors of the Greek translation knew that *arov* meant "mixture," and believed or had a tradition that *arov* was a very small animal, and then picked *kunomuia* because its name is a hybrid. In this way, they were able to interpret *arov* as "mixture."

Another early translation we have is that of Josephus (*Antiquities* II.303), writing around 100 C.E. He translates the plague as "wild

---

129. Aside from *Exodus Rabbah* 11:3, there are many other midrashim that include an interpretation of *arov*. The views expressed in most of these midrashim are similar to that of R. Yehudah (large animals). Some further midrashic sources are *Exodus Rabbah* 11:2 and *Midrash Tehillim* 78:11.

beasts of every species and kind." This translation seems to be based on an understanding of *arov* as "mixture."

So according to perhaps all of the views that I have described so far, the Torah is interpreted as having not described the actual animal involved, but having used a word that meant only "mixture." At first glance, this seems unusual. But perhaps we are dealing with a common ancient idiom and in biblical times everyone understood what particular mixture was implied by the word *arov*.

I should also mention that the church father Jerome (c. 400 C.E.), who was aware of many of the teachings of the Palestinian Amoraim, translated the word with a Latin word that meant "insects."

Many scholars believe that there are a few grounds to prefer the very small animal view and I agree with them.[130] First, the verses in chapter 8 refer to the *arov* entering the houses of the Egyptians. If the animals involved were large ones, the houses could have been secured to prevent them from entering. Also, if the securing would have been to no avail, the text would have described the animals breaking down the premises upon entering. But no such large-scale destruction upon entering is described. Rather, it is simply stated that the *arov* would be sent out and fill the premises.

A second reason to prefer the very small animals approach is that the root ע-ר-ב with the meaning of "mixture" is more naturally applied to small objects. Large objects, each taking up its own space, are inherently less of a mixture. A third reason to prefer the very small animals approach is based on a widespread view that the plagues came in pairs.[131] For example, the first and second plagues, blood and frogs, were both primarily addressed towards the Nile. The seventh and eighth plagues, hail and locusts, were both primarily addressed to the crops. If our fourth plague, *arov*, was meant as a pair to the third plague, *kinim* (=lice), obviously the very small animal interpretation fits better. The *va-yokhlem* of Ps. 78:45 can easily be interpreted metaphorically to include damage inflicted by very small animals.

An altogether different approach to the plague is adopted by Rav S.R. Hirsch. He suggests that the word *arov* derives from the word *aravah* (= wilderness), and that the plague alludes to "animals from

---

130. I am referring here to S.D. Luzzatto, U. Cassuto, and many others.
131. See, e.g., the commentary to Exodus of U. Cassuto, and the *Daat Mikra* commentary, p. 127 and p. 174, n. 77.

the wilderness." I would respond that, although there are verses that refer to animals in the context of an *aravah*, animals do not seem to be a primary characteristic of an *aravah*. It is therefore a leap to claim that the word *arov* alludes to animals from the *aravah*.

An even more speculative approach is adopted by Rashbam. He notes that the Tanakh refers to *ze'evei erev* at Zephaniah 3:3, and to *ze'ev aravot* at Jer. 5:6.[132] These could mean "wolves of the wilderness." But Rashbam suggests that both mean "wolves of the evening" and that the plague *arov* is referring to such wolves, who typically go out and attack at night.

There is, however, an alternative approach to identifying the biblical *arov*. It relies on looking at other ancient languages. For example, in Akkadian there was a word *urbatu* that meant "worm." Some theorize that this was the *arov* of the Bible. But there is a much better suggestion.

Let us meet the beetles. A scarab is a type of beetle.[133] It was called **karabos** in Greek. *Karabos* is very close to the Hebrew *ayin-resh-bet*, due to the guttural sound that the *ayin* made. The "-os" in the Greek word is likely just a Greek addition to a foreign word. The Greek word *karabos* raises the possibility that the beetle was called something like *ayin-resh-bet* in the area of Palestine and nearby areas.

What do we know about the scarab beetle in ancient Egypt? As Isaac Mozeson phrased it, the ancient Egyptians had "beetlemania."[134] They worshipped this particular beetle! In ancient Egypt, the scarab was sculptured on monuments, painted on tombs, and worn around the neck as an amulet. Many of the plagues were attacks on the various deities of Egypt, and this plague would then be another such attack on a deity. In contrast, a plague of "a mixture of animals" is not a clear judgment on an Egyptian deity.

The "scarab" suggestion (originally made by a nineteenth-century British scholar named Marcus Moritz Kalisch) was referred to by Rabbi J.H. Hertz in his note on Ex. 8:17, and was his preferred interpretation.[135] But R. Hertz did not sufficiently explain it. The

---

132. *Ze'evei erev* are also referred to at Hab. 1:8.

133. The English word "scarab" is derived from the Latin *scarabaeus*. The initial "s" in the Latin is just a Latin addition to the Greek word.

134. I. Mozeson, *The Word* (1995), p. 142.

135. See his headline in his commentary (p. 240): "The Fourth Plague: Beetles." Note that the translation at the top in *The Pentateuch and Haftorahs*

suggestion was also referred to without sufficient explanation by R. Aryeh Kaplan in *The Living Torah*. But the suggestion was explained well by Isaac Mozeson in his book *The Word* and in his edenics.net site, entry "scarab." The source I have found that best describes the explanation is a blog entry of March 13, 2012, by Seth Ben-Mordecai, at his site exodushaggadah.com. (He is the author of a book: *The Exodus Haggadah*.)

But there is a weakness to the "scarab" theory. In Egyptian, the scarab was called *kh-p-r*. The theory would be much better if the Egyptian word for the scarab was *kh-r-p*. Perhaps there was such a variant. Such a variant would explain why the name was recorded in Greek the way it was, but I am not aware of any evidence for this variant (yet).[136] Even if there was no such variant in Egyptian, perhaps the K-R-B / A-R-B name for the scarab was so widespread in the region that the Torah could justifiably record the name of the plague as ערב, even if it did not exactly match the way the Egyptians referred to their scarab.[137]

To summarize, a widespread view is that the word *arov* represents some kind of mixture. Perhaps in biblical times, everyone understood the idiom and knew what that mixture was. But if you believe that the Torah was likely referring to a specific animal, then the ancient scarab is an intriguing alternative suggestion.

*

Mitchell First is a personal injury attorney and Jewish history scholar. He enjoys mixtures but is not fond of animals, small or large. He was fond of, but did not worship, The Beatles.

---

is merely a reprint of the 1917 translation of the Jewish Publication Society of America. It is not the translation of R. Hertz himself.

136. Ben-Mordechai writes that there was such a variant in Egyptian: *kh-r-b*. But I think this statement was just a conjecture.

137. Note also that in *The Living Torah* (comm. to 8:17), R. Kaplan wrote that the beetle was called *a̒ov* in Egyptian. I am not aware of his source for this statement and have doubts about its accuracy. But I have done some additional investigation and it seems that aside from *kh-p-r*, there were additional terms in Egyptian for the scarab, like *a-b-b*, and *a-p-y*. I have no background in ancient Egyptian and I leave it to someone else to continue this research.

18. ק-ל-ס: A Root with Two Opposite Meanings?

The root ק-ל-ס is a very interesting one. We all know the root from the Shabbat *shacharit* (just before *Yishtabach*): *le-hodot le-hallel… le-varekh le-aleh u-lekalles*. We also know it from Mishnah *Pesachim* 10:5,[138] and from the *haggadah*. In all of these instances, the verb means: "praise." This verb is often used to mean "praise" in rabbinic literature.[139]

But what happens when we look in Tanakh? The root only appears 8 times in Tanakh. Six of these times, it is obvious from the context that it means "mock." See, for example, Ps. 44:14 (*laag va-keles*). With regard to the remaining two times, at Habakkuk 1:10 there are some who interpret it as "praise," but because it is parallel to מֹשְׂחָק in the verse, it almost certainly means "mock" here. The meaning in the remaining verse, Ezek. 16:31, could go either way.

How did this root, which mean "mock" at least seven out of the eight times it is in Tanakh, end up in rabbinic literature with an additional meaning of "praise"?

Among the suggestions:

- ק-ל-ס meant "praise" at Ezek. 16:31 and this is the source of the "praise" meaning of ק-ל-ס found in rabbinic literature.

---

138. The truth is that although the word is included on most printed editions of Mishnah *Pesachim* 10:5, it is not found in most manuscripts and most likely was not in the original Mishnah. Nevertheless, although the word ק-ל-ס with the meaning "praise" is not found here or in any Mishnaic source, it is found in the *Tosefta* and it is found in many *baraitot*. Therefore, ק-ל-ס with the meaning "praise" is properly considered a word of Tannaitic literature. It is thereafter found with the meaning "praise" throughout the Talmud Bavli and Yerushalmi, and the Midrashim. (On all of this, see the article by Lieberman cited below).

Even though I stated above that ק-ל-ס with the meaning "praise" is not found in any Mishnaic source, the Mishnah in two places (*Betzah* 2:6-7 and *Eduyyot* 3:10-11) refers to the practice of eating a *gedi mekullas*. It is possible that ק-ל-ס with the meaning "praise" is reflected in this latter word. This is at least the view of the Rambam (comm. to *Betzah* 2:6), although most disagree.

139. The "mock" meaning persists in rabbinic literature as well.

- ק-ל-ס merely means "speak" and the speech can be either positive or negative.[140]
- ק-ל-ס developed an opposite meaning. An oft-cited example of such a phenomenon is ב-ר-ך. It is used to mean "curse" several times in Tanakh.[141]
- In rabbinic literature, the root ק-ל-ס also has the meaning "to stamp with one's feet." (See *Moed Katan* 27b). Perhaps this word in rabbinic literature reflects an ancient meaning of the root, and this original meaning developed into "mock" on the one hand and "praise" on the other.

Even though I mentioned all the above suggestions, most likely the answer is a different one. The root ק-ל-ס meant "mock" all 8 times it appears in Tanakh,[142] and the "praise" meaning that is found in rabbinic literature was derived from the Greek word "*kalos*"=beautiful.[143] It has been suggested that this Greek word was used by the Sages because it had an added connotation that the Hebrew or Aramaic words for

---

140. This is suggested by Rashi. See, e.g., his commentaries to Ez. 16:31, Hab. 1:10, and *Sotah* 27a.

141. According to the Even-Shoshan concordance, ב-ר-ך is used to mean "curse" seven or eight times in Tanakh. (For one example, see Job 2:9.) A different example involves the root ח-ט-א. A change in the *binyan* enables the word to mean "remove sin/purify oneself." See, e.g., Num. 19:12: יתחטא.

142. The use of the verb at Ez. 16:31 is a very interesting one. The verb describes what a prostitute does with the money that she is given. Of course, it could mean that she "praises" the money. But if we give ק-ל-ס the "mock" meaning throughout Tanakh, then its meaning here is that she "mocks" the money in an effort to get more! See, e.g., Radak, *Metzudat David*, and Malbim on this verse. See also Radak, *Sefer Ha-Shorashim*, entry קלס.

If the root ק-ל-ס always meant "mock" in Tanakh, what is the first appearance of it as "praise" in Hebrew? The book of Ben Sira represents a transitional book between the Hebrew of the Tanakh and the Hebrew of the Sages. It was probably composed around 200 B.C.E. At Ben Sira 11:4, we have ק-ל-ס with the meaning "mock." But at 47:15, the reading may be "ותקלס" with the meaning "praise." (There is a question as to the proper text here.) I would like to thank Sam Borodach for pointing me to these passages.

143. See, e.g., E. Klein, p. 580, and M. Sokoloff, *A Dictionary of Jewish Babylonian Aramaic of the Talmudic and Geonic periods* (2002), entry קלס. A detailed article on this topic arguing for this position was written by Saul Lieberman, in the volume *Alei Ayin* (1952), pp. 75-81. (It is cited in M. Kasher, *Haggadah Shelemah*, 1967, third edition, p.135, n. 15.)

"praise" lacked. Alternatively, it has been suggested that the word was so familiar to the Sages that they absorbed it into their vocabulary unintentionally.[144]

Many English words, such as "calisthenics" and "calligraphy," are derived from this Greek word.[145]

So now we realize that the biblical root "ק-ל-ס/mock" did not develop an opposite meaning. Rather, the "praise" meaning came from an entirely different source, the Greek language.

That is the first part of the story of this root. The second part of the story relates to the liturgy. Because the root ק-ל-ס meant "mock" many times in Tanakh, there have been Rishonim and Acharonim who objected to including it as a word of praise in the Shabbat *shacharit* and in the *haggadah*.[146] Some examples are Ritva (commentary on the *haggadah* on *u-lekalles*), and R. Barukh Epstein (*Barukh She-Amar*, p. 246).[147]

But more significantly, this same issue arose long ago in the Geonic period in the context of the *Kaddish* prayer. יתקלס is found in some of the early versions of the *Kaddish* prayer. See, e.g., the text of the *Kaddish* prayer in *Siddur Rav Saadiah Gaon* (10th century): *yishtabbach yitpa'ar yitromem yitalleh ve-yitnalsei ve-yitkalles....*[148] We have sources from the Geonic period and from the period of the Rishonim that document a battle for hundreds of years about whether it was appropriate to include יתקלס in the lofty *Kaddish* prayer, given that ק-ל-ס meant "mock" many times in Tanakh. I am now going to provide a small sample of references:

---

144. Both of these suggestions were made by Lieberman.

145. Already in the 11th century, both R. Chananel (comm. to *Shabbat* 108a) and the *Arukh* (entry קלוס) point out that a positive meaning of ק-ל-ס is found in the Greek language. But neither state explicitly that the positive meaning of ק-ל-ס found in rabbinic literature was borrowed from there. It is unclear whether they were of this view.

146. Many of the Rishonim and Acharonim that I will now cite until the end of this article may be of the view that it means "praise" at Ez. 16:31 and Hab. 1:10. But the fact that it certainly has the "mock" meaning several times elsewhere in Tanakh is what is troubling to them.

147. See also M. Kasher, *Haggadah Shelemah*, pp. 134-35.

148. *Siddur Rav Saadiah Gaon*, p. 35.

- *Shibbolei Ha-Leket* (13th century, Italy) quotes a tradition in the name of R. Yehudai Gaon (8th century) that the word should not be included in the *Kaddish*.[149]
- Rambam (d. 1204) was opposed to including it in the *Kaddish*.[150]
- *Sefer Ha-Manhig* (early 13th century) was opposed to including it in the *Kaddish*.[151]

For more sources on this topic, see, e.g., B.M. Lewin, *Otzar Ha-Geonim, Rosh Hashanah*, p. 67, n. 2; *Shibbolei Ha-Leket* (ed. Mirsky), notes to pp. 151-154; and Yaakov Gartner, "*Ha-Me'aneh Ba-Kaddish 'Yeheh Shmeh Rabbah Mevorakh,'* " *Sidra* 11 (1995), pp. 39-53 (at pp. 46-47). The end result is that, while ק-ל-ס survived in prevalent versions of the Shabbat *shacharit* and in the *haggadah*, it did not survive in *Kaddish*

*

Mitchell First is a personal injury attorney and Jewish history scholar. He wonders whether the authors of the word "supercalifragilisticexpialidocious" were using "cali" to mean "beautiful."

19. What is the Meaning of רכב בערבות (Psalms 68:5)?

This phrase is used as a description of God at Ps. 68:5: סלו לרכב בערבות (=extol the one who rides on the *aravot*). But what does *aravot* mean in this verse? Where exactly is God riding?

In an earlier article, "What is the Origin of the Words ערב and בקר?," I have written about the many meanings of the biblical root ע-ר-ב. It has meanings like: "mix," "enter," "guarantor," "pleasant/sweet" and "trade merchandise." The letters ע-ר-ב also underlie the word *aravah*, a desolate, wilderness area. They also underlie the words *aravah*=willow, and *orev*= raven. Of all these meanings, which one fits our phrase at Ps. 68:5?

The only one that might reasonably fit is "desolate, wilderness area." Thus one common translation for לרכב בערבות is "the one who

149. Ed. Mirsky, p. 154.
150. *Ibid.*, p. 151, n. 13.
151. *Sefer Ha-Manhig* (ed. Raphael), pp. 61-62.

rides through the deserts." A similar image is found in *ba-midbar panu derekh Hashem, yashru ba-aravah mesillah*, "clear in the wilderness a way for Hashem, set up in the desert a path for our God" (Isa. 40:3). But God as a rider in a desolate area is still an unusual image. More importantly, רכב usually means mounting an object and superimposing yourself upon it, and not "riding through" something.

In a statement of Reish Lakish at *Chagigah* 12b, the *aravot* of Ps. 68:5 was understood to be one of the seven heavens.[152] (The precise Hebrew words used in the discussion were רקיע and שמים.) But *aravot* does not otherwise mean "heaven" in Tanakh.

Aravot as רקיע or שמים is the understanding adopted in the Geonim and Rishonim as well, and presumably was the understanding of the author of the *Barukh Kel Elyon* song, where our phrase also appears.

Is there another way to interpret רכב בערבות of Ps. 68:5?

The letters ע-ר-פ mean "drip" two times in Tanakh. Also, the word ערפל appears many times in Tanakh with a meaning of "cloud." (Sometimes it merely means "darkness.") A reasonable understanding of the word ערפל is that ע-ר-פ is its root and the ל reflects merely the addition of an ending letter.[153] Therefore, a scholar who thought creatively could suggest that the ערבות of Ps. 68:5 can be understood as if derived from a root ע-ר-פ,[154] and that the image would be God who "rides the clouds."

Supporting the "rides the clouds" interpretation of Ps. 68:5 is that we have such imagery for God elsewhere in Tanakh. It is found in *ha-sam avim rekhuvo*, ("who makes the clouds his chariot" (Ps. 104:4), and *Hashem rokhev al av kal*, "God rides on a swift cloud" (Isa. 19:1). (See also perhaps Deut. 33:26.) Very likely, the "cloud" symbolizes God's chariot. It may be a symbol of glory as well, like the *ananei ha-kavod*. (Many interpretations of the "cloud" symbolism are possible.)

---

152. There is evidence elsewhere that this interpretation of *aravot* preceded Reish Lakish.

153. See also the related word with the root ע-ר-פ at Isa. 5:30.

154. Scholars are often willing to exchange ב with its fellow bilabial consonant פ to help understand a word. Among traditional sources, Rav S. R. Hirsch would often be willing to do this as well. See also Ramban to Ex. 15:10 and Radak, *Sefer Ha-Shorashim*, entry גף.

In another article, I explain that the word הפקר likely derived from the root ב-ק-ר.

Is the "rides the clouds" interpretation of רכב בערבות merely unsupported conjecture? It turns out that with the discovery of Ugaritic, we now have evidence for it. The Ugaritic language first came to light in 1928, based on a discovery in a town in Syria, near the Mediterranean coast. Ugaritic is an ancient Semitic language closely related to Hebrew. The Ugaritic texts cover many centuries and predate the biblical texts. The discovery of Ugaritic has led to many new understandings of difficult terms in the Bible. Relevant to our context is that the phrase *rokhev arafot* with the meaning "charioteer of the clouds" appears 14 times in various Ugaritic mythological texts as an epithet of their most prominent god, Baal. (Baal was believed to control the rainfall. This might be the basis for the metaphor. But other interpretations of the metaphor are also possible. Regarding their spelling *arafot*, there are other examples of Ugaritic "p/f" becoming "b/v" in Hebrew.)

There is a tendency in modern biblical scholarship to overemphasize Ugaritic in interpreting biblical texts. Scholars who believe that Ugaritic has been overemphasized will likely reject this Ugaritic-based interpretation of the biblical רכב בערבות. "Rides through the deserts" is admittedly a possible interpretation of the Biblical Hebrew, they would argue. Why should we create a new biblical word, where *aravot* means clouds? Nowhere else in Tanakh does *aravot* have the meaning "clouds."

So far, I have mentioned the following possible interpretations: (1) a "rides through the desert" interpretation that is consistent with many uses of *aravah* elsewhere in Tanakh (and can be supported a bit by Ps. 68:8), (2) an interpretation of *aravot* as *rakia/shamayim*, and (3) a "rides the clouds" interpretation that has a close parallel in Ugaritic but creates an unusual one-time meaning of *aravot* in Tanakh.[155]

But as stated earlier, רכב usually means mounting an object and superimposing yourself upon it, and not "riding through" something. רכב fits the "clouds" interpretation much better than it does the "desert" interpretation. Also, later in the same psalm, at verse 34, we have the phrase: *rokhev be-shmei shmei kedem*, "He rides on the

---

155. I have not discussed all early interpretations of the word *aravot* at Ps. 68:5, e.g., Septuagint, Targum, and other early sources, Jewish and Christian. That is beyond the scope of this article.

heavens of heavens of old." This serves as a much better parallel to the "clouds" interpretation than it does to the "desert" interpretation. Therefore, I think the "clouds" interpretation is the preferable one. The *Daat Mikra* edition of Psalms is willing to adopt the "rides the clouds" interpretation as its main interpretation in its commentary.

Of course, even though Ugaritic and the Bible may be using the same phrase as a description of God, the metaphor may have a different meaning in each of the two languages. As one scholar has observed in this context, the use of the ancient metaphor in the Hebrew language can be compared to the use of "new wine in an old bottle." Admittedly, the meaning of the metaphor in each language is still not entirely clear.

With regard to the "heaven" interpretation, it probably arose based on a simple reading of our verse, Ps. 68:5. The thinking was probably: If God is *rokhev ba-aravot*, that means *aravot* is likely a heaven. This interpretation could be supported by verse 68:34 which uses the phrase: *rokhev be-shmei shmei kedem*, "He rides on the heavens of heavens of old." But "heaven" still does not fit the word *aravot*.

*

Mitchell First is a personal injury attorney and Jewish history scholar. He has no plans of riding on clouds, and is content riding on the A train.

20. What is the Origin of the Word שאול (Netherworld)?

The netherworld location שאול is mentioned over sixty times in Tanakh. On the simplest level, it is a large place, located deep underground,[156] where the bodies and spirits of dead people dwell, perhaps spending most of their time sleeping.[157] (But some of these

---

156. The verb י-ר-ד is used in conjunction with שאול thirteen times in Tanakh.
157. One scholar has observed that all but a few of the appearances of שאול in Tanakh are passing ones that tell us little. See H. Halkin. *After One-Hundred-and-Twenty: Reflecting on Death, Mourning and the Afterlife in Jewish Tradition* (2016), p. 12. Halkin writes further: "About what took place in this realm, the Bible is silent. There are hints that its only activity was a perpetual sleep from which one might be fitfully awakened."

times, שאול refers only to an individual grave, and other times, it is used merely as a metaphor for distress.)

My question for this article is whether we can relate this place name שאול to our well-known root ש-א-ל which appears almost 200 times in Tanakh with meanings like "ask a question," "inquire," "demand/ask for an object," and "borrow an object"?[158]

שאול as a term for "netherworld" originated in Hebrew (although it is found as a loanword from Hebrew in a few other languages). This means that I will not be able to surprise you with an insight from another language, as I sometimes do.

In the ancient world, dead people were sometimes consulted for advice. (Such consultations persist in our time as well!) Recall the story at 1 Samuel 28, in which Saul goes to a *baalat ov* to bring the deceased Samuel back for consultation. The word שאול is nowhere mentioned in this story, but the fact that Samuel had to be "brought up" is mentioned a few times. This implies that he was located in an underground location. Accordingly, שאול can be viewed as "a place that you consult with." But there is only one such consultation story in Tanakh.

Theological Dictionary of the Old Testament has a long discussion of the root שאול, presenting many possibilities. The most creative approach suggested is that we should not view the ש as a root letter in this word. Rather, it is a prefix and the root of the word is אל. This two-letter word appears many times in Tanakh as a word of negation, and seems to have originally meant "nothing." See, e.g., Job 24:25. With the ש as a prefix, the word could have meant "make into nothing," "belonging to nothingness," or "place of nothingness."

A very interesting suggestion is made by Rav S. R. Hirsch (on Ps. 9:18). He states that the grave is called שאול because it *demands* the body back. Rav Hirsch's comment is very brief, but I would like to expand on it. Perhaps there was an ancient belief that, while we attempt to live on earth, there is an opposing force called שאול which

---

Halkin is a noted expert on the etymology of Hebrew words. But on the etymology of שאול, he writes only (pp. 11-12): "it is a word of obscure origin with no known cognates in Hebrew or other Semitic languages."

158. It is important to remind ourselves that "borrow" is a rare meaning of the root ש-א-ל in Tanakh. See the commentary of Rav Hirsch to Ex. 3:22. (Rav Hirsch writes here that the only time this root means "borrow" in Tanakh is at Ex. 22:13. But it seems to mean "borrow" in a few other passages as well.)

tries to pull us down below, like gravity. שאול is even described as having "cords" to pull people. See Ps. 18:6 (*chevlei Sheol sevavuni*; see similarly 2 Sam. 22:6). But perhaps the primary purpose of those cords was to restrain people from leaving שאול.

I also saw a suggestion that שאול is called this because it is never satisfied and *always asks for more* (i.e., more dead people to absorb.) The idea that שאול is never satisfied is found explicitly at Prov. 27:20 and 30:15-16. (See also Isa. 5:14 and Habakkuk 2:5.)

But the most likely suggestion proposes that שאול derives from the root ש-א-ה and that the final ל is not part of the root.[159] The root ש-א-ה has meanings like "loud noise," "crash into ruins," and "desolation."[160] Although the first two of these meanings would not seem to fit שאול, perhaps "desolation" can be seen as a main aspect of שאול, so שאול can mean "place of desolation."[161] At first, I did not like this suggestion because שאול was probably viewed as a crowded place, since it was the destination of everyone.[162] But perhaps it was viewed as desolate of material objects, or at least desolate of comforting material objects. For example, at Isa. 14:11 it is implied that when one lies down there, one lies on top of maggots and one is covered with worms, i.e., there is nothing to lie down upon there, and no blankets to cover oneself.

Of course, שאול is not described sufficiently in Tanakh, and all of these suggestions are speculative.[163] You are free to reject them

159. There are many examples in Tanakh of words with final *lameds* that are probably not part of the root. See, e.g., כרמל, ערפל, and שמאל. See E. Klein, pp. 287, 487, and 664.

160. Probably, it originally meant "loud noise." See, e.g., *teshuot* (Zech. 4:7), the last verse of the *haftarah* for Hanukkah. Then ש-א-ה encompassed the meaning "crash into ruins" because of the loud noise. Finally, it developed into "desolation," since this is the fate of ruins.

161. Koehler-Baumgartner adopts this interpretation. *Theological Dictionary of the Old Testament* mentioned it and rejected it

162. For example, Halkin writes about his impressions of שאול (from the limited data in the biblical verses): "Sheol is not a place of reward and punishment; all its inhabitants are treated equally. It is a vast subterranean space in which the spirits of kings and paupers, the noble and the villainous, lie side by side" (p. 15).

163. A friend suggested that שאול may have received its name because the individuals walk around there constantly feeling that they are lacking things, i.e., they are constantly "asking." But I think it more likely that the origin of the name would relate to a quality of שאול itself.

and conclude that שאול probably just meant "deep pit" and has no connection to our familiar root ש-א-ל. שאול is parallel to *bor* in many verses in Tanakh. (See, e.g., Ps. 30:4.)

Regarding the story of Saul bringing up the spirit of the dead Samuel for consultation, I would like to make an interesting observation. What was Samuel's first comment on being raised? If I were composing the narrative, I would have had Samuel make a comment like: "It's nice to see some flesh and blood people for a change!" (Or perhaps: "Please get me a tasty slice of ox. I have been longing for one for a while!") Instead, what does Samuel say? *Lamah hirgaztani le-haalot oti*, "Why are you bothering me?" This suggests that שאול, presumably where Samuel was, was viewed (at least by the author of the book of Samuel) as a somewhat restful place. (But note that midrashically, many of the שאול references in Tanakh are interpreted as "Gehinnom," a place of punishment. See, e.g., Rashi to Gen. 37:35.)

It is also very interesting that, when Samuel was brought up, he was wearing his robe (מעיל). This suggests that it was assumed that people dressed in שאול in the same type of clothes that they wore above ground! See also Ezek. 32:27 (warriors go to שאול with their war weapons).

Going back to our word שאול, it is of course ironic that scholars have made extensive efforts *inquiring* about the meaning of the word שאול. This is as humorous as the fact that Ernest Klein, in his *A Comprehensive Etymological Dictionary*, describes the word *safek* (=doubt) as "of uncertain origin"!

Finally, on a homiletical level, perhaps שאול is called this to remind us that we are all on "borrowed time" on this earth![164] We should all use our time here wisely!

*

Another friend suggested that the place received its name because, upon arrival there, one is questioned about one's life!

Finally, there is an old saying that "one does not die from asking a question." In light of שאול being the name for the netherworld, Rabbi Dovid Bashevkin suggested to me that perhaps we should reexamine this old saying!

164. I thank Shulamis Hes for this inspiring thought.

Mitchell First is a personal injury attorney and Jewish history scholar. When he has a large enough number of difficult words, he may consult with שאול and bother the wise king Solomon for a consultation. I hope you enjoyed this deep (!) article!

21. The Multiple Meanings of the Word ש-נ-ה

The root ש-נ-ה has two meanings in Tanakh. On the one hand, it means "to repeat." (Of course, the word *sheni*, "second," comes from this meaning.) On the other hand, it means "to change." A fundamental question is whether these seemingly opposite meanings, "repeat" and "change," originated from the same ש-נ-ה root. A further related question is the origin of the word *shanah* as "year."

Let us answer the second question first. I have seen sources that relate *shanah* as "year" to the "change" meaning. For example, Ernest Klein believes that the year was called *shanah* because it was a "period of changing seasons."[165] But an alternative view, which I prefer, is that the year was called *shanah* because it is fundamentally based on a concept of repetition. Many scholars accept this view. Among traditional Jewish sources, we can find something like this in Radak (*Sefer Ha-Shorashim*), Rav S.R. Hirsch (on Ex. 12:2), and S.D. Luzzatto (on Gen. 1:1).

I also saw a source that believed that the year was called *shanah* because of both the "repeat" and the "change" aspects. It cleverly defined the year as: "the repeating cycle of seasonal change." On the other hand, *Theological Dictionary of the Old Testament*[166] took the position that *shanah* as "year" was a primary noun and did not derive from either the "repeat" or "change" meanings.[167]

Let us now return to our fundamental question. Could שנה as "repeat" and שנה as "change" have come from the same source? In his concordance, Solomon Mandelkern attempts to unify them by pointing out that every time something is repeated, there is always a slight change. I was told, for example, that when the earth rotates

---

165. E. Klein, p. 669.
166. Vol. 15, p. 325.
167. Koehler-Baumgartner, p. 1600, took this position as well.

around the sun, the exact position that the earth travels in its rotation is not the same as the position it traveled the year before.

Also, we all know that when you used to make a copy of a piece of paper, the copy did not look exactly the same as the original. (This was before today's superb technology!) There was once a movie based on this principle. The movie was *Multiplicity*, starring Michael Keaton. In the movie, Michael portrayed a father who realized that the multiple demands on his time were getting too hard for him. He befriended a scientist and they came up with the idea of making two copies of Michael by cloning. This way, Michael could be in multiple places at once (e.g., job and family)! But the premise of the movie was that when you make a copy of something, there is always a slight change. So the movie had one of the clones come out with a more masculine personality than regular Michael, and the other come out with a more feminine personality, creating all kinds of difficulties for everyone! (The two clones also made a copy of Michael from the first clone. The personality of this new clone was really off, because this was a copy made from a copy!)

OK, so should we conclude that the principle set forth by Solomon Mandelkern and reflected in the Michael Keaton movie (=every repetition results in a change) is grounds to conclude that ש-נ-ה as "repeat" and ש-נ-ה as "change" have a common origin?

My intuition tells me that the above principle is not a true explanation for a common origin. But there is another way of looking at the two verbs. Every time you change something, you are doing a repetition. You are just repeating the activity with a change. This sounds like a better explanation for a common origin.

Then I looked at how the scholars treat the two Hebrew roots today. The widespread view is to treat the two Hebrew roots as separate ones. Scholars make this determination based on a review of all of the Semitic languages. For example, I saw the point made that in Aramaic, the verb for "repeat" is תנא, while the verb for "change" is שׁנא.[168] If the roots for "repeat" and "change" had a common origin, it is argued, they would not have gone in separate directions as they did in Aramaic.

Therefore, for a variety of reasons, the widespread view of scholars today is that the Hebrew root שׁנה has combined two different

---

168. This is in Palestinian Aramaic. It is שׁנה in Babylonian Aramaic.

earlier roots. But let us closely analyze the conclusion in *Theological Dictionary of the Old Testament*:[169] "It is possible to say with assurance that two Proto-Semitic roots have coalesced in Hebrew… although we must reckon with the possibility 'that the close relationship between the two meanings suggests that one could have developed from the other, as in Ugaritic….'" In other words, it is clear there that were two different roots for "repeat" and "change" before they coalesced in Hebrew, both using the letters ש-נ-ה. But the author of that essay is still willing to consider the possibility that at some earlier point, one of the two roots developed from the other.[170]

It is important to mention that the "repeat" meaning of *shanah* later developed, in post-Biblical Hebrew, into the meaning "study" and "teach," since the fundamental method of studying and teaching was repetition.

Let us now address a different noun: *shenah* as "sleep." Is this related? This seems to come from a different verb י-ש-ן. But I have seen a claim made that it is related to שנה as "repeat," since sleep is fundamentally an event that is repeated every night!

Finally, let us address the word in modern Hebrew for a small unit of time: *shniah*. This word is based on the English word "second." But why do we use this word in English? The answer (based on what was done in Latin) is that the "second" is meant as the second small part of the hour, in contrast to the "first" small part of the hour, the minute.

*

Mitchell First is a personal injury attorney and Jewish history scholar. Although he repeats a bio at the end of each article, he always changes it a bit as well!

22. The Various Possible Meanings of ושננתם לבניך

As part of the *Shema*, we recite: ***ve-shinnantam** le-vanekha, ve-dibbarta bam* (Deut. 6:7). But what exactly does that first word mean? From the context, we would expect something like "teach" or "make known."

169. Vol. 15, p. 317.
170. But Koehler-Baumgartner is not willing to suggest any such possibility.

How does Rashi explain our word? First, he writes that *ve-shinnantam* has the meaning of *chiddud* (sharpness). Then he explains the idiom. The words should be sharp in your mouth, so that if someone asks you something, you should be able to answer him immediately. (In this interpretation, the prefix *le-* of *le-vanekha* has the meaning of "for the sake of" *vanekha*.)

Why does Rashi provide this unusual interpretation? He does so because this interpretation of our verse is expressed in the Talmud at *Kiddushin* 30a. The interpretation is not recorded in the name of an individual Sage, but as a *tannu Rabbanan*, perhaps giving it even more authority. (This interpretation is also found at *Sifrei Devarim* 34 with a major variant that is probably an error.)

There are two main aspects to this interpretation. First is the interpretation of the root as ן-נ-ש, "sharpen," and second is the idiom that is implied based on this interpretation. It is true that the root ן-נ-ש appears a few times in Tanakh, and it always means something like "sharpen." (Indeed, it is related to the word *shen*, "tooth.")

But what about the idiom that the Talmud and Rashi chose? It is a bit of an unusual one. Therefore, when other commentaries explain *ve-shinnantam*, while they do often view the root as ן-נ-ש and the meaning as "sharpen," they often suggest a different idiom. For example, Seforno believes that the meaning is, "teach them with sharp explanations that explain matters intelligently." Alshikh believes that the meaning is that the words should penetrate the listeners' hearts like arrows. Rav S.R. Hirsch believes that the meaning is "imprint it in short, sharp, concise sentences." A scholarly work, *Brown-Driver-Briggs*, translates it, "teach the words incisively." This expression may reflect the same idea expressed by Alshikh, or perhaps it refers to providing sharp explanations, as suggested by Seforno. The aspect of penetration can be that the idea effectively penetrates the subject matter, or that it effectively penetrates the listener!

Most interesting is Ibn Ezra. He first cites reference to a *chetz shanun*, "a sharp arrow" (Prov. 25:18). But he adds, "it is known how an arrow is sharpened." Most likely, what Ibn Ezra means is that the process of sharpening involves going back and forth over the item. So in effect the instruction of *ve-shinnantam* is an instruction of teaching by repetition. *Theological Dictionary of the Old Testament*, vol. 15, p. 343, interprets *ve-shinnantam* similarly: "incise, engrave (by incessant recitation and explanation)."

Despite my recording all the above suggestions, the purpose of this article is to see if there are other approaches that avoid the ש-נ-ן =sharpen interpretation. Indeed, some of our traditional sources did not follow the "sharpen" interpretation. For example: (1) Targum Onkelos translated *ve-shinnantam* as *u-tetaninun*, "and you shall teach/repeat them," (2) Targum Yerushalmi translated it as *tigmerinun*, "and you shall teach them," and (3) Radak (*Sefer Ha-Shorashim*, entry ש-נ-ן) interpreted it as *ha-dibbur ha-temidi*.[171]

There are two approaches that scholars today take to avoid interpreting ש-נ-ן as "sharpen."

The first approach is based on a finding in Ugaritic, which is another Semitic language, similar to Hebrew. This language first came to light in the early 20th century, based on archaeological finds in Syria. It was discovered that Ugaritic has a verb ת-נ-ן that is the equivalent of the Hebrew ש-נ-ן, and that the Ugaritic ת-נ-ן can have the meaning "repeat." See *Theological Dictionary of the Old Testament*, vol. 15, p. 344. So perhaps "repeat" can be the meaning of our ש-נ-ן at Deut. 6:7.

The second approach is suggested by S.D. Luzzatto. He believes that the word *ve-shinnantam* ultimately derives from the word *shenayim*, "two," but that the doubling of the *nun* in *ve-shinnantam* implies a third repetition and, in effect *multiple* repetitions until the matter is familiar. There are also modern scholars that agree with such an approach. See, e.g., *Theological Dictionary of the Old Testament*, vol. 15, p. 344.

Luzzatto was able to bring some evidence for his approach from a talmudic statement at *Kiddushin* 30a: *al tikri ve-shinnantam ella ve-shillashtam*. This statement effectively interprets *ve-shinnantam* as if it said *ve-shillashtam*. As Rashi explains there, if verse 6:7 meant to instruct to do something exactly twice, the word used would have been *ve-shinitem* (with only one *nun*), and not *ve-shinnantam*.

To summarize, I have offered three different approaches to *ve-shinnantam*. One approach views the root as ש-נ-ן with a meaning of "sharpen," and offers various ways to understand the idiom. A second approach views the root as ש-נ-ן, and believes that this root can

171. See also *Sifrei Devarim* 34, *davar acher*, and R. Saadiah Gaon to Deut. 6:7.

mean "repeat." A third approach views שׁ-נ-ן as implying "continuous repetition and familiarity."

All agree that there is a different root שׁ-נ-ה, which meant "repeat" in Biblical Hebrew.[172] (In post-Biblical Hebrew, it developed into "learn" and "teach," since all this was done through repetition.)

Finally, it is possible that the root שׁ-נ-ן as "sharpen" derives from the root שׁ-נ-ה, "repeat." As alluded to by Ibn Ezra above, there is a close relationship between the two verbs, as sharpening is produced by way of repetitive actions.

Postscript: At Deut. 28:37, the Torah uses the word *sheninah*. Rashi writes the following there: *leshon ve-shinnantam, yedabru bekha*. In interpreting this word *sheninah*, Rashi seems to be telling us that it has the same meaning as the *ve-shinnantam* of Deut. 6:7 and that it means "speak about you." He does the same thing in his comments on *sheninah* at 1 Kings 9:7. But there is no mention of *chiddud* in either of these two comments. So what happened to Rashi's interpretation of *chiddud*, "sharpness"? He certainly did not forget that he offered this interpretation at Deut. 6:7!

Of course, it is possible that Rashi changed his mind and no longer believed in his *chiddud* interpretation. (See, e.g., his comments quoted in Rashbam's commentary to Gen. 37:2. Here Rashi admits that if he had time, he would revise his commentaries, due to the new understandings that arise every day.) But we would like to assume that Rashi did not change his mind between the time he composed his commentary to the sixth chapter of Deuteronomy and the time he composed his commentary to its twenty-eighth chapter. (Another example of an inconsistency between two different comments of Rashi in *Chumash* is found in Rashi's interpretation of the root *lamed-hei-tet*. He gives a certain interpretation of *lahat* at Gen. 3:24. Then, at Ex. 7:11, he gives a different interpretation of the *lahat* of Gen. 3:24.[173])

It seems that we just have to admit that Rashi gives himself some freedom to express different word interpretations in different

---

172. It also means "change" in Biblical Hebrew. I discuss this root in a separate article.

173. Also, on the place name *bakha*, compare Rashi to Ex. 14:3 with Rashi to Ps. 84:7. I would like to thank my brother-in-law Nochum Efroymson for pointing out these inconsistent Rashi's on *lahat* and *bakha* to me.

places in *Chumash*. He likely had an underlying reason to prefer each interpretation in its place. We are just going to have to live with this.

*

Mitchell First is a personal injury attorney and Jewish history scholar. His children consider him to be very sharp. But his wife instructs that things must often be repeated to him.

23. What Are the שׂרפים of Isaiah Chapter 6?

In the book of Isaiah, chapter 6, the prophet has a vision in which he sees God sitting on a throne, with *seraphim* above him. Each has six wings. With two wings, they cover their face, with two wings they cover their legs, and with two wings they fly. They call to one another: *kadosh, kadosh, kadosh*…. One of them uses a tong to take a burning coal from an altar and touches Isaiah's mouth, purifying him.

What exactly were these *seraphim*? The meaning of the term is of interest because *seraphim* are referred to many times in our liturgy (usually in the context of the *Kedushah* prayer).

A widely held view is that they were angels made of fire. This view is expressed, for example, by Rambam (*Yesodei Ha-Torah* 2:4) and Radak (*Sefer Ha-Shorasim*). (But query, if the *seraphim* were made of fire, why was that tong necessary?[174]) Another source I saw (an anonymous commentary on Rambam's *Hilkhot Yesodei Ha-Torah*) suggests that the word *seraphim* alludes to the fact that whoever looked at them was burned. Taking a completely different approach, Ibn Ezra notes that one of them touches Isaiah's mouth with a burning coal. He suggests that they were all called *seraphim* due to this mission. Finally, the vision also recorded that the area was filled with smoke (likely from the altar, and not from the *seraphim*). This allows Malbim to suggest that this smoke was an allusion to the future burning of the First Temple that these angels would have a role in. This explains why they were called *seraphim*.

But if we look at all the other references to *saraph* or *seraphim* in Tanakh, we find something completely different. The references at

---

174. I would like to thank Ze'ev Atlas for this observation.

153

Num. 21:6 and 21:8, and Deut. 8:15 are to serpents. The references at Isa. 14:29 and 30:6 are also to serpents, serpents that fly (*saraph me'ofef*).[175]

Thus, outside of Isaiah chapter 6, *saraph* and *seraphim* always refer to serpents!

This gives us reason to suspect that this may be its meaning in Isaiah chapter 6 as well. A divine/royal figure surrounded by serpents? Have any of us ever heard of something so unusual? We all have. In ancient Egypt, the uraeus serpent, standing on its coil, was the symbol of royalty of the pharaohs and of the gods. Archaeology has discovered numerous depictions of ancient Egyptian pharaohs (and their wives!) with the uraeus serpent on their foreheads. It seems that the uraeus was a symbol of protection of the pharaoh and of the sacred objects. (There was also a belief that it breathed fire on enemies!) Images of the uraeus as a royal symbol have also been found in ancient Israel from around the time of Isaiah, as Egyptian artistic motifs spread to Israel.[176]

The *seraphim* of Isaiah 6 have wings, legs, and a face, and are able to talk. One can argue that this makes it difficult to view these *seraphim* as serpents. But the implication of the word *seraphim* may be merely that they are angels which in some significant way resemble serpents. They can be composite figures that have both serpentine and human features.

In our "serpentine angel" interpretation, we now have a completely different picture of the throne scene in Isaiah 6. Many scholars adopt this interpretation.[177]

I am not claiming that the Tannaim and Amoraim understood the *seraphim* of Isaiah 6 in this way.[178] I am just trying to be an "original

---

175. Such creatures may never have actually existed. This deserves an article in itself.

176. See the material in Joines below.

177. See, e.g., K. Joines, "Winged Serpents in Isaiah's Inaugural Vision," *Journal of Biblical Literature* 86 (1967), pp. 10-15, Joines, *Serpent Symbolism in the Old Testament* (1974), and Koehler-Baumgartner. There is also an ancient source that adopted this interpretation: Enoch 20:7.

178. For a midrash on Isa. 6:2, see *Sifrei Haazinu* 306: *ha-seraphim, she-echad mei-hem yakhol lisrof et kol ha-olam kullo....* See also *Deut. Rabbah*, 11:9 which refers to *sarfei lehavah* and is probably giving an interpretation of Isa. 6:2. See also *Ex. Rabbah* 15:6.

intent" scholar and determine what the word may have meant at the time of Isaiah in the 8th century B.C.E.

We can attempt to rebut the "serpentine angel" interpretation by citing a point made by S.D. Luzzatto in his commentary to Isa. 6:2. Luzzatto has an answer to the argument that all the other references to *seraphim* in Tanakh are to serpents. Fiery *seraphim* are not mentioned anywhere in Tanakh precisely because they have a body of fire and are too dangerous to have contact with humans. Fiery *seraphim* are the highest levels of angels and attend only to God. Since they are confined to that heavenly locale, we would not expect them to be mentioned anywhere else in Tanakh! In this way, we can accept that most of the references in Tanakh are to serpentine *seraphim*, while the ones in Isaiah 6 are to fiery *seraphim*.

But there is a subtle problem with Luzzatto's approach. If our fiery *seraphim* did not exist anywhere but in the heavens, how did Isaiah know what to call them? Isaiah says he saw *seraphim*. This implies that he is describing an object that he already recognized.[179]

Therefore, in my view, the "serpentine angel" interpretation of Isaiah 6 is compelling. As I stated at the outset, in the rest of Tanakh and even elsewhere in the book of Isaiah, *saraph* and *seraphim* always refer to serpents.[180]

P.S. I also have to address the reason that serpents are called *seraphim*. I have seen it suggested that it was due to the burning sensation at the time of the bite, or the burning of the subsequent skin inflammation or fever. See also Rashi to Num. 21:6, *Tanchuma* 19, and *Numbers Rabbah* 19:22 (*she-sorfin et ha-nefesh*).

Finally, my etymological research reveals that it is only coincidental that the word "serpent" resembles the words *saraph* and *seraphim*.

*

Mitchell First is a personal injury attorney and Jewish history scholar. He is careful to avoid both serpents and fiery angels.

---

179. I would like to thank Fred Schulman for this observation.
180. The "serpentine angel" interpretation did make its way into one of the notes of the *Daat Mikra* commentary on Isaiah 6.

B. General Articles About the Language of Tanakh

1. Words that Appear Only One Time in Tanakh

There is a special term for words that appear only one time in Tanakh. They are called *hapax legomena*. (This is Greek for "once said.") There are about 1300 such words in Tanakh. Of course, a form of a word might appear only one time, but the root itself may appear many times. An example of this is עמדתו, "standing place," found at Micah 1:11. We all know the root ע-מ-ד, so there is no problem in understanding this one-time word. The more interesting words are words that appear only one time and do not share a related three-letter root with other known words. There are about 400 such words.[181]

Both the *Encyclopaedia Judaica* and the older *Jewish Encyclopedia* include an entry for *hapax legomena*. But the *Jewish Encyclopedia* entry also includes a proposed list of such words. Many of the *hapax legomena* are words for animals, plants, and diseases. Others are loan words from foreign languages.

Sometimes the meaning of these words can be guessed at from the context. If not, sometimes we can find help in one of the other Semitic languages. Other times we can find the word in Hebrew from a later period such as the Mishnah. We can also look to how the word was translated into Greek in the Septuagint in the Second Temple period.[182] Finally, we can sometimes make a reasonable conjecture that the word is related to another Hebrew root that shares some of its root letters.

The *Jewish Encyclopedia* lists fifteen *hapax legomena* in the book of Genesis. I will now go through some of them. (For brevity, I will shorten the term to *hapax*.) You will see that for many of these words (and with regard to any list that is proposed), there is a question as to whether or not the particular word should be considered a *hapax*.

181. As you will see from reading this article, determining which words should be considered *hapax legomena* and which words should not is not an exact science. Therefore, we cannot give an exact number of all such words. 182. Of course, our surviving Septuagint manuscripts are not that early. Moreover, the Septuagint translators did not have a good knowledge of Biblical Hebrew. The Pentateuch was translated into Greek in the 3rd century B.C.E. The translation of the Prophets and Writings seems to have been completed by the end of the 2nd century B.C.E.

- 41:43 אברך: (used regarding Joseph: *va-yikreu le-fanav avrekh*): I have discussed this word in my article "Egyptian Words in Tanakh." As I explain there, very possibly this word is of Egyptian origin and is an imperative that meant "attention!"[183] But most of our Rishonim and many scholars believe that it is a Hebrew word that is related to the word for knee (ברך) and meant "bend down, kneel." If so, it should not be considered a *hapax*.

- 43:11 בטנים: (sent by Jacob to Joseph): Since it is followed by the word ושקדים, a reasonable guess is that בטנים are a type of nuts. Based on Akkadian, the meaning seems to be "pistachios."[184]

- 6:14 גפר: This is a type of wood that was used to make Noah's ark.[185]

  A different word with the same root letters, *gafrit,* appears many times and means "sulphur." If *gofer* and *gafrit* would be related, then *gofer* should not be considered a *hapax*. But admittedly a relationship between the two seems unlikely.

- 25:30 הלעיטני: (used by Esau when asking to be fed): Although the root ל-ע-ט appears nowhere else in Tanakh, it does appear in the Mishnah and Tosefta. We can deduce from these sources that the root means, "to swallow." הלעיטני is in the *hifil* construct, so it literally means "cause me to swallow." As is clear from the context, Esau is asking to be fed.

- 15:2 משק: (*u-ven meshek beiti hu Damesek Eliezer*). It seems that the reason this unusual word was chosen was a play on words with *Damesek* (even though *Damesek* has a *sin*). Scholars today still have difficulty with the origin and precise meaning of this word.[186] From the context, it seems that it means something like "support" (Rashi, Targum) or "manage" (S.D. Luzzatto).

  Another difficult word, ממשק (*mimshak*), appears at Zephaniah 2:9. If it would be related to משק, then we should not consider either one a *hapax*. But ממשק seems to be a totally

---

183. H. Tawil, p. 5, seems to prefer an Akkadian origin for the word, pointing to the word *abarakku*, "steward."

184. See H. Tawil, p. 48. Even though בטנים only appears once, בטן (=stomach) appears many times. S. Mandelkern had suggested that בטנים are called this because they have the shape of a stomach. If this conjecture would be correct, then בטנים should not be considered a *hapax*.

185. According to Koehler-Baumgartner, p. 200, the species is still unknown.

186. Koehler-Baumgartner, p. 652, writes that it is "unexplained."

unrelated word. Even if its root is מ-שׁ-ק, it is reasonable to consider both *meshek* and *mimshak* as one-time words.[187]

- 24:21 מִשְׁתָּאֵה: (*ve-ha-ish mishtaeh lah*) The אִישׁ refers to Eliezer and the לה refers to Rebecca. But what exactly was Eliezer doing?

  The root here is שׁ-א-ה. This root does appear elsewhere in Tanakh. It has the meanings of "loud noise," "crash into ruins," and "desolation." The author of the *Jewish Encyclopedia* list included מִשְׁתָּאֵה on his list because he believed that the underlying שׁ-א-ה root here is not related to the other שׁ-א-ה root.

  But Rashi and many others do relate מִשְׁתָּאֵה to the "crash into ruins" and "desolation" meaning of שׁ-א-ה. They believe that from "crash into ruins" and/or "desolation" developed a meaning of "confused, silent, and deep in thought." If so, we should not consider מִשְׁתָּאֵה a *hapax*.[188]

Looking outside of Genesis, here are some of my favorite *hapax*:

- מַעֲקֶה (Deut. 22:8): The Torah commands us to build a *maakeh* for our roofs, so people will not fall. But what is a *maakeh*? Solomon Mandelkern put this word in its own entry under the root ע-ק-ה, implying that it is a *hapax*.[189] From the context, we understand that it must mean some kind of wall or protection at the edge of the roof, to protect people from falling off. There are also similar words in Arabic that mean "deter" and "hold back."[190]

---

187. But it is possible that that our word מֶשֶׁק derives from the biblical root נ-שׁ-ק which meant "equip, arm." We could then understand מֶשֶׁק as if it was written מִנְשַׁק and the נ dropped. If this would be the case, then מֶשֶׁק would not be a *hapax*.

188. I have discussed this word at length in a separate article. I argue there that the best way to understand it is to take a different approach. We should understand it as if it was spelled with an ע, and the root was שׁ-ע-ה/look. The meaning of מִשְׁתָּעֶה, a word in the *hitpael* construct, would be "continually looking."

189. This is not an exact science. Most view the root ע-ק-ה as related to the root ע-ו-ק. This should not prevent מַעֲקֶה from being considered a *hapax* with the root ע-ק-ה. There are two other words in Tanakh, עָקַת (Ps. 55:4) and מוּעָקָה (Ps. 66:11), that one could argue also belong in the root ע-ק-ה. But Mandelkern includes these with the root ע-ו-ק. An alternative approach might include מַעֲקֶה as well within the root ע-ו-ק. In this scenario, it would not be a *hapax*.

190. See Koehler-Baumgartner, p. 615.

- מְשַׂקְּרוֹת (Isa. 3:16: *u-mesakrot einayim*): According to the context of the verse, this is something that haughty women do with their eyes. The root is שׂ-ק-ר. But wait a minute, the root שׁ-ק-ר (to lie) appears over 100 times. Why did the post-talmudic Masoretes put the dot on the left here and create this *hapax*? Why did they not make things simple for us and put the dot on the right like all the other times?

  I have discussed this issue in a different article.[191] As I point out there, there are some who believe that the dot on this word should be on the right, in which case we would not have a *hapax*. There are even texts of the Tanakh that have the dot on the right.

  If the root really is שׂ-ק-ר, some attempt to deduce its meaning from the root in early Rabbinic Hebrew ס-ק-ר, which itself has two different meanings: "paint red," and "look."

- הָאֲחַשְׁתְּרָנִים בְּנֵי הָרַמָּכִים (Esther 8:10): Here we have two one-time words. This is a well-known phrase because an Amora in the Talmud (at *Megillah* 18a) seems to admit that even the Amoraic Sages did not know the meaning of the phrase. רמכים is found in Mishnah *Kilaim* 8:5, and is a kind of horse, so perhaps the Amoraic statement was really focused on the first word. The solution to אחשתרנים was found in the mid-19th century, when ancient Persian cuneiform was deciphered. אחשתרנים means "royal/governmental."[192]

There are words that appear twice in Tanakh but effectively appear only once. This occurs when an identical passage is repeated in two different books of the Tanakh. An example is שנהבים (ivory), found only at 1 Kings 10:22 and its repetition at 2 Chron. 9:21. (שנהב is a combination of שן, "tooth," and הב, "elephant."[193]) Another interesting word is אמתחת (sack), repeated 14 times in Genesis 42-44, but found nowhere else!

---

191. "Original *Shin* and Original *Sin*."

192. See E. Klein, p. 18, and Z. Ron, "*Ha'achastranim Bnei Ha'ramachim*: Translating Esther 8:10," *The Jewish Bible Quarterly* 36:1 (Jan.-Mar. 2008), pp. 33-38.

193. הב is not in Tanakh with the meaning "elephant." But it is close to the Egyptian word for elephant.

Finally, there is a very unusual root, טאטא that appears only twice in Tanakh, both times at Isa. 14:23 (in slightly different forms). It means "sweep" and "broom." According to the Talmud (*Rosh Hashanah* 26b), the Sages only learned the meaning of this word by overhearing it being used by the handmaid of Rabbi Yehuda Ha-Nasi!

*

Mitchell First is a personal injury attorney and Jewish history scholar. He regrets not having used any *hapax legomena* in the title of this book.

2. Original *Shin* and Original *Sin*

Today, we pronounce the letter שׂ the same way as the letter ס. Was this always the case? And why do שׁ and שׂ share the same letter form? The only difference between שׁ and שׂ is the location of the dot, but the dots are markings that did not arise until the post-talmudic period.

To answer the first question, scholars today realize that שׂ and ס were not pronounced the same way in biblical times. A scholar who wrote his dissertation on this in 1974 was Dr. Richard Steiner, who later taught at Yeshiva University for decades. His dissertation was *The Case for Fricative Laterals in Proto-Semitic*. (Have I lost you already?!) Steiner showed that originally the letter שׂ was pronounced "SL."

This original "SL" pronunciation explains many phenomena. For example, the Tanakh refers to an ancient people called כשׂדים. Yet in other ancient sources they are called "Chaldeans." What happened to the "L" sound in the Hebrew? Now we understand that Hebrew did not omit it. It was built in all along with the שׂ.

A few generations ago scholars believed that שׂ was merely a later development from שׁ. But this view has been discarded. Now scholars believe that the letters were originally separate root letters. They were able to make this determination based on a review of the other Semitic languages.[194] Since שׁ and שׂ originated as separate letters, we

194. See, e.g., E.Y. Kutscher, *A History of the Hebrew Language* (2d. ed., 1984), p. 13.

should normally not attempt to equate roots in which one root has a שׂ and the other has a שׁ.[195]

A very interesting question is why Hebrew utilizes an alphabet in which one letter has to do "double duty." The answer suggested by scholars today is somewhat surprising. The background is that Hebrew is one of several languages that arose from an original language that scholars call Proto-Semitic. The assumption is that Proto-Semitic had 29 consonants. Over time, in the Hebrew language that number was reduced to 23. Reduction occurs when sounds disappear due to similarity and merger. At the stage where Hebrew began to be written down and needed an alphabet, it borrowed an alphabet from another people (the Phoenicians) that had only 22 letters. But rather than add a new letter, Hebrew decided to employ one sign for both the *shin* sound and the *sin* sound, since their pronunciations were not that different.[196]

Over the centuries, everyone who has written a Hebrew dictionary or concordance has been faced with a dilemma. Do the letters שׂ and שׁ warrant separate entries or one merged entry? Now that we realize that the letters originated as separate root letters, it would seem that they deserve separate entries. But some books are attempting to be easy to use by non-Hebrew speakers. An example is Ernest Klein, *A Comprehensive Etymological Dictionary of the Hebrew Language for Readers of English* (1987). Here this very scholarly book merged all the שׂ and שׁ words into one long entry. Another work that merged all the שׂ and שׁ words into one entry was the dictionary of Marcus Jastrow. Perhaps when this work was published at the end of the 19th century, it was still thought that the letters were related.[197]

Now I will address an interesting word related to the topic of שׂ and שׁ. At Isa. 3:16, we find the word מְשַׂקְּרוֹת. Here God talks about punishing the daughters of Zion, because "they are haughty and walk

---

195. Of course, admittedly sometimes one of the letters may have evolved into the other.
196. E.Y. Kutscher, *A History of the Hebrew Language* (2d. ed., 1984), p. 13.
197. The Even-Shoshan concordance also merges the two entries, unlike the Mandelkern concordance. I suspect that Even-Shoshan was following the precedent of some earlier concordances. Also, perhaps he too thought this would be more user-friendly.

with stretched-forth necks [*netuyot garon*] and are מְשַׂקְּרוֹת עֵינָיִם...."
The root of מְשַׂקְּרוֹת is שׂ-ק-ר. In all of Tanakh this root only appears
here, so we are faced with the difficult issue of determining what it
means.

But wait a minute. We all know the root שׁ-ק-ר, to lie. This root
appears over 100 times in Tanakh. When the dots were added in the
post-talmudic period, why was it decided to put the dot on the left
here, and create a unique root? Why could they not have dotted it on
the right like they did all those other times?

One possibility is that they had a strong tradition that the letter
was שׂ. Alternatively, perhaps they could not fathom a reasonable
interpretation of an expression "lying with their eyes."[198]

How have our commentaries dealt with this word מְשַׂקְּרוֹת? This
is a very relevant question because our verse with מְשַׂקְּרוֹת עֵינָיִם is the
source for the שִׂקּוּר עַיִן line in the *al chet* prayer.

Note that in the early versions of the *al chet* prayer, the line was
spelled סִקּוּר עַיִן.[199] That is why it is found today in the position of the
samekh line in the acrostic. The spelling was later changed in most
versions to שִׂקּוּר to reflect the שׂ spelling of the biblical word מְשַׂקְּרוֹת.[200]

Rashi on Isa. 3:16 offers two interpretations of מְשַׂקְּרוֹת עֵינָיִם:
"looking," and "putting red make-up on their eyes."[201] The basis for
these interpretations is that in early Rabbinic Hebrew there was a
root in Hebrew ס-ק-ר that had two different meanings: "looking," and
"painting red." Probably, Rashi's thinking was that one of these was
the original meaning of שׂ-ק-ר, even though the spelling changed over
the centuries to ס-ק-ר. Some of the other Rishonim interpret *mesakrot*

---

198. The "Lying Eyes" song by the Eagles had not yet been composed!
199. See, e.g., the version found in the Cairo Genizah published by M. Zulay,
in *Piyutei Yannai* (1938), p. 322, and *Machzor Vitry*, p. 391 (ed. S. Hurwitz).
200. We know that the original phrase סִקּוּר עַיִן was derived from the phrase
מְשַׂקְּרוֹת עֵינָיִם of Isa. 3:16 because the previous line in the *Al Chet* prayer
addresses the sin of נְטִיַּת גָּרוֹן, also derived from Isa. 3:16.
201. These are also the two main possibilities presented at Koehler-
Baumgartner, p. 1350.

It has also been suggested that שׂקר may be a methathesis of שׂרק.
See Koehler-Baumgartner, p. 1350. שׂרק may mean "red" in Tanakh. See
perhaps Zech. 1:8 and elsewhere. See Koehler-Baumgartner, pp. 1361-62
and E. Klein, p. 683.

einayim to mean "winking with their eyes," as a form of seduction. But this is just a guess from the context.

Most interesting is the approach taken by S.D. Luzzatto. He points out that there are some texts of Isa. 3:16 that have מְשַׁקְּרוֹת (i.e., second letter is a *shin*). He suggests that this was the original reading. He theorizes that, since the context of the verse was a criticism of haughtiness, "lying with one's eyes" meant seeing people and pretending not to see them.

I now believe I understand why the post-talmudic Masoretes put the dot on the left. A possible idiom of "lying with their eyes" was unclear to them. What was clear to them were two different meanings with a שׂ (looking, and painting red). Even though they had to assume that the original שׂ in one or both of these roots evolved into a ס, this was preferable to them than creating a difficult idiom. (Or alternatively, perhaps they did have a strong tradition that the letter was a שׂ.)

Going back to the *al chet* prayer, there are really two separate questions that are raised by the סקור עין line. One is: what was the meaning of the phrase מְשַׁקְּרוֹת עֵינַיִם at Isa. 3:16? The other is what did the post-talmudic author of the *al chet* prayer have in mind when he composed the line סקור עין? We have seen that the first question is a hard question, due to the uniqueness of the root שׂ-ק-ר. But the second question is easier. We know what the root ס-ק-ר meant in the talmudic and post-talmudic periods: "looking" or "painting a red stripe." Since the latter does not fit the context in the *al chet*," סקור there must have something to do with "looking." And based on sources such as *Genesis Rabbah* 18:2, it seems that the transgression referred to is looking around too much with one's eyes, i.e., prying into the affairs of others.

*

Mitchell First is a personal injury attorney and Jewish history scholar. If he ever publishes a concordance or a dictionary, he will make sure it has separate entries for שׂ and שׁ.

3. Some Interesting Words in *Parashat Miketz*

Parashat Miketz includes many interesting words. I thought it would be interesting to discuss some of them:

- אברך: This word appears only at Gen. 41:43 (*va-yikreu le-fanav avrekh*). Most of our commentators see the letters ברך and translate it as something like: "bend the knee." (But Rashi takes a different approach.) There is a widely quoted suggestion that the word is of Egyptian origin and means "attention!" Hayim Tawil, in his *An Akkadian Lexical Companion for Biblical Hebrew*, mentions this suggestion but would rather use Akkadian to explain the word. He points to the Akkadian word *abarakku*, "steward."[202]
- אחו: grass or reed (as food for cattle). This word appears twice in *Parashat Miketz*. It only appears one other time in Tanakh, at Job 8:11. It is a word of Egyptian origin.
- אמתחת: bag, sack. This word appears 15 times in Tanakh (in various forms). But all of its appearances are in *Parashat Miketz*! There is a verb מ-ת-ח that appears one time in Tanakh (at Isaa 40:22) and means "spread out." Some relate אמתחת to this verb. The suggestion is that it is a sack that spreads over two sides of the animal. But Tawil relates אמתחת to an Akkadian word that means "carry, pick up."
- זמרת: At verse 43:11, Jacob tells his sons to take from *zimrat ha-aretz* as a present to Joseph. We all know that the root ז-מ-ר means "to sing." There are also a few occasions in Tanakh where the root means "to cut, prune, trim." (See Lev. 25:3-4 and Isa. 5:6.) But neither of those two meanings fit Gen. 43:11. (Yes, we could force the "cut" meaning into the term, but it is a stretch.) How do we solve this difficulty?

  We all know the verse in אז ישיר where God is described as עזי וזמרת (Ex. 15:2). The second word should be understood as if it were written זמרתי.[203] Now we would ordinarily translate the

---

202. H. Tawil, p. 5. אברך eventually became a title for young rabbinic scholars. This is based on the statement of R. Yehudah quoted in Rashi: *av be-chakhmah ve-rakh be-shanim.*
203. See my article: "Some Interesting Words in אז ישיר."

entire phrase as, "The Lord is my strength and my song." But in the early 20th century the ancient language of Ugaritic was discovered (based on excavations in Syria). Then we realized that in this Semitic language, the root ז-מ-ר could also mean "strength." Now Ex. 15:2 makes much better sense! It is a poem with two parallel words for "strength. We can use this "strength" meaning in Gen. 43:11 as well. Jacob is telling his sons to take from the strongest, i.e., best, produce of the land.

- חרטמים: This word is found in Genesis, Exodus, and Daniel, and is always in the plural. Some relate it to the Hebrew root ח-ר-ט, "engrave." But most likely, the word is of Egyptian or Akkadian origin and meant something like "soothsayer priest,"[204] "magician," or "interpreter of dreams."[205]

- טף: child. This word appears in *Parashat Miketz* and throughout Tanakh. Its root is טפף. (See Isa. 3:16.) But what does that three-letter root mean? It means "to toddle" (= to walk in an abnormal way.) So we see that it is not only in English that children are called "toddlers." They are called this in Biblical Hebrew as well!

- מליץ: translator. The root of this word is ליץ. But this root also means "scoff, mock." In Italian, there is an expression *traduttore traditore*, "every translator is a traitor"! Does the Hebrew language include a similar assumption, that every translator is a mocker, someone who alters the truth? Solomon Mandelkern, in his concordance, takes this position and combines all the words with root ל-י-ץ into one entry.[206]

But most scholars take the position that the two ל-י-ץ roots do not have a common origin. One clue to this is that מליץ does

---

204. This is a priest who recited spells and hymns during temple rituals and official ceremonies.

205. See, e.g., Koehler-Baumgartner, p. 353, and H. Tawil, p. 120. For some interesting older interpretations of חרטמים, see, e.g., the commentary of S.D. Luzzatto to Gen. 41:8.

206. People who author concordances, like S. Mandelkern, are constantly faced with a dilemma. Do they put words which have identical three-letter roots in the same entry? If the words seem to have a common origin, they do. If not, they set up two separate entries for the root. But often it is unclear whether the two words with the same three-letter root have a common origin.

not only mean "translator." It also means "intercessor, advocate." See, e.g., Job 33:23: *im yesh alav malakh melitz*....[207]

- צפנת פענח: According to many scholars, this looks like an Egyptian word, as the last three letters resemble the Egyptian word for "life." The meaning seems to be "the god has said: he will live!"[208]

- שאול: This is the biblical word for the "netherworld." But what does it mean? Is it a reflection of the fact that dead people are sometimes *asked* for advice, as in the story of Saul and the witch of En Dor?[209] The Hebrew root ש-א-ל has various meanings such as: "ask a question," "inquire," "demand an object," "ask for an object," and "borrow an object." Can we use any of these to explain this place name? Are there other alternatives? I have discussed this word at length in a separate article.

- שבר (shever): This word means "grain." But where does it come from? Is it related to ש-ב-ר, "break"?

  Some relate שבר as "grain" to the similar word בר. Others relate it to ש-ב-ר as "break" and think it originally meant "broken or threshed food." Alternatively, perhaps grain was called this because it "breaks out easily from the husk."

  We can also speculate that food in general may have been called שבר because it breaks one's hunger. (See similarly Ps. 104:11, referring to drink as "breaking" the thirst of animals.) Even in English we have the word "breakfast," i.e., food breaks ones fast. Also, in Modern Hebrew, to eat after a fast is "*lishbor et ha-tzom*."

  Nevertheless, Tawil concludes that most likely, the two ש-ב-ר words "break" and "grain" are not related. He notes that *shibru* is a type of flour in Akkadian. *The Hebrew and Aramaic Lexicon of the Old Testament* (=Koehler-Baumgartner) also concludes that the connection with "breaking" is improbable and unclear, and

---

207. This verse should sound familiar, as we recite it in our *kapparot* ritual.
208. See Koehler-Baumgartner, p. 1049. I have seen other translations by scholars as well. See, e.g., E. Klein, p. 518.

R. Aryeh Kaplan, in *The Living Torah* (1981), provides an illustration of how the words would have been written in Egyptian. He offers three translations: "Lord of life," "Neth speaks life," and "The God speaks and [this man] lives."
209. I read somewhere that the name of the character Endora on the TV show *Bewitched* may have been based on the biblical place En Dor!

raises the possibility that שבר as "grain" may have derived from a non-Hebrew root.

I will now kiss this article goodbye with the following discussion:

- ישק: Pharaoh tells Joseph (at Gen. 41:40): *ve-al pikha yishak kol ammi.* Most commentaries relate ישק to the word משק at Gen. 15:2.There Eliezer is described as the *ben meshek* of the house of Abraham. Of course, we do not know what משק means.[210] But from the context, it is evident that it means something like feed, support, or manage. (See, e.g., Onkelos, Rashi and S.D. Luzzatto.) It is possible that that word משק is derived from the biblical root נ-שׁ-ק which means "equip, arm." We can adapt most of these understandings to the ישק of Gen. 41:40.

  The *Daat Mikra* mentions the משק approach to ישק approvingly but then argues alternatively that ישק may mean "kiss" here. It states that to kiss someone can sometimes be a *neshikah shel gedulah* and suggests an analogy to Samuel's kissing Saul upon anointing him. (See 1 Sam. 10:1.) I did not find this analogy convincing, so I disagree with his suggestion that Pharaoh was alluding to Joseph metaphorically kissing all the Egyptian people!

  *

Mitchell First is a personal injury attorney and Jewish history scholar. From his youth, he remembers Ibn Ezra's sharp comments on צפנת פענה (Gen. 41:45): "If this is an Egyptian word, we do not know its meaning; if it is a translation, we do not know Joseph's name." As he got older, he has spent much time "inquiring" about the meaning of Sheol.

4. Some Interesting Words in אז ישיר

There is much to discuss in this biblical poem. I am limiting myself to a brief selection:

---

210. Koehler-Baumgartner, p. 652, writes that it is "unexplained."

- עזי וזמרת י-ה: It is very reasonable to understand the second word as if it was written וזמרתי, and that we just have an abbreviated form here.[211] As to its meaning, traditionally the root ז-מ-ר has been translated as "song" here, so that entire phrase would mean, "God is my strength and my song" But in the early 20th century the ancient language of Ugaritic was discovered (based on excavations in Syria) and it was realized that in this Semitic language, ז-מ-ר could also mean "strength." That is certainly its meaning here,[212] since it would form a perfect parallel to עזי. Parallelism is typical in ancient biblical poetry.

- ירה: "The chariots of Pharaoh and his army, God cast (*yarah*) into the sea." The word תורה also has the root י-ר-ה, derived from the "proclaim/instruct" meaning of י-ר-ה.[213] So this verb י-ר-ה has at least two different meanings: (1) throw/cast/shoot, and (2) proclaim/instruct.[214]

---

211. See, e.g., the commentaries of S.D. Luzzatto and *Daat Mikra* on our verse.

For a very interesting alternative theory to explain why we should read the word וזמרת as if there is a *yod* at the end, see: S.D. Luzzatto, comm. to Gen. 27:46, J. H. Hertz, comm. to Lev.1:1, R. Margaliot, *Ha-Mikra Ve-Ha-Mesorah* (1964), pp. 66-70, and I .O. Lehman, "A Forgotten Principle of Biblical Textual Tradition Rediscovered," *Journal of Near Eastern Studies* 26 (1967), pp. 93-101.

212. Strength" is also probably the meaning of the root ז-מ-ר in the phrase *mi-zimrat ha-aretz* (Gen. 43:11). Jacob is telling his sons to bring Joseph a present from the strongest, i.e., best, produce of the land. The root ז-מ-ר also has another meaning in Tanakh: "cutting, pruning."

213. When the *yod* is in the first position in the root, it usually changes to *vav* when the verb becomes a noun.

214. *Theological Dictionary of the Old Testament*, vol. 6, p. 330 and 339.

It also has a third meaning as a verb, "to water." But according to many scholars, this is just a by-form of ר-ו-ה = to drink/be saturated. Most likely, this third meaning is the basis for the biblical words יורה and מורה: "early rain." See Koehler-Baumgartner, pp. 404 and 436 and *Theological Dictionary of the Old Testament*, p. 336. See similarly *Taanit* 6a, second explanation, and Rashi to Deut. 11:14.

Of course, one can alternatively view the early rain as moisture that is "thrown" to the earth. It has also been suggested that the early rain provides "instruction" on some level. (See, e.g., *Taanit* 6a, first explanation). But this explanation seems farfetched.

It seems unlikely that these two י-ר-ה meanings have a common origin. But it is interesting to mention some of the creative attempts that have been made to connect them. One suggestion is that both are a form of guiding. Another suggestion is that a teacher casts the stone of wisdom into the heart of his student![215]

Finally, I cannot resist mentioning Rav S.R. Hirsch's creative alternative understanding of the root of תורה. In his commentary to Gen. 16:5, he suggests that the root is ה-ר-ה, since teaching means "to plant a spiritual seed in someone."[216]

- שלישיו (shalishav): The word שליש as some kind of military/ governmental officer or advisor appears seventeen times in Tanakh, but the Tanakh is vague as to the precise role of the shalish. One of these seventeen times is Ex. 15:4. In Akkadian, the third man in a chariot is called tashlishu. Some want to interpret shalish here in this way.[217] But all the other times that shalish appears in Tanakh, it does not seem to be referring to officers/ advisors on chariots.[218]

Another possible explanation for the origin of shalish is that it originally meant something like "third-level advisor," after the king and his main advisors.[219] Then perhaps it expanded to mean any kind of advisor.

Note that in Ex. 15:4, shalishav is parallel to markevot Paroh ve-cheilo, so the parallel can be to either markevot (chariots) or to cheilo (his army).

---

215. This was suggested by S. Mandelkern.
216. Also of interest is the suggestion in Brown-Driver-Briggs that the root of the word תורה was perhaps י-ר-ה with the meaning "casting lots"!
217. In this scenario, it has been suggested that the "third man in the chariot" acted mainly in an advisory role and then the term expanded to become a general term for an advisor.
218. See, e.g., Ex. 14:7: ve-shalishim al kullo, where Rashi gives shalishim the meaning שרי צבאות. The shalishim here seem to be on a higher level than chariot riders. See also 2 Chron. 8:9 (ve-sarei shalishav ve-sarei rikhbo) and 1 Kings 9:22 (ve-shalishav ve-sarei rikhbo). Two different categories are being described.
219. See similarly Ibn Ezra to Ex. 14:7.

Scholars have also searched for the origin of the word *shalish* in Hittite, Egyptian, and Ugaritic. [220]

- טבעו: I always knew that the root ט-ב-ע meant something like "sink down." That is the meaning here: "sunk down into the *yam suf.*" But what about the word טבעת, "signet ring, seal"? I always thought that this word came from the root ט-ב-ע, because a signet ring/seal was used to press down on something. This is certainly a widespread view. But Thomas Lambdin, in his *Egyptian Loan Words in the Old Testament*, suggests an alternative approach, that טבעת is a word of Egyptian origin. [221]

- יכסימו (*yekhasyumu*): My question here relates to the end of the word. Later on in the poem we have the words *yokhleimo, timlaeimo, torisheimo, tivlaeimo, yochazeimo, tivieimo,* and *titaeimo.* These words all end with ו. So why not: *yekhasyumo*? Here are the interesting comments of S.D. Luzzatto (taken from the translation of Daniel Klein):

Hebrew grammarians...as well as Rashbam say that the [letter *mem* in *yekhasyumu*] is vocalized with a *shuruk* in order to match the pronunciation of the preceding *yod*, which is also vocalized with a *shuruk*.... I say that the reason for the *shuruk* [in *yekhasyumu*] is to portray to the listener's ear the

---

220. For further reading, see *Theological Dictionary of the Old Testament*, vol. 15, p. 125, Koehler-Baumgartner, pp. 1525-26, and the detailed article by M. Vervenne in *Ugarit-Forschungen* 19 (1987), pp. 355-73.

Regarding the evidence from Ugaritic, the relevant root is *t-l- t*. This root would evolve into *sh-l-sh* in Hebrew. *Daat Mikra* writes (comm. to Ex. 14:7) that the Ugaritic word refers to soldiers who fight from chariots. But this is very misleading. All we really know from the Ugaritic is that *t-l- t* is mentioned near the Ugaritic word *mrkbt* (chariot) in a certain repeated passage. But the Ugaritic *t-l-t* may not mean "chariot" or "chariot soldiers" in this passage. For example, it may mean "three" or "bronze/copper." The article by Vervenne cites many different interpretations of the Ugaritic *t-l-t* in the relevant passage. (Based on the "bronze/copper" meaning, some suggest it means "armored soldiers.")

221. T. Lambdin, "Egyptian Loan Words in the Old Testament," *Journal of the American Oriental Society* 73 (1953), pp. 145-55. Koehler-Baumgartner, pp. 368-369, in its entry for טבעת, mentions both possibilities for the origin of the word.

sinking into the depths and the submerging under the water, for the function of the *u* sound seems to be to arouse in us an impression of darkness and depth…. Only with another *shuruk* preceding it does the final *shuruk* have the power to arouse such an impression.[222]

- נערמו: "With a breath from Your face, the waters piled up." The root here is ע-ר-ם which means "pile." But wait a minute. Don't we know this root ע-ר-ם elsewhere as meaning "cunning/smart"? For example, at Gen. 3:1, the *nachash* is described as ערום.

   It is hard for me to believe that the words "cunning/smart" and "pile" are connected. Nevertheless I always found the following attempt by Rav S.R. Hirsch at Genesis 2:25 to be exceptionally clever and worth mentioning:

   We find the root ערם elsewhere having the two meanings: cunning, subtle… and as ערמה a heap of grain. The connection between these two is easily found…Every subtle plan is a joining up of single arrangements to achieve an ultimate purpose…. The subtle one does various things which are unnoticed, the single little grains have no importance, but together they make the heap.[223]

   Surprisingly, Onkelos translates "נערמו מים" as חכימו מיא, "the waters became intelligent." He is using the "cunning/smart" meaning of ע-ר-ם here, instead of the "pile" meaning! In his view, the meaning is something like the water used its intelligence and figured out how to defeat the Egyptians.

- ירגזון: This word means "tremble" here ("the nations heard and trembled"). It is parallel to "חיל" in this verse, which also means "tremble." But don't we know the root ר-ג-ז elsewhere as meaning "anger"? S.D. Luzzatto suggests an explanation.[224] The root ר-ג-ז originally meant "shaking" or "trembling," as it does here. But

---

222. Klein suggests an analogous example in English: "doom and gloom."
223. In the methodology of Rav Hirsch, roots with three identical letters are *always* connected. Therefore, he must always attempt to find a connection.
224. See his commentaries to Gen. 45:24 and Ex. 15:14.

it was then transferred to denote other emotional tumults or agitations, such as "sorrow"[225] and "anger."

Any discussion of the root ר-ג-ז reminds me of one of my favorite translations in *The Living Torah* (1981) of R. Aryeh Kaplan. At Gen. 45:24, after Joseph has revealed his identity to his brothers, he bids goodbye to them with the phrase אל תרגזו בדרך, "do not be agitated while you are traveling." In the introduction to *The Living Torah*, R. Kaplan writes that he was trying to produce a translation that was among other things "modern" and "readable " Here he decided on: "Have a pleasant journey!"

*

Mitchell First is a personal injury attorney and Jewish history scholar. He never gets angry. (But his family members have a different recollection.)

5. Some Interesting Words in the Daily *Amidah*

Compared to some of our other prayers, the Hebrew in the daily *Amidah* is fairly straightforward. Nevertheless, there are some interesting words. I will now present a selection (in the order the words appear in the *Amidah*):

- גומל: In Tanakh, the root ג-מ-ל has several meanings. Sometimes it means "ripen." Other times, it means "wean a child from its mother's milk." (Both of these meanings are probably related to the root ג-מ-ר.)

  However, other times ג-מ-ל means something completely different: "give/pay back" (e.g., giving someone back what they deserve).

  The interesting issue is this "give/pay back" meaning. For years I had assumed that this meaning must be related to the word *gamal* as "camel." I thought that perhaps it meant giving something that you had stored up, like camels store water. Or perhaps the fact that it often connoted a "payback" came from the fact that camels went back and forth.

  Now that I have gotten older (and hopefully wiser), I am less willing to make the connection from the "give/pay back"

---

225. See, e.g., 2 Sam. 19:1.

meaning to "camel." I see that most scholars do not make it and believe that it is just coincidence that the verb ג-מ-ל for "give/pay back" has the same letters as the word for camel. I vividly remember attending a *shiur* on the *Amidah* where the presenter began: "What does it mean to be **camel** *chesed*?" But I do not think that this is a relevant inquiry anymore. (Of course, I may be wrong. There are no clear answers here.)

I will also note that the giving and actions that are done via ג-מ-ל in Tanakh sometimes affect people favorably and other times affect them unfavorably.

- משיב: The root of this word is נ-שׁ-ב. This root means "blow." We are supposed to understand *mashiv* as if it was written *manshiv*. The *nun* dropped out from the initial position, as often happens in Biblical Hebrew.[226] This root only appears three times in Tanakh, and at two of these times, Gen. 15:11 and Ps. 147:18, the *nun* is not even there. The one time the *nun* is there is at Isa. 40:7. The root does appear in the Rosh Hashanah service: *ruach noshavet*. *Mashiv* (=*manshiv*) is in the *hifil* construct. It means "causes to blow," i.e., God causes the wind to blow.

- מכלכל: The word כלכל appears in Tanakh a few times in various forms. I have seen two different approaches to it. One view sees it as derived from the root כ-ל-ל as "to complete" (and its derivative כל= all), and sees the meaning as "to provide with everything."[227] This is what I had always thought.

  But I have seen other scholars take a different approach. There is a biblical root כול, which means something like "contain." It is used, for example, in the case of vessels that contain things. These scholars suggest that כלכל derives from this root. Since the original meaning "contain" is the equivalent of "holding something within," this evolved into a "sustain, support" meaning.[228]

  (With regard to the doubling of the letters, going from כל to כלכל, this usually reflects some form of intensification.)

---

226. I have discussed this phenomena in a separate article: "Searching for Omitted *Nuns*."

227. See, e.g., M. Jastrow, p. 643, and Rav S.R. Hirsch on Gen. 45:11.

228. See, e.g., Koehler-Baumgartner, pp. 463-464, E. Klein, p. 278 and S. Mandelkern, entry כול .

- מתיר אסורים: God does not permit the forbidden! Rather, the explanation is as follows. The root א-ס-ר means "bind," so אסורים here means "bound individuals." (Related to this is the word אסור, "a binding obligation.")

  But what does מתיר mean? It turns out that its root is נ-ת-ר, which means "release." The *nun* dropped from the initial position. The word is in the *hifil* construct and should be understood as *mantir*, "causes to be released." The two words together mean that God releases bound individuals.

- סלח, מחל: I have discussed these words extensively in an article in Ḥakirah, vol. 18 and in my book *Esther Unmasked*. I will just reiterate some highlights here:

  מ-ח-ל never appears as a verb in Tanakh. (Admittedly, there are several names in Tanakh that seem to derive from the letters מ-ח-ל. But most likely these מ-ח-ל names were based on the "joy" meaning of the letters מ-ח-ל, which ultimately derives from a different root, either ח-ל-ל or ח-ו-ל.) The letters מ-ח-ל with a meaning like "forgive" first appear in a text of the Dead Sea Scrolls. Later the word is found in the Mishnah.

  ס-ל-ח is the word for "forgive" in Tanakh. But in Tanakh it is always God doing the forgiveness or being asked for forgiveness. How did individuals ask other individuals for forgiveness in the time of Tanakh? We do not know! Unless of course, the verb מ-ח-ל was used but never made its way into Tanakh.

  When we look at the letters מ-ח-ל in this word, a main issue is whether that initial מ is a root letter. Perhaps the root was ח-ל-ל, with its meaning "open space" or "emptiness." Alternatively, Tanakh includes a root מ-ח-ה with a meaning like "erase, remove." Perhaps מ-ח-ל was derived from this root.

  From the Cairo Genizah we learn that the Palestinian version of the daily *Amidah* did not include the words מחל or מוחל in the *selichah* blessing (in contrast to the prevalent version today). After the initial phrase beginning with סלח, the next phrase began with מחה.

- יהמו: Regarding various types of righteous people (and ourselves!), we ask *yehemu rachamekha*. It is evident from the context that it means "may your mercy be aroused." But what precisely does the root ה-מ-ה mean? This root is found various times in Tanakh, including in the well-known verse at Jer. 31:19: "Is Ephraim a darling son to me? ... Therefore *hamu meiai lo*. I will surely have compassion on him...."

To answer the question, I would first like to quote from Solomon Mandelkern's statement at the beginning of his entry for the root ה-מ-ה: *yesodato havarah tiv'it she-motziim baalei chayim be-shaat ha-hitpaalot ve-ha-hitragshut*, "its essence is a *natural noise* that living things emit at a time of activity and feeling." Then, please forgive me, but I will rely on Homer Simpson. I have not had a TV in my house for over ten years but I still have vivid memories of Homer enjoying the smell of his anticipated dinner and murmuring joyously: "Hmmm, rump roast!" This "Hmmm" sound is undoubtedly the meaning of ה-מ-ה. It surely is an onomatopoeia (a word that sounds like what it is).[229] So asking *yehemu rachamekha* is, literally, asking for an arousal of God's mercy with some accompanying sound signifying the arousal. Of course, by the time the *Amidah* was composed, the word probably merely meant "arouse," without any implication of an accompanying sound.

- תמגר: The root מ-ג-ר means "cast down." The root appears in Tanakh at Ps. 89:45, Ezek. 21:17, and at Ezra 6:12 (in a section of Tanakh that is in Aramaic).[230]

I will close with an interesting observation. According to most scholars, the daily *Amidah* was composed and instituted around the late first century C.E.[231] Much of the Mishnah dates from this same period. Yet the Mishnah includes hundreds of words derived from Greek and Latin, while all such foreign words are lacking in the *Amidah*. Evidently, as suggested by the Israeli scholar Moshe

---

229. I looked in Koehler-Baumgartner (p. 250) and was hoping that this work would mention the suggestion that this root was an onomatopoeia. But it did not. Nevertheless, it clearly views the root as one which is related to making a noise/sound.

230. But some believe the word at Ez. 21:17 is from a different root. See, e.g., Rashi.

231. See, e.g., A. Friedman, "The *Amida*'s Biblical and Historical Roots: Some New Perspectives," *Tradition* 45:3 (2012), pp. 21-34.

Bar-Asher, there was a desire to compose the prayer in pure Hebrew, drawing exclusively on words with roots in Tanakh.[232]

*

Mitchell First is a personal injury attorney and Jewish history scholar. He tries not to get too distracted by interesting words when reciting the *Amidah*.

6. Searching for Omitted *Nuns*

No, this is not an article about *Ashrei*. (I have written about that elsewhere![233]) I am now going to write about *nuns* that are root letters that have dropped out, and that need to be "restored" in order to understand the words.

Let me start with something I discovered only recently (at age 59!). What is the meaning of the word מֵשִׁיב in the phrase מַשִּׁיב הָרוּחַ? In order to know the meaning, you must first know the root. But what is the root of this word? The root of this word is not מ-שׁ-ב (there is no such root), י-שׁ-ב (sit), or שׁ-ו-ב (return). Rather, the root of this word is נ-שׁ-ב. This root means "blow." We are supposed to understand מֵשִׁיב as if it was written מַנְשִׁיב.

It is not your fault that you did not know נ-שׁ-ב as a root in Tanakh. It only appears three times, and two of those times, at Gen. 15:11 and Ps. 147:18, the *nun* is not even there. The only time the *nun* is there is at Isa. 40:7. (But the root does appear in the Rosh Hashanah service: *ruach noshavet.*)

As I mentioned, נ-שׁ-ב means "blow." מֵשִׁיב (to be understood as מַנְשִׁיב) is in the *hifil* construct. Therefore it means "causes to blow," i.e., God causes the wind to blow. Most likely this is how you understood the phrase anyway, even though you did not understand how you arrived at this understanding!

232, The only foreign word in the *Amidah* is the word *ligyonot* (=legions). This word derives from Latin and is part of the *Nachem* insertion for Tisha b'Av. But the *Nachem* insertion may be Amoraic in origin. See JT *Berakhot* 4:3.

233. See the article: "The Most Important Dead Sea Text: A Lost Paragraph from the Book of Samuel!"

Just like נ-שׁ-ב means "blow," so does נ-שׁ-ף (e.g., *nashafta be-ruchakha*, Ex. 15:10). Also, נ-שׁ-ם means "breathe." This is some evidence that Hebrew roots were originally two letters.

Every day in *Pesukei De-Zimra* (Psalms147:18), we recite: *yashev rucho, yizlu mayim*, "He blows His wind, the waters flow." Not only does the *nun* need to be restored in *yashev*, it also needs to be restored in *yizlu*. *Yizlu* should be understood as *yinzlu*. Its root is נ-ז-ל, "flow."

I have now given you several examples of *nun* root letters that dropped from the first position. This was a very common occurrence in Biblical Hebrew. The *nun* dropped from the first position for reasons related to ease of pronunciation.

As long as we were talking about the *Amidah*, let me give you another example there: אסורים. מתיר אסורים here means "bound individuals." (Related to this is the word אסור, "a binding obligation.") But what does מתיר mean? Its root is נ-ת-ר, which means "release." It should be understood as מנתיר, "causes to be released."[234]

Now I am going to give you many more examples:
- הביט (*hibbit*): This word and its variant forms appears many times in Tanakh. But only once, at Isa. 5:30, does that *nun* actually appear. We have to pretend it is there all the time! Every *hibbit* should be understood as *hinbit*. The root is נ-ב-ט. The meaning of *hinbit*: to cause oneself to see. (God left that *nun* in one place to help us see the light here!)[235]
- הגיד (*higgid*): The root here is נ-ג-ד, "next to." Every *higgid* should be understood as *hingid*. It means, "to cause an idea to be next to someone else." The closest synonym in English would be "to present."[236]
- הגיע (*higgia*): Every *higgia* should be read as *hingia*. The root is נ-ג-ע, "touch." The meaning is "cause to touch." When you are caused to touch, that is when you have "arrived."

---

234. מותר, "permitted," is also from the root נ-ת-ר and should be understood as מונתר.

235.. The Akkadian cognate to the Hebrew root נ-ב-ט means "to shine brightly." See H. Tawil, p. 232.

236. Similarly, *ve-higgadeta le-vinkha* (Ex. 13:8) does not mean "tell your son a long story." Rather, it too comes from נ-ג-ד, and implies only the presentation of an idea to your son.

- הכה (*hikkah*): הכה appears many times in Tanakh. The root is נ-כ-ה, which means "damage." Every *hikkah* should be read as *hinkah*. The meaning is: "to cause damage."
- מבול: Many sources (e.g., Radak, Seforno, S.D. Luzzatto) believe that this word should be understood as מנבול. They believe that the root is נ-ב-ל, with its meaning "destroy, decay, fall." (But Umberto Cassuto, *Daat Mikra* and others, including myself, believe that the root is actually י-ב-ל, "flow." I have addressed this in a separate article.)
- מגפה: plague. This should be understood as *mangefah*, from נ-ג-ף, "strike."
- מתנה: gift. This should be understood as *mantanah*, from נ-ת-ן, "give."
- מטה (*matteh*): rod. This word derives from the root נ-ט-ה and its meaning "extend." It should be understood as *manteh*. It is a rod that is used to extend one's reach. This is as opposed to a *mishan*, which is a rod that is leaned on (from the root ש-ע-ן).[237]
- מטה (*mittah*): bed. This should be understood as *mintah*. It derives from the root נ-ט-ה and its meaning is "incline." (Both the "extend" and the "incline" meanings of נ-ט-ה are related.)
- מצבה (*matzevah*): pillar. This word should be read as if it were *mantzevah*. It derives from the root נ-צ-ב, which means "stand." In Modern Hebrew people always ask about the מצב. This is from *mantzav*. The literal meaning of *mah ha-matzav* is "how do we stand?"
- An interesting word in Modern Hebrew with an omitted first position *nun* is the word מגבת, "towel." This word was coined by Eliezer Ben-Yehuda from the root נ-ג-ב which means "dry" (like the Negev!).[238] A related word is מגב, "a mop or windshield wiper."

I once saw a very interesting edition of Tanakh. The author printed the accepted text and added in all the root letters that had dropped out. But he added them in a different font, so you would realize that they were not in the accepted text. Hundreds of *nuns* and *yods* (and other letters) were added! (Admittedly, a lot of conjecture

---

237. Other biblical words for rod are שבט and מקל. The word שבט is also the source of the word שרביט. The etymology of מקל remains unclear.
238. See E. Klein, p. 314.

went into this work.) When I looked at this work, it was extremely enlightening. Unfortunately, this work was self-published and has not been widely circulated. But I have been thinking that if Judaism ever put me in charge, just like the ArtScroll Stone Chumash replaced the Hertz Pentateuch, I would consider replacing the ArtScroll Stone Chumash with this edition. (OK, only temporarily!) (Also, on Simchat Torah, I would add an alternative dancing circle that sings 100 מנשיב הרוח times!)

I would also like to explain how one can develop the skill of finding dropped initial *nuns*. It can be developed by using the concordance of Solomon Mandelkern (originally published in 1896). Mandelkern organized his concordance by roots and was very strict about it. So what happens when you look up a word like מתיר, "release"? There is no entry מ-ת-ר. You must then speculate what the missing root letter is! When you engage in this frustrating task time after time you begin to realize how often there was a *nun* that dropped in the first position![239]

Once in a while, Mandelkern has mercy on his users. For example, he includes an entry in the location מבול, even though he knows that מבל or מבול is not the root of this word. In this entry, he gives you the several candidates for the root. (Most likely, the root is נ-ב-ל or י-ב-ל, see above.) Mandelkern writes explicitly that he made this exception and created this entry so that it would be easier for his users to find the word.

My friend Rabbi Moshe Yasgur once gave me some very important advice regarding the Mandelkern concordance. You must use the editions published in 1955 or later. These usually include an appendix authored by a later professor that tells you where to find the words whose roots are difficult to discern.

I want to discuss one more omitted *nun*. מקבת is a hammer or a stonecutter's tool. This comes from the root נ-ק-ב, "pierce." So *makkevet* should be understood as *mankevet*. As I have written elsewhere,[240] "Maccabee" was initially a nickname for Judah only, and then, in the 2nd century C.E. came to be used by the church fathers as a nickname for the entire family. Almost certainly, Judah's nickname

---

239. Admittedly, an easier way to develop this skill is to look for a *dagesh*. A *dagesh* in a letter often indicates that a preceding letter was dropped.
240. See my article: "The Meaning of the Name 'Maccabee.' "

"Maccabee" was originally spelled with a ק and came from the word מקבת. So perhaps we should be calling the group the "Mankabees"!

By the way, everything I wrote above is אמת. This word comes from the root א-מ-ן. Here, the *nun* must be restored to the **third** position!

Finally, the book of Esther tells us in two places that Achashverosh reign from *Hodu* to *Kush*. But where exactly is *Hodu*? (These are the only two times in Tanakh that *Hodu* is mentioned.) The answer is that *Hodu* is the Tanakh's word for *Hindu*, i.e., it is the area of ancient India. The *nun* that should have been in the Hebrew transliteration (הנדו), and perhaps was there initially, was dropped here as well![241]

*

Mitchell First is a personal injury attorney and Jewish history scholar. This may be an appropriate time to disclose that his real first name is "Mintchell."

7. Wordplay in Tanakh

One of my favorite examples of wordplay in Tanakh is at Gen. 18:23, where Abraham is negotiating with God about the destruction of Sodom. Abraham says: *ha-af tispeh tzaddik im rasha*? The literal translation is: "will you *even* destroy righteous people with evil people?" But *af* also means "anger," so the statement simultaneously means: "will your *anger* destroy righteous people with evil people?" Rashi presents both interpretations as if they are alternative choices, but one does not have to choose between them. Both can be present simultaneously. That is the function of wordplay.

Now let us deal with a different kind of wordplay. At Gen. 2:25, Adam and Chavah are described as ערומים. In the next verse, 3:1, the nachash is described as ערום. The word ערומים means "naked," from the root ע-ר-ה=bare (like the word ערוה). ערום, on the other hand, means "wise" or "cunning." The text has cleverly used two similarly spelled words that have different meanings,[242] teasing us a bit, but without any substantive import.

---

241. See E. Klein, p. 140.
242. One source that believes that both words are used here with the same meaning is Targum Yonatan. It interprets the 2:25 reference as meaning "wise."

Ibn Ezra is one commentator who comments on the wordplay here. He points out some similar instances of wordplay in Tanakh. For example, he cites Judg. 10:4. Here we are told that Yair the Giladite had thirty sons that rode on thirty עירים, and they had thirty עירים. The first *ayarim* means "donkeys." The second *ayarim* means "cities." Both are spelled exactly the same way! These words are certainly not related.

A similar example of wordplay is found at Num. 25:8. Pinchas follows the male and female sinners into the *kubah* (inner room in the tent). A few words later we are told that he stabs the female *el kovatah* (through her stomach).[243] Both *kubah* and *kovatah* superficially appear to be related words. But they are not related.[244]

Going back to Gen. 2:25-3:1, I have to mention a humorous comment by the post-talmudic Masoretes. The first מ in ערומים has a *dagesh* in it, strengthening it, while the מ in ערום has no *dagesh*. These Masoretes, who were responsible for the *dagesh* and other such symbols, had an interesting mnemonic here: "The 'wise' are weak and the 'naked' are strong!"

Another example of wordplay is at Ruth 2:10. Here Ruth says to Boaz: Why have I found favor in your sight *le-hakkireni, ve-anokhi nakhriah*? Here the wordplay is subtler, since there is no visible *nun* in להכירני (since the original root *nun* dropped). But both הכירני and נכריה have the same root: נ-כ-ר, yet they have opposite meanings: "recognize" and "strange."[245]

Now I am going to mention a wordplay that will surprise you because it is generally unnoticed, even though it is literally right under our noses. I am referring now to the biblical text regarding the commandment of ציצת. At Numbers 15, the word ציצת is used three times: *ve-asu lahem tzitzit... ve-natnu al tzitzit ha-kanaf... ve-hayah lakhem le-tzitzit u-re'item oto....*

---

243. See Deut. 18:3.
244. S. Mandelkern lists them both under ק-ב-ה, but provides two separate entries and explanations of origin. Both Koehler-Baumgartner, p. 1060, and E. Klein, p. 559, view *kubah* as having a different root altogether: ק-ב-ב.
245. Whether these roots have a common origin or not is still debated. *Theological Dictionary of the Old Testament*, vol. 9, p. 424 prefers to assume that they do not, while Koehler-Baumgartner, p. 699, prefers to assume that they do.

One theory for a common origin is based on the idea that the process of recognizing something begins with recognizing its strangeness/uniqueness. See E. Klein, p. 416.

The word צִיץ has various meanings, all related. One of its meanings is something that protrudes outward and blossoms. Another meaning is something that is visible, (e.g., the צִיץ on the forehead of the high priest). While the first and second uses of צִיצַת in *parashat tzitzit* are referring to the literal *mitzvah* object (which protrudes outward), the third use is relying primarily on the other meaning: something that is visible. Now all of a sudden we understand the flow of the sentence: *ve-hayah lakhem le-tzitzit, u-re'item oto u-zekhartem…* (The conventional translation: "And it shall be for you *tzitzit*" is obviously awkward.)

One commentator who noted the wordplay was Rashbam. See his comment on the third צִיצַת reference at 15:39: *petil ha-tzitzit ha-zeh yihiyeh lakhem le-reiah she-tiru oto.*

The English translations are faced with a dilemma here. Even though some probably realize that there is a wordplay here, they cannot show it. Because the three uses of the word צִיצַת are in close proximity to one another, they feel the need to translate the word צִיצַת the same way throughout (whether as "tassels" or "fringes," or merely as "tzitzit").

(I will also note that Rashi, in his comment on the first use of צִיצַת, mentions both the "protruding" meaning of צִיצַת and the "visible" meaning. But it is Rashbam, by making his comment on the third use of צִיצַת, who clearly points out that there is a wordplay here with the third instance having a different meaning.)

A most dramatic wordplay is found in the story of Joseph and his interpretations of the dreams of the chief butler and baker at Genesis 40. When Joseph interprets the dream of the chief butler, Joseph says that in three days *yissa Paroh et roshekha* and he will return you to your position. But a few verses later, when Joseph interprets the dream of the chief baker, Joseph says that in three days *yissa Paroh et roshekha me-alekha* "and he will hang you on a tree"! The term *yissa et rosh* (literally: "lift the head") has a few different meanings and the text has dramatically juxtaposed a positive one with a negative one!

Finally, another wordplay is the reference to the *nachash ha-nechoshet* at Num. 21:9. Almost certainly, the Hebrew words *nachash* (snake) and "*nechoshet*" (bronze or copper or brass) are not related to one another.[246] What we have here is mere wordplay.

Whether נחש as "snake" is related to נחש as "divination" is a separate issue. A suggested connection is that the ritual was perhaps originally done with snakes. But most scholars today reject this connection.[247]

I will end with an example of a different type of wordplay, a wordplay involving sound. At 1 Samuel 15, Saul was commanded to destroy the entire people of Amalek including its animals. But Saul spared Agag and some of the Amalekite animals. When Samuel came to meet Saul thereafter, Samuel's first words to Saul were: *u-meh kol ha-tzon ha-zeh be-oznai....* Most likely that *meh* was meant as an allusion to the sound of sheep that Samuel was hearing![248]

*

Mitchell First is a personal injury attorney and Jewish history scholar. He is thinking of a third profession, a diviner, to finally determine whether snakes are an integral part of the ritual.

---

246. See, e.g., *Theological Dictionary of the Old Testament*, vol. 9, p. 370. The suggestion that copper was called נחשת because its color was reminiscent of the color of snakes is mentioned and rejected here.

Since we just mentioned copper, I am reminded of the English word "cop" for policeman. I had always wondered about this word and imagined, without any basis, that it was an abbreviation for "commander of police." Then I came across an article in the *Wall Street Journal* which reported that originally each policeman in New York City wore a copper star and that this led to "coppers" and finally to "cops." But then I found out that there is an alternative view that "cops" comes from a verb "to cop," meaning "to seize, to capture." Of course, perhaps both explanations are correct, each one explaining what happened in a different region (New York City vs. England). But this all deserves more research.

247. See, e.g., *Theological Dictionary of the Old Testament*, vol. 9, p. 357. What is often suggested instead is that נחש as "divination" is related to the root ל-ח-ש, "whisper." *Ibid.*, p. 357, Koehler-Baumgartner, p. 690, and E. Klein, p. 412.

Aramaic has the root נ-ח-ש for "divination" but does not have the word נחש for "snake." This also supports that there is no connection between the two.

I also saw a suggestion that the divination was originally done with metal/נחשת. This suggestion is mentioned at Koehler-Baumgartner, p. 690.

248. For another example of a wordplay based on sound, see my discussion of the word *yekhasyumu* in the article: "Some Interesting Words in אז ישיר."

8. Akkadian Words in Tanakh

Although we are used to thinking of the Tanakh as entirely Hebrew, sometimes words from other languages creep in. One of the languages that sometimes creeps in is Akkadian. Akkadian was the language of the ancient Assyrians and Babylonians.

In 2009, the scholar Hayim Tawil published a book titled, *An Akkadian Lexical Companion for Biblical Hebrew*. This book helps us with some of these Akkadian words. It also helps with Hebrew words in cases where the Hebrew words did not occur often enough in Tanakh to deduce their meaning, since we now have some of these words, or cognates to these words, in Akkadian sources. Akkadian is considered one of the Semitic languages. It is undeniably related to Hebrew, even though it was written in cuneiform, and not in an alphabetic script like the other Semitic languages.

There are many profound insights in Tawil's book. But because it is organized in alphabetical order and not by *parashah*, you have to slowly go through the entries to find the pearls of wisdom. (An idea for a book is for someone to go through this book and present something on each *parashah*!) I have done some of the digging and will present some of my findings:

- אוב: This term and its plural appear many times in Tanakh, usually parallel to ידעני. A ידעני (from the Hebrew י-ד-ע) is a soothsayer, someone who claims to know the future. So how did אוב come to mean something like this? In Akkadian, the word *apu* means an "opening into the ground." Tawil writes that "אוב is an ancient term employed in most Near Eastern languages for a ritual pit through which mortals communicated with chthonic deities." ("Chthonic" deities are those who dwell under the earth. Surely, you knew that!) So from an original meaning of "an opening into the ground," אוב evolved into a reference to someone who goes to such an opening to communicate with underworld deities! Tawil suggests that we can see the "pit" meaning of אוב at Isa. 29:4.
- אלול : In Akkadian, *ullulu* means "to purify." This may be the meaning of the name of the month.[249] In ancient Assyrian times,

---

249. But Tawil is not certain and suggests another scenario as well.

their goddesses had their annual cleansing in the sacred river in this month.

- אֲרֶשֶׁת: This word appears only once in Tanakh, at Ps. 21:3: *va-areshet sefatav*. We all know it from the Rosh Hashanah *musaf*, where the phrase *areshet sefateinu* is recited. (It appears that the authors of the High Holiday payers enjoyed utilizing difficult, rarely appearing words! There are many examples of this, such as *dibarnu dofi. Dofi* appears only one time, at Ps. 50:20.)

   The Complete ArtScroll Machzor: Rosh Hashanah translates *areshet* as "utterance." They are here following the view of Rashi and most Rishonim. But Tawil points out that there is an Akkadian verb *erēshu*, "to desire," and a noun *erishtu*, "desire." Therefore, most likely, the word in Psalms means "the desires of." Indeed, the "desire" meaning is confirmed by the parallel phrase in the earlier part of the verse in Ps. 21:3: *taavat libbo*. (Finding a parallel word in the same verse is the best method of determining the meaning of a rare word in Tanakh.)

   ArtScroll's *Sefer Tehillim* (ArtScroll Tanach Series) commentary on the *areshet* of Ps. 21:3 includes the following passage: "This 'utterance' expresses a deep wish or desire. The word may be related to *erusin*, the initial act of marriage." So this work came to the correct conclusion, not by parallelism (*taavat libbo*) and not through the use of Akkadian, but by suggesting a similarity to *erusin*, even though the root for this word in Tanakh is with a *sin* (ארש), unlike אֲרֶשֶׁת. Interestingly, modern scholars do consider it likely that there is a relationship between ארשׁ and אֲרֶשֶׁת,[250] even though fundamentally *shin* and *sin* are two separate root letters.

   Finally, even though *areshet* is generally considered a word that appears only one time in Tanakh, Tawil also sees it as the meaning of the word *yerushat* at Ps. 61:6, where "inheritance" does not fit the context.

- הֵיכָל: From the many times this word appears in Tanakh, it is evident that it means something like a palace or temple. Some

---

250. See, e.g., Koehler-Baumgartner, pp. 91-92, and E. Klein, p. 57.

   It seems from Koehler-Baumgartner that the Hebrew ארשׁ represents a later evolution from the original word which had the "sh" sound, as in the Akkadian.

might see the root of this word as the Hebrew י-כ-ל (=to be able to). In this view, a היכל originally would have been a "place of ability/power." But this seems farfetched. Rather, Tawil points out that Akkadian has a word *ekallu* (derived from Sumerian) which means "big house" or "palace." Most likely, this is origin of the word היכל.

- הסכת: At Deut. 27:9, Moses declares: *hasket u-shema Yisrael*. If the root is ס-כ-ת, this root only occurs here. The Targum, Rashi, and Radak suggest that הסכת means something like: "listen, pay attention." This is also the view implicit at *Berakhot* 16a. Ibn Ezra writes regarding this word: אין ריע לו (=it has no friends). This is one of the colorful ways he describes a unique root! Tawil points out that the Akkadian equivalent of this root, *sakātu*, means "be silent." This certainly fits the context in the verse.

- כבד: At Exodus 4:10, Moses is described as being כבד פה and כבד לשון. There is much disagreement among the commentators as to whether these terms imply a speech impediment or are an idiom for a lack of eloquence/inability to persuade. [251] Based on evidence from the Akkadian cognate to כבד, Tawil believes that the terms do imply a speech impediment.

- שגל: This root appears as a verb four times in Tanakh. Each time, there is a *ketiv/kri* to prevent the actual word from being read. Evidently, the Masoretes believed that the root ש-ג-ל was so offensive that it should not be read. What they proposed instead was a word from the root ש-כ-ב. It would seem that the Masoretes understood ש-ג-ל as an offensive term for sexual relations,[252] and ameliorated it with the blander term ש-כ-ב.

But if those three letters ש-ג-ל, are so offensive, how come *sheigal* is used as the term for the queen at Neh. 2:6: *ve-ha-sheigal yoshevet etzlo*? Some attempt to get around the problem by claiming that the reference at Nehemiah is not to the queen, but to the chief concubine. But let us look at another instance of this noun in Tanakh, Ps. 45:10. Here, the verse reads: "Kings'

---

251. I address this topic in a separate article.
252. How do modern scholars understand the offensive word? Koehler-Baumgartner opines that the etymology of the word is uncertain, but that it is "obviously an uncouth word." It suggests that it may come from the root ג-ל-ה, "reveal," with the addition of an initial ש. Alternatively, it suggests that it is related to an Akkadian word that means "confiscate, seize."

daughters are among your favorites; at your right hand stands the *sheigal* in gold of Ophir." A *sheigal* in the choicest of gold sounds more like a queen than a chief concubine!

Also, the parallel to King's daughters sounds like we are talking about a queen. Nouns with the root שׁ-ג-ל also appear three times in Daniel 5, in the Aramaic section of the book.[253] What is going on here? Are we reciting offensive words in Psalms, Nehemiah, and Daniel?

I mentioned earlier that the word for "palace" in Akkadian is *ekallu*. A proposed explanation is that the biblical noun *sheigal* is not related to the offensive biblical verb שׁ-ג-ל. Rather, it derives from the Akkadian *sha ekalli*, which means "the one of the palace," and which was used in Akkadian for the "queen."[254]

But we are still left with the question of why the Masoretes were not bothered by the root in Neh. 2:6, Ps. 45:10, and three times in the book of Daniel. Surely they did not know a solution based on Akkadian (a language not rediscovered until the 19th century!). Perhaps they just viewed nouns with the letters שׁ-ג-ל as reflecting an unrelated root.

*

Mitchell First is a personal injury attorney and Jewish history scholar. He is still afraid to read out loud the verses at Ps. 45:10, Neh. 2:6, and Dan. 5:2, 3, and 23.

---

253. The Aramaic section of the book of Daniel includes the term מלכתא for the queen. Thus it is evident that in the Aramaic section of the book of Daniel, the nouns from the root שׁ-ג-ל meant something less than the queen, i.e., some other type of royal wife or concubine.

254. Tawil adopts this suggestion. It is also mentioned in Koehler-Baumgartner. Koehler-Baumgartner also mentions that *sh-g-l* was the name of an ancient deity.

In the Aramaic section of the book of Daniel, we can explain that the word meant "one of the palace," but not the "queen."

9. Egyptian Words in Tanakh

Did you ever wonder which words in Tanakh are not Hebrew but are Egyptian? Others have been wondering as well! In 1953, an important article on this topic was published by Thomas Lambdin.[255] Lambdin was a professor of Semitic Languages at Harvard for many years.

Of course, identifying Egyptian words in Tanakh is not an exact science. We must distinguish between: (1) words that are definitely or almost certainly of Egyptian origin, (2) words that have a significant possibility of being of Egyptian origin, and (3) words for which an Egyptian origin has been suggested but the suggestion is very unlikely. For the most part, Lambdin's article avoids words in the third category.

I am going to present to you the words that Lambdin included. Usually, the suggested original Egyptian word does not completely match the Hebrew word. But scholars are capable of making educated guesses about which kinds of discrepancies are to be expected.

Egyptian is not a Semitic language, unlike Hebrew, Aramaic, Akkadian, Arabic, and several others.

Here are the words that Lambdin included in his article:

- אביון: poor, needy, wretched. I had always thought that it came from the Hebrew root: א-ב-ה, "want," but Lambdin suggests an Egyptian origin for it.[256]
- אבנט: girdle or sash. Lambdin writes that it is possibly connected to Egyptian *b-n-d*.
- אברך: This word appears only at Gen. 41:43, *va-yikreu le-fanav avrekh*. Lambdin comments that the possible Egyptian origin of

---

255. See T. Lambdin, "Egyptian Loan Words in the Old Testament," *Journal of the American Oriental Society* 73 (1953), pp. 145-55. Lambdin's *Introduction to Biblical Hebrew* is often used as a textbook in advanced Hebrew classes at Yeshiva University. He is connected to a book whose title I always found intriguing: *Working with No Data: Semitic and Egyptian Studies Presented to Thomas O. Lambdin*" (1987).

256. After researching further, I found that many agree with what I thought originally, and that other suggestions for the origin of the word have been made as well. *Theological Dictionary of the Old Testament*, vol. 1, p. 27, concludes that the origin of the word is still uncertain.

this word has led to an immense number of suggestions, almost all of which are baseless. But he does allow for the possibility that the word is Egyptian. The suggestion that he takes most seriously is that it is an imperative that means "attention!"[257]

- אח: fireplace. This word appears only two times, at Jer. 36:22-23.
- אחו: grass or reed (as food for cattle).
- אחלמה: This word only appears at Ex. 28:19 and 39:12. If we substitute an Egyptian "N" for the Hebrew "L," it is similar to an Egyptian word which is the name of a precious stone. Lambdin is willing to make this substitution. (See also לשם below.)
- אטון: red linen. This word appears only at Prov. 7:16.
- אי: island. We all know this word from Gen. 10:5 and Esther 10:1. It appears many other times in Tanakh.
- איפה: measure.
- בהט: This word appears only at Esther 1:6 (floors made of *bahat* and *shesh*). Lambdin first suggests an Egyptian origin for this word, a type of stone, but then raises a difficulty with the suggestion.
- בוץ: linen. We all know this word from its appearance twice in the book of Esther. It appears six other times in Tanakh. Lambdin discusses this word at length. He believes that an Egyptian origin is possible but very questionable.
- בחן: This word appears at Isa. 28:16 (*even bochan*). The meaning of *bochan* in Egyptian is a particular type of stone, perhaps close to granite. (If *bochan* had a Hebrew/Semitic origin, *even bochan* would have the meaning: "stone of testing" or "well-tested stone.")
- בחן: castle or fortress. This word (*vachan*) appears at Isa. 32:14. See also Isa. 23:13.

---

257. Most of our commentators see the letters ברך and translate it as something like "bend the knee." (Rashi takes a different approach.) H. Tawil, p. 5, writes that the etymology of the word is still uncertain. He mentions the suggestion that it is a loanword from Egyptian and means "attention." But he seems to prefer an Akkadian origin for the word, pointing to the word *abarakku*, "steward." Koehler-Baumgartner writes that the meaning of the word is uncertain and mentions the suggestions "watch out" and "kneel down."

- גמא: reeds. We all know this word from Ex. 2:3. But it also appears twice in Isaiah and once in Job.[258]
- הובנים : ebony. This word only appears at Ezek. 27:15.
- הין: a liquid measure.
- זרת: a unit of measure. Based on Egyptian, it seems to be related to "hand" or "handful."
- חניכיו: We all know this word from Gen. 14:14. Abraham took this category of men with him when he went to rescue Lot. Based on Egyptian, the meaning seems to be "armed" men. (If the word would be Hebrew/Semitic, the meaning would be something like "trainees," from the root ח-נ-ך.)
- חרטמים: This word is found in Genesis, Exodus, and Daniel. It is always in the plural. Lambdin views it as very likely that this word is of Egyptian origin, but he cannot prove it.[259]
- חותם: seal, signet ring. We all know the Hebrew verb ח-ת-ם/seal. But since the noun חותם is Egyptian, this means that the Hebrew verb is derived from the noun. (Typically in Hebrew, the verb precedes the noun. The noun is usually formed by taking the three-letter root of the verb and adding a *mem* or a *tav* as the initial letter.)
- טבעת: signet ring, seal. Lambdin cites a similar, but not exactly similar, word in Egyptian and believes it explains this word.[260]
- טנא: basket. This word only appears in Deuteronomy (four times).
- יאור: Originally, this was the word for "the Nile." Later, the meaning became "a river."
- כתם: valuable type of gold. Lambdin believes that the word is foreign to both Hebrew and Egyptian and originally came from Sumerian.
- לשם: This word occurs only at Ex. 28:19 and 39:12. If we substitute an Egyptian "N" for the Hebrew "L," it is similar to

---

258. Others believe that this word may be from the Hebrew root ג-מ-א and means "the plant that swallows water." See Klein, p.102.

259. I have discussed this word further in another article: "Some Interesting Words in *Parashat Miketz*."

260. The alternative view, that טבעת came from the Hebrew/Semitic root ט-ב-ע/press down is still possible and adopted by many. See, e.g., E. Klein, p. 240, which only mentions this view. Koehler-Baumgartner, pp. 368-369, mentions both views.

an Egyptian word that is a type of precious stone. Lambdin is willing to make this substitution.

- מרח: to anoint a wound. It is found only at Isa. 38:21.
- נפך and פוך: The latter is a shorter variant of the former. Each appear a few times. The meaning is "turquoise" or "malachite stone."
- נתר: This word appears two times, at Prov. 25:20 and Jer. 2:22. The meaning is "natron," which is a natural soda consisting essentially of sodium carbonate and sodium bicarbonate.
- סוף: fresh-water reed, seaweed.
- פח: Sometimes this word means a trap used to trap chickens. Other times it is a thin sheet of metal. Both are of Egyptian origin.
- פרעה: This word is certainly of Egyptian origin and originally meant "great house."
- צי: ship. This word appears only four times in Tanakh.
- קוף: ape, monkey. This word only appears two times in Tanakh (both in the plural).
- קלחת: pot, kettle. This word only appears two times in Tanakh. The Egyptian original is something like *k-r-ch-t*.
- קסת: an ink vessel. This word appears only three times in Tanakh, all in Ezekiel 9.
- שושן: a type of flower. (I had always thought the word was Hebrew and originated as a "flower with six petals."[261])
- שטה (almost always in the plural, *shitim*): acacia.
- שכיות: ships. This word only appears at Isa. 2:16. Those assuming it was Hebrew thought it came from the root שׁ-כ-ה, "look," with a meaning like "objects to be looked at" or "images." But at Isa. 2:16, it is parallel to אניות (ships). Thus, the Egyptian etymology fits much better!
- שסה: to plunder. We should all know this root from *Lekha Dodi*: *ve-hayu li-meshisah shosayikh*, "they that spoil thee shall become spoil." The original Egyptian noun, which led to the verb, is *shasu*, "nomads, marauders."
- שעטנז: Lambdin suggests that this difficult word, which only appears two times in Tanakh, is of Egyptian origin. Kohler-

---

261. Koehler-Baumgartner agrees with Lambdin. It does mention the above suggestion of Hebrew origin but views it as less likely.

Baumgartner agrees and concludes that the explanation is not yet established. Kohler-Baumgartner mentions a few suggestions including one that Lambdin had offered: a combined word, comprising the elements of "weaving" and "threading."

- שׁיש: white marble. שׁיש appears at 1 Chron. 29:2. The same word in a different form, שׁש, appears twice at Esther 1:6 and once in Song of Songs. The Egyptian word meant "alabaster."
- שׁש: fine linen. This word appears many times in Tanakh.
- תחרא: This word appears at Ex. 28:32 and 39:23. It is a type of garment. Lambdin mentions a scholar who suggests an Egyptian origin but he doubts that the suggestion is correct.

Now, if anyone asks you how many Egyptian words there are in the Tanakh, you know that there are not just a handful. But neither are there 100 (unless you count the repetitions as added examples). As Lambdin realizes, some of the suggestions that he included are probably not correct. On the other hand, for the most part, he did not include words that had an Egyptian origin suggestion that he viewed as very unlikely. But some of those unlikely suggestions may be correct. So the actual number of Egyptian words in Tanakh is probably around three or four dozen.[262]

*

Mitchell First is a personal injury attorney and Jewish history scholar. He was once able to (barely) read ancient Persian cuneiform. He admits he knows nothing about ancient Egyptian.

262. One thing I do not understand is why he did not include צפנת פענח in the article. This is usually understood to be an Egyptian name with a meaning like: "the god has said: he will live!" Probably he left it out because it was a name. I have discussed צפנת פענח in my article "Some Interesting Words in *Parashat Miketz*."

IV. Jewish Holidays and the Calendar

1. The Origin of the Jewish Count from Creation (presently 5779)

Nowhere in Tanakh is anyone counting the year from creation. What is the origin of this counting method?

As further background, if one looks at how Jews dated events in the Amoraic and Geonic periods, we see a contrast between the Jewish community of Palestine and that of Babylonia. In Amoraic and Geonic Palestine, Jews counted mainly from the second *churban*. Either 69 or 70 C.E. was year 1. We know this from many Jewish tombstones from the town of Zoar (south of the Dead Sea). For example, one reads: "May the soul rest of Shaul...who died on the first of the month of Marcheshvan of the first year of the *shemitah*, **the year 364 after the *churban beit ha-mikdash*.**"[263] There are many more tombstones from this site, mostly from the fourth and fifth centuries C.E., and all use a date on the *churban beit ha-mikdash* count. Another example of a *churban beit ha-mikdash* count in Palestine is a 6th century inscription found at a synagogue in Kefar Neburaya in the Galilee which states that the synagogue was built *arba meot ve-tishim ve-arba* (=494) *shanah le-churban*.[264]

In contrast, in Amoraic and Geonic Babylonia, the main dating system used by the Jews was *minyan shetarot* (="the count of contracts"). This was a counting system used in much of the secular world at the time; its name in the secular world was "the Seleucid Era." Its year one was 312 B.C.E., due to a military victory in Gaza by Seleucus I in that year. (In some regions, 311 B.C.E. was year one on this system.) Seleucus I had been a general to Alexander the Great.

---

263. See B. Wacholder, "The Calendar of Sabbatical Cycles During the Second Temple and the Early Rabbinic Period," *Hebrew Union College Annual* 44 (1973), pp. 53-196, at p.180 This article publishes the first three Jewish tombstone inscriptions discovered from Zoar. These were discovered in the first half of the 20th century. Many more were discovered thereafter. See S. Stern, *Calendar and Community* (2001), p. 88.

See also S. Stern, *Time and Process in Ancient Judaism* (2003), pp. 76-77, on all the issues that I am now discussing.

264. See L. Levine, *Ancient Synagogues Revealed* (1981), p. 137.

We do have evidence from the Talmud that there was knowledge of the Jewish year from creation in the Amoraic period in both Palestine and Babylonia, but it seems not to have been the most commonly used method of dating in either region. (The Talmud, at *Avodah Zarah* 9b, also refers to one source from the late Tannaitic period, an anonymous *baraita*, that uses the year from creation.)

How did the Jews in the late Tannaitic and Amoraic periods get their knowledge of what year it was from creation? The starting point is the work *Seder Olam*, put into final form by R. Yose ben Chalafta in the 2nd century C.E. Although this work does not give the total of the years from creation, it gives the length of time for each of the individual periods mentioned in Tanakh, and it gives the length of the Second Temple period. From the data conveniently collected in this work, a Jew could easily calculate the year from creation. For example, *Seder Olam* starts with the following passage: "From Adam to Noach, 1656 years." Here, the work has conveniently added up all the years listed at the beginning of Genesis.

Although the lengths of all the different periods from Adam to the second *churban* are listed in *Seder Olam*, it seems that R. Yosi did not intend that people total them up and start using a count from creation based on his work.[265] The conclusion of the work instructs people in Palestine to date from the second *churban*. It also remarks that people in the *golah* (=Babylonia) date on the *minyan shetarot* system.

But over time, the count from creation, based on the data in *Seder Olam*, came to be used more and more. Eventually, in the period of the Rishonim, it became the main count used by most Jewish communities. (Interesting is a passage in the Rambam, writing in Egypt in the late 12th century, where he provides the count on each of the three systems. See his *Hilkhot Shemittah ve-Yovel* 10:4.)

We do not have enough sources to understand why the Jews slowly began to favor the count from creation. It has been theorized that it was a response to the fact that the Christians began using their own count from creation starting in the 7th century.[266] (They calculated a different year from creation than us.) The result of the

265. See E. Carlebach, *Palaces of Time: Jewish Calendar and Culture in Early Modern Europe* (2011), p. 252 n. 19 (citing C. Milikowsky).

266. A leading expert on ancient Jewish chronology, Chaim Milikowsky, believes that this suggestion is a very reasonable one. See his *Seder Olam: Mahadurah Maddait, Peirush U-Mavo* (2013), vol .1, p. 20 (introduction).

spread of the use of the Jewish count from creation among world Jewry was that world Jewry began to slowly unite behind one counting system. Perhaps this was one of the motivating factors for the shift to this count as well. The Jews in Babylonia had no tradition of a count from the second *churban* and the Jews in Palestine seem to have abandoned the Seleucid era count after the second century. The count from creation, in contrast, was something that both societies were familiar with, even though it had not been in wide use.

Interesting are tombstone inscriptions from a Jewish community in Venosa, Italy from the 9th century. (In general, the Jewish customs in Italy followed the customs of Palestine.) All twenty-three surviving inscriptions bear a date from the second *churban* but three bear an additional date on the count from creation.[267] These inscriptions show that the date from the second *churban* was still the dominant chronology in the 9th century C.E. in the areas under the influence of Palestine, but the count from creation was slowly making headway.

It is unfortunate that, out of the three possible schemes, it was the count from creation scheme that became the mostly widely used one; it is the most problematic of the three. With regard to the other two, there is no dispute how long it is today from the second *churban*, and no dispute how long it is today from the beginning of the Seleucid era. (I am ignoring trivial issues of 1-2 years.) The count from creation scheme, on the other hand, has difficulties with it.

I am here only going to discuss the major difficulty with it.[268] When R. Yose in the 2nd century C.E. had to figure out the length of the Second Temple period, where did he get his data? The Tanakh gives the data for the biblical period, but the biblical period only spans up to the mid- 5th century B.C.E. It stops in the middle of the Persian period. To get the length of the entire Second Temple period, R. Yose had to rely on a prediction in the ninth chapter of Daniel, which refers to a future period of 490 years, the endpoints of which are ambiguous. R. Yose interpreted this prediction as referring to a 70-year exilic period and a **420**-year Second Temple period. He

---

267. See Carlebach, p. 191. These inscriptions were published by M.D. Cassuto in *Kedem* II (1945), pp. 99-120. (They were published earlier by G.I. Ascoli.)

268. I authored a book on this topic: *Jewish History in Conflict: A Study of the Major Discrepancy Between Rabbinic and Conventional Chronology* (1997).

accordingly assigned 420 years to the Second Temple period. In truth, the Second Temple period spanned **589** years, from approximately 520 B.C.E (2nd year of Darius) until 70 C.E. (There is no year zero.) This means that our count from creation lacks 169 years if we focus solely on the Second Temple period. (On the other hand, R. Yose assigns 410 years to the First Temple period, and this is about 29 years too big. The First Temple period spanned approximately the years 967 B.C.E.-586 B.C.E.) A sixteenth-century Italian Jewish scholar, Azariah de Rossi, wrote much about the error in the count from creation due to the discrepancy with regard to the length of the Second Temple period, causing much controversy in his time.[269]

Fortunately, in some contexts we use the phrase *le-minyan she-anu monin kan*, which would seem to cover ourselves for errors, i.e., we are not claiming that our count is accurate, only that we are giving this specific date according to the way we count.

I mentioned earlier that in the Amoraic and Geonic periods in Palestine, the surviving sources mainly reflect a count from the second *churban*. There is one notable exception. A synagogue mosaic in the town of Susiya, in southern Judea, uses the count from creation. Unfortunately, the precise year inscribed has not survived. But a paleography expert has estimated the date of this particular mosaic inscription to be the 6th or 7th century.[270]

Finally, the system of counting that counts the present year as 2018 was invented by a Christian monk named Dionysius Exiguus (the latter word means "the humble") in the early sixth century C.E. He did not like the system in use in his time which was pegged to Roman emperors who were notorious for persecuting Christians. Accordingly, he invented a system where year 1 was the year that Jesus was born. (But he was wrong in his assumed year of Jesus' birth; Jesus was born a few years earlier.) It took about two hundred years for the counting system of Dionysius to become the standard one.

*

Mitchell First is a personal injury attorney and Jewish history scholar. Since the Jewish count from creation is significantly incorrect and the 2018 count has a Christian origin, he thinks that we should consider going back to dating from the second *churban*.

---

269. See his *Meor Einayim*.
270. See Milikowsky, vol. 1, p. 20.

2. **What is the Meaning of יום תרועה?**

The Torah gives very little explanation of the holiday that we call today "Rosh Hashanah." The Torah calls it only *yom teruah* (Num. 29:1) and *zikhron teruah* (Lev. 23:24). What are the meanings of these brief terms *yom teruah* and *zikhron teruah*? What is the plain sense understanding of the meaning of this holiday? Neither of the above biblical sections even mention the word *shofar* or the concepts of judgment or new year![271]

The word *teruah* (root: רוע) points us in various directions. While it clearly means a loud sound, sometimes it is a loud sound of war or threats,[272] and other times it is a loud sound of joy or praise.[273]

I am now going to give a sample of the different approaches to understanding the *yom teruah/zikhron teruah* holiday within traditional sources.[274]

S.D. Luzzatto (on Lev. 23:24) takes the approach that the fundamental meaning of the holiday is that a *teruah* is blown to announce the new year. He notes that in the case of the jubilee, the Torah records a blowing of *shofar teruah* in Tishrei (on the tenth) to declare the beginning of that special year. So by analogy, our blowing of a *teruah* in Tishrei is also likely done to proclaim a new year. (As to *zikhron*, Luzzatto interprets it to mean something like "declaring," citing Isa. 12:4.)

Radak (on Ps. 81:4) suggests that the blowing of a *teruah* can symbolize the freeing of slaves, since it does so in the case of the jubilee year at Lev. 25:9. There is a tradition in the Talmud (*Rosh Hashanah* 10b-11a) that our ancestors in Egypt were freed from work on the first day of Tishrei, six months before they left in Nisan. He

---

271. Nevertheless, it is likely that the month that we now call Tishrei was considered the beginning of the new year. We can deduce this from the fact that the blowing of the shofar to declare the beginning of the jubilee year took place in this month, on the tenth. See Lev. 25:9.

272. See, e.g., Josh. 6:5, Zeph. 1:16, Amos 1:14, and Jer. 4:19.

273. See, e.g., 1 Sam. 4:5, Job 8:21, Ezra 3:11, and Ps. 150:5. The word *teruah*, in its various forms, appears over thirty times in Tanakh.

274. A separate issue is how the Karaites understood this vaguely described biblical holiday. See P. Miller, "Karaite Perspectives on *Yôm Těrû'â*," in *Ki Baruch Hu: Ancient Near Eastern, Biblical, and Judaic Studies in Honor of Baruch A. Levine*, eds. R. Chazan et al (1999), pp. 537-541.

believes that this event is what our blowing on the first day of Tishrei was enacted to commemorate.

Rav S.R. Hirsch translates *zikhron teruah* as a *teruah* that causes one to retrospect on one's life. Just as the seventh day of the week invites us to reflect weekly, so too this holiday on the seventh month was set up for reflection and introspection. The yearly *teruah* on this day calls us to a spiritual *yovel*, just as the *teruah* of the fiftieth year calls us to a social *yovel*. Our yearly *teruah* is a call for repossession of those spiritual measures that were originally our very own and that we have parted from. Since the day is in essence one of self-introspection, the verses need to state only little about it.[275]

Ramban (commentary to Leviticus 23:24) first focuses on the phrase "*zikhron teruah*." He observes that, at Numbers 10:10, the Torah refers to the Israelites' blowing of *chatzotzrot* with their holiday sacrifices and states that this blowing will result in a *zikaron* before God.[276] By analogy, Ramban suggests that the phrase *zikhron teruah* in our context must also be a reference to a blowing which produces a *zikkaron* before God.

Then he asks the obvious question. The Torah has not explained why we have to produce a *zikkaron* before God on this day. But because the holiday is in the same month as Yom Kippur, he concludes that we are producing this *zikkaron* because it is a *yom din*. (The idea of Rosh Hashanah being a *yom din* is found in Mishnah *Rosh Hashanah* 1:2.[277]) Ramban does not say it explicitly, but he implies that the purpose of the *zikkaron* that we are producing is to act as a reminder to God to judge us favorably on this day of *din*.[278]

Note that in our prayers, Rosh Hashanah is called *yom ha-zikkaron*. This term for the holiday is very ancient. It is already found

---

275. See his commentaries to Lev. 23:24 and Num. 29:1.

276. See similarly the "*ve-nizkartem*" of Num. 10:9.

277. In most Jewish communities, Rosh Hashanah is observed as a holiday of joy, while Yom Kippur is observed with great solemnity. It seems that this attitude is wrong for both of these holidays. If Rosh Hashanah is the Day of Judgment and Yom Kippur is the day of Forgiveness, it is the former that calls for fear and trembling and the latter that calls for rejoicing.

278. See similarly *Bereshit Rabbah* 56:9.

Daat Mikra to Lev. 23:24 suggests that the opposite approach is possible as well. The *zikkaron* is produced so as to remind Israel to remember Hashem and serve Him with a full heart.

in the Dead Sea Scrolls and may even have originated centuries before this. It is possible that whoever inaugurated the use of this term for our holiday had something like the Ramban's understanding in mind.[279]

Many others also view the words *zikhron teruah* as the key to understanding the holiday. But they interpret the words differently. They interpret them as indicating that the holiday is in essence a commemoration of that famous earlier *shofar* blast described at Exodus 19, the one associated with the giving of the Torah. This interpretation is first found in Philo (1st century C.E.), and many others over the centuries have taken this approach. Of course, a major difficulty with this approach is that Exodus 19 does not use the word *teruah*.

It bears pointing out that the root זכר can mean both "mentioning/proclaiming" and "remembering." Some of the above approaches are focusing on a meaning like "mentioning, proclaiming" and others are focusing on a meaning like "remembering."

I would now like to mention a completely different approach to understanding the Torah's brevity when it comes to this holiday. I first saw this approach in an article by Rabbi Michael Berger, "The *Mo'adim* of *Parashat Emor*," *Alei Etzion* (5756), pp. 7-23. But it is also implicit in the Rambam in his *Moreh Nevukhim*. The suggestion is that the Torah does not give a specific theme to this holiday on the first day of the seventh month because the holiday is, in its essence, merely an adjunct and preparatory holiday for Yom Kippur. The Torah recognizes that we cannot prepare properly for Yom Kippur without a ten-day period of repentance. *Yom Teruah* is merely the inauguration of this period and the beginning of preparation for Yom Kippur. That is why no independent theme is expressed for the holiday! The concept of the Ten Days of Repentance, in this reading, is already implicit in the Torah itself.

Here are the words of the Rambam in his *Moreh Nevukhim*: "The day is, as it were, a preparation for and an introduction to the day of the Fast, as is obvious from the national tradition about the days between New-Year and the Day of Atonement."[280]

---

279. But without knowing in what early century and by what early group the term *yom ha-zikaron* first came into use, it is hard to definitively get into the minds of its authors.

280. Translation from the Arabic by M. Friedländer (part III, ch. 43, p. 353).

I will close with one more insight. When one opens up a standard daily *siddur*, e.g., *The Complete ArtScroll Siddur*, p. 110, one sees the following choices for the recitation of *yaaleh ve-yavo*: Rosh Chodesh, Pesach, and Sukkos. But do you think it is possible that *yaaleh ve-yavo* might have been composed for one particular holiday first, and was later adjusted so it could include the others? What particular holiday could that have been? Let us look at its text: *ve-**yippaked** ve-**yizzakher** zikhroneinu u-**fikdoneinu** ve-**zikhron** avoteinu ve-**zikhron** mashiach ben David avdekha ve-**zikhron** Yerushalayim... ve-**zikhron** kol amkha... **zakhreinu** Hashem Elokeiu bo le-tovah u-**fakdeinu** bo le-verakha...*

It seems evident from the above language that this prayer was originally composed for *Yom Ha-Zikkaron!*[281]

Although we have no direct proof of this, we have some circumstantial evidence. Today we do not recite *yaaleh ve-yavo* in the *zikhronot* section of the *Amidah*, but it is found in the *zikhronot* section of the *Amidah* in the *Siddur Rav Saadiah Gaon* (10th century). This makes us realize that it perhaps began as a prayer originally composed for the *zikhronot* section of the Rosh Hashanah *Amidah*.[282]

*

Mitchell First is a personal injury attorney and Jewish history scholar. He wishes everyone a meaningful *yom teruah* and *zikhron teruah*, in whatever interpretation they adopt for these terms.

---

281. I first saw this insight in an article by Meir Bar-Ilan. See his *"Kivuy Yesod Le-Hithavutah Shel Ha-Kedushah Ve-Gibushah," Daat 25,* 1990, pp. 5-20. Very likely, others had suggested it earlier.

I quoted the text of *yaaleh ve-yavo* above from *The Complete ArtScroll Siddur,* since this is the text that most of us are familiar with. Here is the relevant passage in our earliest text of *Yaale Ve-Yavo,* the *Siddur Rav Saadiah Gaon* (p. 223): *ve-yippaked le-fanekha zikhroneinu ve-zikhron avoteinu zikhron Yerushalayim irkha zikhron mashiach ben David avdekha zikhron amkha... zakhreinu Hashem Elokeiu bo le-tovah fakdeinu bo le-verakhah....* As you can see, this text is substantially the same.

282. We also have evidence of an old Geonic tradition that on Rosh Hashanah it was only recited in connection with the *zikhronot* of *musaf* and not recited in *shacharit.* See the statement of R. Paltoy Gaon (9th century) quoted in *Sefer Ha-Manhig,* p. 310. I would like to thank Rabbi Avrohom Lieberman for this reference.

Yaaleh ve-yavo was perhaps inspired by the brief passage, in the context of Rosh Hashanah, at Tosefta *Rosh Hashanah* 1:12.   .

3. Some Interesting High Holiday Words

Many interesting words come up in the context of the high holidays. (Many of the *paytannim* enjoyed using rare words!) I will discuss a few of them.

- דפי: *Dibarnu dofi*, from the *Ashamnu* prayer. This word appears only one time in Tanakh, at Ps. 50:20: "You sit and speak about your brother; regarding the son of your mother you give דפי." From the context, it seems to be a type of slander. But what is its root and what exactly does it mean? Some relate it to the root ג-ד-ף (blaspheme, defame, scorn). But why would the *gimmel* drop? Some relate it to the root ה-ד-ף (push). The meaning would be "words that push someone away." Some relate it to the word ד-ב-ה, which means "slander" (see Num. 14:36). (The origin of this word is itself an interesting issue!)

  Whatever its root, we do see from its use in Aramaic in the Talmud that דפי means some type of defect.[283] Accordingly, Koehler-Baumgartner defines the biblical word דפי as "blemish, fault."[284]

- סלד: This root appears many times in the high holiday liturgy. For example, we have the phrase: "*viysaledu ve-chilah panekha.*" This is translated in *The Complete ArtScroll Machzor: Rosh Hashanah*: "in your presence they will **pray** with trepidation."[285] But is this translation correct?

  The root ס-ל-ד appears only one time in Tanakh, at Job 6:10. The Targum translates it with a word derived from the Aramaic root ב-ע-י, which means "request, pray." Based on this, the word is used by the *paytannim* throughout the liturgy as if it is a synonym for pray." But we know the root ס-ל-ד from the Mishnah and the Talmud. It is found in the expression *yad soledet bo*. Most likely, it means something like "jump up," both in this expression (the hand jumps up from the heat) and at Job. 6:10.[286] It does not mean "request, pray."

---

283. See, e.g., *Pesachim* 60b and M. Jastrow, p. 287.

284. P. 229.

285. P. 496 (1985).

286. See Koehler-Baumgartner, p. 756. It is also suggested here that it is related to the root ס-ל-ל which means "raise."

- כפר: Rashi (on Gen. 32:21) understands this root as having a fundamental meaning of "wiping away and removing." In contrast, S.D. Luzzatto (commenting on the same verse) understands this word as having a fundamental meaning of "covering." This same debate exists among modern scholars. There is a detailed article on this subject by the scholar Michael Brown.[287] He concludes that the root is used in both ways in Tanakh and that the only real issue is whether these different meanings of the root כ-פ-ר come from a common source. (This issue, he believes, can never be resolved.)

  Of course, whether our sins are "wiped away and removed" or are merely "covered" is a major difference theologically.[288]

- תעתענו: This is the last word in the *Ashamnu* prayer. Words with the four letters תעתע appear four times in Tanakh. The most famous instance is the statement of Esau at Gen. 27:12: "*ve-hayiti be-einav ke-metate'a.*" From the four instances, we see that the root of the word is either תעע or תעה.[289] The meaning is either "deceive" or "mock."[290] Accordingly, תעתענו means "we have mocked" or "we have deceived."

  Yet *The Complete ArtScroll Machzor: Yom Kippur* translated it: "You have led us go astray."[291] Why would they do this? The explanation is that the sin specified before this one in the *Ashamnu* prayer is תעינו "we have strayed." The proximity of the תעינו and תעתענו sins in this prayer seems to have led ArtScroll astray (!) into interpreting תעתענו in light of תעינו.[292]

---

287. M. Brown, "Kippēr and Atonement in the Book of Isaiah," in *Ki Baruch Hu: Ancient Near Eastern, Biblical and Judaic Studies in Honor of Baruch A. Levine* (1999), pp. 189-202.

288. On a related note, I would like to add that the English word "atonement," however we understand it now, has an interesting origin. It meant to be "at one" with God. The implication was to be reconciled with God, and united with Him and at peace. See W. Funk, *Word Origins and Their Romantic Stories* (1978), p. 268.

289. For the former, see, e.g., Koehler-Baumgartner, p. 1770 and E. Klein, p. 711. For the latter, see, e.g., Ibn Ezra to Gen. 27:12. Of course, these roots are probably related.

290. E. Klein, p. 711.

291. P. 853 (1986).

292. Admittedly, the truth is a bit more complex. The explanation that ArtScroll offered came from an earlier source, *Etz Yosef.* See his commentary

- שׁקוּר: *Sikur Ayin*, from the *Al Cheit* prayer. I have discussed this word in the earlier article "Original *Shin* and Original *Sin*."
- מחל: I have discussed this word in the earlier article: "Some Interesting Words in the *Amidah*."

I will now conclude with my favorite high holiday word:

פּשׁפּשׁ: The Rema writes (*Shulchan Arukh, Orach Chayyim* 603) that during the ten days of repentance *yesh le-khol adam le-chappes u-le-fashpesh be-maasav*. We all know that those last two words mean "examine his deeds." But where exactly did this root פּשׁפּשׁ come from?

It turns out that פּשׁפּשׁ is the word for bedbug! It is found in Mishnah *Terumot* 8:2 and in both Talmuds.[293]

In his *A Comprehensive Etymological Dictionary of the Hebrew Language for Readers of English* (p. 535), Ernest Klein writes that the verb פּשׁפּשׁ is usually connected with the word משׁמשׁ (touch, feel, examine, search), from the root מ-שׁ-שׁ. But he concludes that it is more probable that the verb פּשׁפּשׁ comes from the noun for "bedbug," and that the original meaning of the verb was "he searched for bedbugs." From this, arose the meaning "he searched in general." Whoever would have imagined![294]

I have to point out that the term *le-fashpesh be-maasav* did not originate in the High Holiday context. The Talmud, *Berakhot* 5a, uses the term as the recommended course for someone who sees that troubles have come upon him. See similarly Tosefta *Negaim*, chapter 6. Nevertheless, since the Rema and his predecessors the Meiri and the Maharil have all used the term in the context of the High Holiday period, there is justification for my including this term in this article!

---

in *Siddur Otzar Ha-Tefillot*, p. 1117. It was the second explanation he offered there. In his first explanation, he implied that the word meant "we have mocked." But ArtScroll chose to present his second explanation. Fortunately, years later, ArtScroll gave a better translation in their interlinear edition: "we have scoffed."

293. See Jastrow, p. 1248 (*pishpash*).
294. See also Jastrow, pp. 1248 and 185.
   Menachem Shapiro pointed out me that we have an analogous case of meaning expansion in English. The word "nitpicking" has expanded from its original meaning of removing "nits"!

*

Mitchell First is a personal injury attorney and Jewish history scholar. In preparation for the High Holidays, he searches the *machzor* for interesting words!

4. Hanukkah: A Survey of the Ancient Sources

The holiday of Hanukkah is mentioned only briefly in the Mishnah and the Talmud. In fact, the names of the sons of Matityahu are not mentioned. How do we know the background to this holiday? The purpose of this article is to describe three of the main sources that we have and to understand the differences between them. These sources are 1 Maccabees, 2 Maccabees, and *Megillat Antiochus.*

1 Maccabees spans the period from the beginning of the reign of Antiochus IV (the Antiochus who persecuted the Jews) until the death of Shimon, son of Matityahu. These are the years 175-134 B.C.E. (The persecution by Antiochus took place during the years 167-164 B.C.E.)

The author of 1 Maccabees is unknown, but it is evident that he was a Jew who was an admirer of Matityahu and his sons. 1 Maccabees was probably composed sometime after the death of John Hyrcanus (son of Shimon) in 104 B.C.E.

The work was originally composed in Hebrew, but the Hebrew has not survived. What has survived is a Greek translation from the Hebrew. The church father Jerome (4th cent.) reports that he saw the original Hebrew.

Another early church father refers to 1 Maccabees by the title *sarbêthsabanaiel.* But what does this garbled title mean? Probably, it is connected to the nickname for the priestly order Yehoyariv, the order that Matityahu came from. The nickname for this order was something like מסרביי. See JT *Taanit* 4:5. Probably, the original title was something like *sefer beit sarbanei el* = the book of the dynasty of God's resisters.[295]

2 Maccabees is an entirely different work. It was composed in Greek, likely in the Diaspora (perhaps in Alexandria). The unknown author tells us that his work is an abridgement of the work of

295. See J. Goldstein, *I Maccabees* (The Anchor Bible) (1976), pp. 16.

Jason of Cyrene. (Cyrene is a city on the northern coast of Libya.) Unfortunately, this Jason is unknown. But it is widely agreed that Jason wrote very close in time to the events he described.

2 Maccabees covers a shorter time period than 1 Maccabees. It begins in the years before the reign of Antiochus IV and ends with Judah's victory over the general Nicanor in 161 B.C.E.

Both 1 and 2 Maccabees were preserved because they were incorporated into the canon of the early church. Probably, the books were canonized by the early church because they modeled steadfastness in the defense of God, and because the persecuted Jews were seen as forerunners of Christian martyrs.

With regard to why 1 Maccabees is not included in Tanakh, probably the biblical canon was considered closed by Jewry even before 1 Maccabees was composed. For example, Sid Z. Leiman, in his authorative work *The Canonization of Hebrew Scripture* (1976), takes the position that the Jewish biblical canon was already closed in the middle of the 2nd century B.C.E. But even if this canon was still open at the time 1 Maccabees was composed,[296] 1 Maccabees was probably never a candidate for canonization. It did not claim to be a book composed before the period of prophecy ended. With regard to 2 Maccabees, it would never have been a candidate for canonization since it was composed in Greek.

The third work that I mentioned at the outset is *Megillat Antiochus.* This work is familiar to many in modern times because a Hebrew text of this work was included in the Birnbaum Siddur. But this work was originally composed in Aramaic, and the Aramaic text has been recovered. There are several important contradictions between this work and 1 and 2 Maccabees and the work is generally viewed as very unreliable. See, for example, the discussion of this work in the *Encyclopaedia Judaica* 14:1046-47. Most likely, it was composed in the Geonic period.[297]

---

296. See, *e.g.*, L. Schiffman, *Reclaiming the Dead Sea Scrolls* (1994), pp. 162-169.

297. See A. Kasher, "The Historical Background of *Megillath Antiochus*," *Proceedings of the American Academy for Jewish Research* 48 (1981), pp. 207-30, and Z. Safrai, "The Scroll of Antiochus and the Scroll of Fasts," in *The Literature of the Sages*, vol. 2, eds. S. Safrai, et al (2006), pp. 238-241. According to the latter, linguistic analysis of the Aramaic indicates that the scroll dates from sometime between the 6th and 8th centuries.

Interestingly, in some communities in the time of the Rishonim and even later, *Megillat Antiochus* was read on Hanukkah. See the article in Daniel Sperber's *Minhagei Yisrael*, vol. 5, pp. 102-113, for some references. The earliest reference to a practice of reading *Megillat Antiochus* on Hanukkah is a statement by R. Saadiah Gaon (10th century). In his introduction to *Megillat Antiochus*, R. Saadiah writes that "most of the nation read it." R. Saadiah does not state that it was read as part of a Hanukkah ritual, but that would be a reasonable interpretation of the passage.

One interesting example of a difference between 1 Maccabees, 2 Maccabees, and *Megillat Antiochus* is with regard to their understanding of what motivated Antiochus to issue his decrees against the Jews. According to 1 Macc. 1:41-42, Antiochus had a grand plan to unify his empire through Hellenism but the Jews resisted his plan. 2 Maccabees does not mention any such grand plan of Antiochus. Rather, according to this work, the decrees were merely a response by Antiochus to what he erroneously perceived as a revolt by the Jews of Judea. See 2 Macc. 5:11. Finally, according to *Megillat Antiochus*, Antiochus announces to his ministers, without any particular provocation, that the Jews need to be eliminated, and that the rituals of Shabbat, Rosh Chodesh and *milah* must be abolished. The king's complaint was that the Jews do not sacrifice to his gods or follow his laws, and someday hope to rule the world. I have written a detailed article on the topic of what motivated Antiochus decrees.[298] Almost certainly, the approach taken by 2 Maccabees is the correct one.

Another ancient source that discusses the background to Hanukkah is Josephus. But he is largely relying on 1 Maccabees. (It seems that he did not have 2 Maccabees.) With regard to non-Jewish sources, Antiochus' persecution of the Jews is mentioned in ancient sources such as Diodorus and Tacitus but the references are very brief. They are collected in Menahem Stern's classic work, *Greek and Latin Authors on Jews and Judaism* (1974-84).

It is only through sources like 1 and 2 Maccabees that we can determine the probable original Hebrew spelling and meaning of the

---

298. See my article in *Ḥakirah*, vol.16 (2013), "What Motivated Antiochus to Issue his Decrees against the Jews?," pp. 193-2011 (available online at hakirah.org) and *Esther Unmasked* (2015), pp. 94-117.

term "Maccabee" (the nickname for Judah), a term not found in the Mishnah or Talmud or classical midrashim. Most likely, it was spelled with a ק. I discuss this in the next article.

*

Mitchell First is a personal injury attorney and Jewish history scholar. He is still hoping that the original Hebrew of 1 Maccabees can someday be found so that it can be read in *shul* on Hanukkah.

5. The Meaning of the Name "Maccabee"

The name "Maccabee" is not found in classical Tannaitic or Amoraic literature. But this is not surprising. The name was originally an additional name for Judah only and there are no references to Judah by name in classical Tannaitic or Amoraic literature.[299]

The earliest sources that include the name in some form are works preserved by the Church: 1 Maccabees and 2 Maccabees. (These are not the original titles of these works.) 1 Maccabees was originally written in Hebrew, but what has survived is a Greek translation from the Hebrew. 2 Maccabees, an entirely different work, was written in Greek. In the early Church, 1 and 2 Maccabees were considered part of the Bible.

1 Maccabees tells us that Mattathias (=Matityahu) had five sons, and that each had another name. For Joudas (=Judah), the name was Makkabaios (Gr: Μακκαβαῖος.) (As is evident, Greek often adds an "s" at the end of foreign names.)

To determine whether the earliest spelling of the name in Hebrew was with a כ or a ק, one must guess from the double *kappa* (κκ) in Μακκαβαῖος what the original Hebrew letter (or letters) would have been.

Fortunately, this is not hard. Although there are exceptions, there is a general pattern in the Greek translation of the Bible of transliterating כ with *chi* (χ), and ק with *kappa* (k). Usually ק is

---

299. A story is told about Judah in the Jerusalem Talmud, in the second chapter of *Taanit* and in a parallel passage in the first chapter of *Megillah*, but he is not mentioned by name. With regard to the reference to Judah in *Megillat Antiochus*, I am not considering this to be classical rabbinic literature.

transliterated with one *kappa*, but sometimes two *kappas* are used. A transliteration of כ with two *kappas* is very rare. These same patterns hold true in 1 and 2 Maccabees.

Thus, the spelling of *Makkabaios* with two *kappas* points strongly to a ק in the original Hebrew or Aramaic name, and does not mandate assuming a קק.[300] Based on this spelling, it seems reasonable to agree with the oft-proposed suggestion that the name is related to the Hebrew word מקבת (*makevet*) and its Aramaic cognate מקבא (*makava*).[301]

מקבת/מקבא is usually assumed to mean a "hammer" used as a military weapon. Therefore, a reasonable suggestion is that the name was an allusion to Judah's physical strength or military prowess. [302] Before Mattathias died, he described Judah as having been "a mighty warrior from his youth."[303]

But there is an alternative view that the name reflects the appearance of Judah's head or body in some way. Perhaps something resembled a hammer. Interestingly, the Mishnah at *Bekhorot* 7:1 lists one of the categories of disqualified priests as המקבן, and the term is explained in the Talmud as meaning one whose head resembles a מקבא. (See *Bekhorot* 43b, Rashi's text.) Naming men according to physical characteristics was common in the ancient world.

However, our task of determining the original spelling and meaning of the additional name of Judah is not that simple, since we do not know whether the authors of 1 and 2 Maccabees knew how Judah himself, who died in approximately 160 B.C.E, spelled his name. With regard to 1 Maccabees, which covers the period 175-134 B.C.E., this work was probably composed after the death of John Hyrcanus in 104 B.C.E., or at least when his reign was well-advanced.

300. Also, the best manuscripts of *Megillat Antiochus* spell the word מקבי. This work probably dates to the Geonic period. See my article "Our Sources on Hanukkah."

301. מקבת is found in the Tanakh at Judg. 4:21and Isa. 51:1. It is also found in Tanakh in the plural. It is usually viewed as deriving from the root נקב, since it is a tool which is used to penetrate.

302. But מקבת /מקבא can also refer to a stonecutters' tool. See, e.g., Mishnah *Kelim* 29:7, which refers to a מקבה used by stonecutters.

303. See 1 Macc. 2:6. This was even before Judah's leading his brothers to victory over the army of Antiochus IV.

With regard to 2 Maccabees, we are told by the unknown author that it is an abridgement of an earlier work by someone named Jason of Cyrene. He is otherwise unknown, so he was not necessarily a contemporary of Judah. But even if we adopt the prevailing view that he was a contemporary of Judah, this does not necessarily mean that he knew how Judah himself spelled his name.

The second issue is that the name is written *Machabaeus* in the Latin translation of 1 and 2 Maccabees composed by the church father Jerome (c. 400 C.E.). There is a question whether this spelling reflects Jerome's own spelling choice, which was perhaps made after he consulted the original Hebrew of 1 Maccabees, or whether this was the conventional spelling of the name in the earlier Latin translations made from the Greek, which Jerome simply let stand. If this spelling was Jerome's own *and* he made it after consulting with the original Hebrew of 1 Maccabees, this would strongly suggest that the Hebrew text that he had before him spelled the name with a כ. In his translation of the Bible into Latin, Jerome almost uniformly used *ch* to represent כ.

Alternatively, if the *ch* spelling originated in the Latin translations before Jerome, or if it originated with Jerome, but not in consultation with the original Hebrew of 1 Maccabees, it would seem to be based on a Greek text which spelled the name with *chi*. This too would seem to reflect an original Hebrew spelling of the name with a כ.

Thus, although we saw earlier that the double *kappa* in the Greek translation of 1 Maccabees suggests a ק in the original Hebrew, the evidence from Jerome's Latin translation points in the opposite direction. Perhaps already in an early stage there were two different Hebrew spellings of the name. If the Hebrew name was spelled with a כ, one suggestion that has been made is that the meaning was "the extinguisher."

The spelling of Maccabee with a כ that is prevalent in Jewish sources today is not evidence of an original כ spelling. It is only the consequence of the spelling found in the book of Yosippon. [304] This spelling influenced the Rishonim thereafter.

---

304. Yosippon is a medieval Jewish historical work that was based in large part on a Latin translation of the works of Josephus. It also utilized a Latin translation of 1 and 2 Maccabees. Here Judah's additional name was spelled *Machabaeus*. Based on this, the book of Yosippon spelled the name with a כ.

There never was a group by the name Maccabees in ancient times. How did the references to this non-existent group ever arise and how did the books get their titles? 2 Maccabees focuses in large part on Judah. Jonathan Goldstein, the author of *I Maccabees* and *II Maccabees* in the Anchor Bible series, explains further:

> Clement of Alexandria and Origen, the earliest of the Church Fathers to mention the books by name, call them Ta Makkabaïka, "Maccabaean Histories," from which title persons who spoke loosely probably turned to call all the heroes in the stories "Maccabees." The first datable occurrence of such use of "Maccabees" for the heroes is in Tertullian... ca. 195 C.E.

Conclusion

The two *kappas* in the name in the Greek translation of 1 Maccabees suggest that the original Hebrew from which this translation was made spelled the name with a ק. This spelling would suggest that the name is related to the Hebrew word מקבת. Most likely, the name was assigned to Judah based on his physical strength or military prowess. But it is also possible that the name alluded to his physical appearance in some way.

But it is possible that neither the authors of 1 or 2 Maccabees nor Jason knew how Judah spelled his own name. Also, the fact that the name is spelled with a *ch* in Jerome's Latin translation suggests that there may also have been a Hebrew version of 1 Maccabees that spelled the name with a כ.

At present, there are archaeologists in Israel working on locating the actual tombs of Judah and his brothers. Perhaps the issue of the spelling of the name may soon be resolved![305]

*

Mitchell First is a personal injury attorney and Jewish history scholar. He knows that, after he is gone, there will be people who erroneously spell his last name as "Furst."

---

305. The above was an abridgement of an article published in *Esther Unmasked*.

6. Dec. 4 and *Tein Tal U-Matar*: Some Insights into the Calendar

The Balfour Declaration was issued in England on Nov. 2, 1917. But it preceded the 1917 October Revolution in Russia by a few days. How could this be? If it was November in England, was it not November in Russia?

Actually, it was still October in Russia. At that time, Russia was still following the Julian calendar, even though much of the world had already moved on to the Gregorian calendar. The Gregorian calendar was instituted in 1582 when Pope Gregory XIII decided to drop ten days from the calendar, as part of a long-needed calendar correction. Aside from the dropping of the ten days, it was also decided that leap years would be eliminated in years that were not divisible by 400.

In the new Gregorian calendar, the day after Thursday, October 4, 1582, was declared to be Friday, October 15. England and its colonies (including America) adopted the Gregorian calendar in 1752.[306] But Russia did not change over until 1918, *after* the 1917 October revolution. Today, we take it for granted that all countries use the same calendar date. But as we have just seen, this is only a relatively recent phenomenon.

Those omitted ten days in 1582 have an important ramification for us in the context of the *tein tal u-matar* request in the ninth blessing of the *Amidah*. According to the Talmud (*Taanit* 10a), the time for this request in Babylonia (which the entire Diaspora now follows) is 60 days after the autumnal equinox. The autumnal equinox usually falls on Sept. 22 or 23. If it fell on Sept. 22, the sixtieth day after would be Nov. 20. So why do we Diasporans today not commence the recitation until the *maariv* of Dec. 4? The loss of those 10 days in 1582 is one of the factors that causes our present request date to be long after Nov. 20.

The other factor that changes the *tein tal u-matar* date is that the Gregorian calendar eliminated the leap years in years that were not

---

306. Because England was a Protestant country, it took them a while to be willing to adopt the Pope's new calendar.

This 1752 calendar correction has an interesting ramification for Americans today. George Washington was born on Feb. 11. It was only because of this calendar correction in 1752 that the date of his birthday was changed to Feb. 22.

divisible by 400. The result is that the *tein tal u-matar* date (which corresponds with the Julian calendar) moves forward 3 days every 400 years. It moved forward one day in the years 1700, 1800, and 1900, but not in the year 2000. It will move forward one day again in 2100, 2200 and 2300, but not in 2400.

Since 1900, the date for the beginning of the *tein tal u-matar* insertion has been *maariv* of Dec. 4.[307] But in 2100, the date will be Dec. 5 and in 2200, it will be Dec. 6, continuing to progress forward 3 days every 400 years.

It turns out that the Artscroll publishers were very fortunate. Since there was no adjustment in the year 2000 (because it was a leap year in the Gregorian calendar as well as the Julian calendar), all those *siddurim* that they published at the end of the 20th century will have the correct *tein tal u-matar* date for 120 years! Eventually, approximately 35,000 years from now, the date for the recital of *tein tal u-matar* in the Diaspora will be Passover time! This Diaspora problem is of course another incentive to move to Israel! (But presumably the Messiah will have arrived long before then!)

A very interesting issue that arose in connection with the date for *tein tal u-matar* is what date the Jews in the non-Babylonian Diaspora should begin saying it. The accepted date for its recital in Palestine became 7 Marchesvan (based on the view of R. Gamliel, Mishnah *Taanit* 1:3), and the Talmud records that in the *Golah* (i.e., Babylonia) the recital would not begin until 60 days from the autumnal equinox.[308] But there is no guidance in the Talmud as to what Jews in other countries should do. This was of little concern in the talmudic and Geonic periods, when most of world Jewry lived in either Palestine or Babylonia. But as Jews spread throughout the world, the issue arose.

The *Rosh*, writing in the 13th century, admitted that the widespread custom in his time in Europe was to follow the Babylonian *tein tal u-matar* date. But he admits that he does not understand why, as most

---

307. The date is Dec. 4 only for the first three years of each four-year cycle. In the fourth year, it moves to Dec. 5. It then reverts back to Dec. 4 for the next three years. This cycle repeats throughout each four-year set. This is because in the fourth year of each cycle, by the time the *tekufah* falls, it is already after dark and is considered the next day. Similarly, in the 22nd century, the date will be Dec. 5 for the first three years, and Dec. 6 for the fourth year.
308. *Taanit* 10a.

lands needed rain long before the 60th day from the autumnal equinox, even if Babylonia did not. The *Rosh* mentions that he saw a custom in Provence of following the 7 Marcheshvan date and that this custom was *yashar meod* in his eyes. Also, the Rambam, in his commentary on Mishnah *Taanit* (first chapter) wrote that each country should begin the recitation of *tein tal u-matar* at the time appropriate for their specific country. But Rambam changed his mind in *Mishneh Torah, Hilkhot Tefillah* 2:16, and most other authorities also felt that the Babylonian date was the appropriate date for the entire Diaspora. This was R. Yosef Caro's ruling in *Orach Chayyim* 117.[309]

Regarding the name of the second month, I called it "Marcheshvan," because that was its original name, not "Cheshvan." מרחשון is always how it is written in the Mishnah. It is the Akkadian form of what would be in Hebrew: *yerach shemonah* (eighth month). The reason people do not realize that the original name of the month is "Marcheshvan" is that the name of this month did not make it into Tanakh. A few of our other present month names also never made it into Tanakh: Tishrei, Iyyar, Tammuz and Av. (Although Tammuz is in Tanakh as the name of an ancient God! See Ezek. 8:14.)

Yemenite Jewry has a different pronunciation of מרחשון. They pronounce it "Marach-sha'wan." This sounds closer to *yerach shemonah* and is probably a more accurate pronunciation than our pronunciation.

Regarding the name of the first month, Yemenite Jewry pronounces it "Tishri." Just as in the case of Marchesvan, the reason a variant tradition for the name of the first month exists is that the name of the month is not in Tanakh. If it were, we could all point to the word in Tanakh and its vocalization and resolve the issue. Here too, probably Yemenite Jewry preserves the more accurate tradition than our "Tishrei."

*

Mitchell First is a personal injury attorney and Jewish history scholar. He thinks we should put back those 10 days removed in 1582.

---

309. For further material on issues relating to *tein tal u-matar*, see A. Lasker and D. Lasker, "The Jewish Prayer for Rain in Babylonia," *Journal for the Study of Judaism*, vol. XV (June 1984), pp. 123-144 and "The Strange Case of December 4: A Liturgical Problem," *Conservative Judaism*, vol. 38(1), Fall 1985, pp. 91-99.

7. Yes, We Can Identify
Achashverosh and Esther in Secular Sources!

I spent many years researching this topic. It is time to get everyone up to speed.

Until the 19th century, a search in secular sources for a Persian king named Achashverosh would have been an unsuccessful one. Our knowledge of the Persian kings from the biblical period was coming entirely from the writings of Greek historians, and none of the names that they recorded were close to Achashverosh. The Greek historians (Herodotus, mid-5th cent. BCE, and the others who came after him) described the following Persian kings from the biblical period: Cyrus, Cambyses, Darius, Xerxes, and Artaxerxes.

It was only in the 19th century that we were able to solve our problem, as a result of the deciphering of inscriptions from the ancient Persian palaces and from the inscription on the rockface at Behistun. It was discovered that the name of the king that the Greeks had been referring to as "Xerxes" was in fact: "Khshayarsha" (written in Old Persian cuneiform).[310] The Greeks did not properly record his name because they did not have a letter to represent the *shin* sound. "Khshayarsha" is very close to the Hebrew אחשורוש. In their consonantal structure, the two names are identical. Both center on the consonantal sounds *kh*, *sh*, *r* and *sh*. The Hebrew just added two *vavs* and an initial *aleph*.[311] (Sometimes the Megillah spells the name with only one *vav*, and once, at 10:1, with no *vav*s.)

Identifying Khshayarsha/Xerxes with Achashverosh thus makes much sense on linguistic grounds. Moreover, it is consistent with Ezra 4:6 which implied that Achashverosh was the king between Daryavesh

---

310. Many people today think that Achashverosh never existed. Yet 2500 years later there are still people in Iran (and the U.S.) with the first or last name "Khshayarsha," or a name derived from it, like "Khashayarsha," or "Khashayar." I found this out because a friend of mine who is a physician met an Iranian-born patient who bore the name "Khashayar." The patient knew that the name had its origin in the name of an ancient Persian king. (Names derived from "Khshayarsha" are not used by Jews in Iran, although they do name their children after Koresh and Daryavesh.)

311. Both the Elamite and the Akkadian versions of the name also have an initial vowel sound. In Elamite, the name has an initial "i" sound. In Akkadian, the name usually has an initial "a" sound."

(=Darius I), mentioned at 4:5, and Artachshasta (=Artaxerxes I), mentioned at 4:7-23. This is exactly when Xerxes reigned.

Now that we have identified Achashverosh with Xerxes, we can construct main elements of his biography, as Herodotus includes much material about him. Xerxes' father was Darius and his mother was Atossa, daughter of Cyrus. Xerxes reigned from 486-465 B.C.E., when the Temple was already rebuilt. It was rebuilt in the reign of his father Darius I in 516 B.C.E. One of the main things we learn from Herodotus is that Xerxes led an invasion of Greece and was defeated. He returned in the fall of his the 7th year. This would have been a few months before Tevet of his seventh year, when the Megillah tells us (2:16) that he took Esther.

Reliefs depicting the Persian kings have survived in the Persian palaces. There are some that scholars believe may depict Xerxes.[312] But we cannot take these depictions "at face value." There was a tendency to depict all the various kings so that they looked identical.

But what does Herodotus tell us about the wife of Xerxes? He only mentions one wife, "Amestris." Close examination of the name "Amestris" supports its identification with Esther. The "-is" at the end was just a suffix added to turn the foreign name into proper Greek grammatical form (just as "-es" was added at the end of "Xerxes"). When comparing the remaining consonants, the name of the wife of Xerxes is recorded in the Greek historians as based around the consonants M, S, T, and R, and the name as recorded in the Megillah is based around the consonants S, T, and R. Out of the numerous possible consonants in these languages, three consonants are the same and in the same order! Probability suggests that this is not coincidence and that the two are the same person. [313] (Most likely, her Persian name was composed of the consonants M, S, T, and R, and the M was not preserved in the Hebrew.)

There is one main issue with identifying Esther with Amestris. According to Herodotus, Amestris was the daughter of a military commander named Otanes. In contrast, the Megillah gives the name of Esther's father as אביחיל. But it is easy to postulate that Herodotus

---

312. See, e.g., the photos at Y. Landy, *Purim and the Persian Empire* (2010), pp. 15 and 46.

313. It bears pointing out that if Esther is Amestris, then Artaxerxes I was the son of Achashverosh and Esther.

simply erred regarding her ancestry. Herodotus traveled widely in the 450's, but he never set foot in Persia. He had to rely only on what he heard. Every scholar knows that he could not possibly have been correct on a very large percentage of the details that he records. Also, the impression that one receives from the Megillah is that Esther did not disclose her true ancestry from the seventh year until the twelfth year. Whatever rumors first arose about her ancestry may have been what made their way to Herodotus. It is also striking that אביחיל is very close to אב-חיל, "commander of the military."[314]

The author of the introduction to the Megillah in Mossad HaRav Kook's *Chamesh Megillot (Daat Mikra)* realized that Achashverosh was Xerxes. But unfortunately he did not understand how easy it was to get around the issues raised by the identification of Esther and Amestris. Therefore, he took the farfetched position that Esther was never the main wife of Xerxes, but was one of other wives of a lesser status. But this cannot be reconciled with verse 2:17: *va-yasem keter malkhut be-roshah, va-yamlikheha tachat Vashti*. Moreover, Esther is called *ha-malkah* 17 times thereafter!

We do not have evidence in secular sources for the main plot of the Purim story, the threat to destroy the Jews in the twelfth year of Xerxes (3:7). But this is to be expected. Our main source for the events of the reign of Xerxes is Herodotus and his narrative ends in the seventh year of Xerxes.[315] (His main interest in Xerxes related to his invasion, which ended at this time.) From sources after Herodotus, we learn practically nothing about what happened between year 7 and year 21, Xerxes' last year. But we do learn (not from Herodotus) that Xerxes died by assassination!

Once we realize that Achashverosh is Xerxes, it becomes evident that the one who was exiled at Esther 2:6 cannot be Mordechai. King

---

314. Also, perhaps Avichayil had another name which included the sounds "T." and "N." The Megillah tells us that Esther seems to have had both a Hebrew name and a Persian name (Hadassah).

I have to mention that both Herodotus and the later Greek historian Ctesias give an unflattering picture of Amestris. But scholars today realize not to believe the tales told by the Greek historians about the Persian royal women. The Greeks and Persians were enemies. I have discussed all of this in detail in my book *Esther Unmasked* (2015).

315. There are a few scattered references to events after the seventh year of Xerxes, but they are only tangential to the main narrative.

Yechanyah was exiled in 597 B.C.E. If Mordechai was old enough to have been exiled with King Yechanyah, he would have been over 120 years old when appointed to a high position in the twelfth year of Xerxes. Moreover, Esther, his first cousin, would not have been young enough to have been chosen queen a few years earlier. A reasonable alternative interpretation is that the individual exiled was Mordechai's great-grandfather, Kish.[316]

It is also of significance that a later Greek historian, Ctesias, writing circa 400 B.C.E., mentions an important advisor to Xerxes whose name was either Matacas or Natacas. This may be a reference to Mordechai.[317]

Admittedly, the identification of Achashverosh with Xerxes does not fit with the view of the Talmud. According to the Talmud, *Megillah* 11b (and followed by numerous midrashim), Achashverosh reigned between Koresh and Daryavesh, i.e., he reigned before the Temple was rebuilt in the reign of Daryavesh.

Why are there two divergent views as to when Achashverosh reigned? I will explain.

The book of Esther nowhere mentions which Persian king preceded or followed Achashverosh. We have to look outside the book of Esther for a clue. The clue is found in Ezra chapter 4, where Achashverosh is mentioned in the context of other Persian kings. The problem is that this chapter is very unclear. Achashverosh is mentioned at verse 6. The Daryavesh in whose reign the Temple was rebuilt is mentioned at verse 5 and again at verse 24. This leads to two ways of reading the chapter. In one reading, we can understand Achashverosh (mentioned in verse 6) as preceding Daryavesh (mentioned in verse 24). In another reading, we can understand Achashverosh (mentioned in verse 6) as following Daryavesh (mentioned in verse 5). The correct way to read the verses was

---

316. See A. Koller, "The Exile of Kish: Syntax and History in Esther 2:5-6," *Journal for the Study of the Old Testament* 37:1 (2012), pp. 45-56. See also *Chamesh Megillot (Daat Mikra)*, comm. to Esth. 2:6.

317. I have discussed this all at length in my book. Very briefly, a name with the consonants M-T-C could easily be a reflection of an original M-R-D-C. (A contemporary parallel is that the name Mordechai is often shortened to "Moti.") The "as" at the end of the name "Matacas" is almost certainly a Greek addition. If "Matacas" is Mordechai, this would confirm one of the main elements of the plot of the Purim story.

only determined once it was realized that linguistically the name Achashverosh was a match to the name Khshayarsha (=Xerxes). Once this identification was made, it was realized that the correct reading was the one that understood Achashverosh (mentioned in verse 6) as following Daryavesh (mentioned in verse 5), and understood verses 4:6-23 as a digression to a later period[318] and verse 4:24 as a resumption of the main narrative in the reign of Daryavesh.

The Talmud (and *Seder Olam* which preceded it) had a reasonable interpretation of the difficult fourth chapter of Ezra. But it turns out that a different interpretation is now to be preferred. Today, there is no reasonable basis to deny the identification of Xerxes and Achashverosh.[319]

(The above is an abridgement of an article published in my 2015 book *Esther Unmasked.*)

*

Mitchell First is a personal injury attorney and Jewish history scholar. He recalls an interesting competition in *New York Magazine* decades ago. You were asked to add one letter to a word, and then redefine it. A winning entry was: "Xeroxes: Persian copy king."

8. Two Books to Read for Purim

The book of Esther jumps immediately into the reign of Achashverosh, but provides little background. Fortunately, we get some background from the book of Ezra. There we learn that, after defeating the Babylonians, the Persian king Koresh gave permission to the Jewish exiles to return and build their Temple. The returnees start work,

---

318. The author or editor of the book of Ezra decided to digress and supplement the reference to accusations made against the Jews in the reigns of Koresh through Daryavesh with mention of further accusations against them in the reigns of the subsequent kings, Achashverosh (Xerxes) and Artachshasta (Artaxerxes). But this digression confused everyone for centuries.

319. With regard to the king who reigned between Koresh and Daryavesh, he was called Cambyses by the Greeks. It has since been discovered that his name was "Kabujiya" in Persian and כנבוזי in Aramaic. He did not reign long enough to be Achashverosh. Nor did he reign over *Hodu* (=India). His reign is alluded to in the word *ve-ad* at Ezra 4:5.

but run into opposition from people already in the land. They have difficulties from the time of *Koresh melekh Paras ve-ad malkhut Daryavesh melekh Paras* (Ezra 4:5). Later, in the second year of Daryavesh (=Darius I), they resume their work. Since it is now 19 years later,[320] the Persian governor asks them who gave them permission for this rebuilding work. The returnees respond that Koresh had given them permission. King Daryavesh is notified and he orders a search which locates the initial decree of Koresh. Accordingly, Daryavesh renews the permission and the work on the Temple is completed in his reign. There is also a one sentence reference to Achashverosh in the book of Ezra. Finally, the book of Ezra and the book of Nehemiah describe the activities of Ezra and Nehemiah and the assistance that king Artachshasta (=Artaxerxes I) provided to them.

What if you wanted to learn more about kings Koresh, Daryavesh, Achashverosh and Artachshasta? Where would you go? In 1990, Edwin Yamauchi, a professor in Ohio, published a book titled *Persia and the Bible*. It is easy to read, with many pictures and charts, and gives us all the background that we need. You see from the title of the book that is meant for us, readers of the Bible. It is not a dry general history of ancient Persia. (For that, you would read Pierre Briant, *From Cyrus to Alexander*.) Yamauchi presents, in a clear and organized manner, all that ancient historians and archaeology teach us about the reigns of kings Cyrus, Cambyses, Darius I, Xerxes (=Achashverosh) and Artaxerxes I.[321] (With regard to Cambyses, he

---

320. This length of time is not in the text but we can calculate it. The initial permission was given by Koresh in approximately 539 B.C.E. and we are told in Tanakh that the work commenced again in the second year of Daryavesh. This would be approximately 520 B.C.E.

321. The king after Artaxerxes I was Darius II. Most likely, the "Daryavesh" referred to at Neh. 12:22 is this king. Theoretically, Yamauchi should have had a chapter on him as well. But since he is only mentioned briefly and tangentially, it is understandable that Yamauchi did not include him. Of course, Yamauchi could have chosen to omit any discussion of Cambyses as well. Unlike Daryavesh=Darius II, Cambyses is not mentioned by name in Tanakh. But the story of the reign of Cambyses is an integral part of the story of the period from Cyrus to Artaxerxes I, so we would not have been able to forgive Yamauchi had he omitted a chapter on Cambyses!

is not mentioned by name in Tanakh, but his reign is alluded to in the word *ve-ad* that I cited above.[322])

With regard to Cyrus, Yamauchi summarizes all the legends about his life reported in the various Greek historians (Herodotus and others). We also learn about one of the most important biblical archaeological finds ever: The Cyrus Cylinder. This was an inscription of Cyrus that revealed that it was not just the Jewish returnees who were permitted by Cyrus to return and build their Temple. Rather, Cyrus gave such a permission to many of the peoples under his rule whom the Assyrians and Babylonians had exiled. This was part of his plan for benevolent rule. This was a dramatic insight. All of a sudden, Cyrus' permission to the Jewish returnees described in the book of Ezra became understandable!

Yamauchi then moves on to Cambyses, summarizing the data in Herodotus, the later Greek historians, and archaeology.

Yamauchi then deals with Darius I. The extra-biblical material about Darius I is voluminous. First, we learn the most important story in the history of ancient Persia: the story of how Darius became king. Herotodus tells us that Darius was not the son of Cambyses, but was a distant relative. (Cambyses had no children.) Someone who pretended to be Cambyses' brother reigned for about seven months. (The real brother of Cambyses was already dead.) Darius and six others joined in a conspiracy to kill the impostor. After the conspiracy was successful, Darius was installed as king. (I have here oversimplified a very long story![323])

Then Yamauchi focuses on the many inscriptions of Darius I. The most important is the trilingual inscription (Old Persian, Elamite, and Akkadian) in Behistun that largely confirms the above story told by Herodotus.[324] Then we are told about the canal that Darius built between the Nile and the Red Sea, his expeditions against the Greeks and other military adventures, and his work building the palace at Shushan. Finally, we learn about his tomb and his several wives.

---

322. The word *ve-ad* implies that Koresh and Daryavesh were not adjacent kings. If they were, the text would have recorded that the Jews had difficulties in the reigns of *Koresh melekh Paras ve-Daryavesh melekh Paras.*

323. I have given further details in the article "Archaeology Sheds Light on King Darius."

324. Behistun is in Western Iran.

Then comes a fifty-two page chapter devoted to Xerxes, followed by a thirty-seven page chapter on Artaxerxes. There are also chapters on the palace at Shushan and the other ancient Persian palaces.

As I have discussed in the previous article, it is clear that Xerxes is to be identified with Achashverosh. This was discovered in the middle of the 19th century when Old Persian cuneiform was deciphered and the original Old Persian names of the kings came to light. Once Old Persian was deciphered, it was discovered that the king the Greeks were calling "Xerxes" had the name "Khshayarsha" in Old Persian. This name is structured around the consonantal sounds Kh-Sh-R-Sh. These are the same consonantal sounds as in the name Achashverosh.

Xerxes reigned from 486-465 B.C.E. This was after the work on the building of the Second Temple was completed in the reign of his father Darius I in 516 B.C.E. From Ezra 4:6, where Achashverosh is mentioned in a context, we see that Achashverosh was the king who reigned between Daryavesh (=Darius I), mentioned at 4:5, and Artachshasta (=Artaxerxes I), mentioned at 4:7-23.[325] This is exactly when Xerxes reigned.

Yamauchi writes all about Xerxes' military expedition against the Greeks which took place in the early years of his reign. But he can tell us practically nothing about what happened in the reign of Xerxes after that. Why not? Because Herodotus and the Greek historians after him wrote practically nothing about the events of Xerxes after year seven, when Xerxes returned from his expedition defeated. This is important because skeptics always point out that the Greek historians do not refer to the Purim story, the plot to destroy the Jews in the twelfth year of Xerxes' reign (3:7). But the Greek historians refer to practically nothing in the reign of Xerxes after year seven until his assassination in year twenty-one. (Of course, even if the Greek historians had described some events of years eight through twenty-one, it would hardly have been surprising if one brief plot to destroy the Jews was not mentioned.)

---

325. I am being a bit misleading here. The order of the Persian kings presented in the fourth chapter of the book of Ezra is a complicated topic. I have discussed it in the previous article. Because the fourth chapter of the book of Ezra was written in the confusing way that it was, *Seder Olam* and the Talmud were misled into to taking a different view of the order of the Persian kings. They placed Achashverosh before Darius I.

There is only one flaw in Yamauchi's book for our purposes. Xerxes' wife was referred to by the Greek historians as "Amestris." Yamauchi has a section suggesting that Amestris may be Vashti. But nowhere does he consider that Amestris may be Esther. (The "-is" at the end of "Amestris" is likely only a Greek addition to her original Old Persian name, which must have been something like M-S-T-R.) I argue strongly for the identification of Esther with Amestris in my book, *Esther Unmasked*.

The other book I recommend is Yehuda Landy, *Purim and the Persian Empire* (Feldheim, 2010). This book is of a completely different nature. It is a book with wonderful color photos of archaeological findings that helps one visualize the palace at Shushan, and many of the other items mentioned in the Megillah. The author is an Orthodox rabbi and educator in Israel. He knew very little about ancient Persia until around 2006, when he visited a special exhibit on this subject at the British Museum. He was shocked at how much archaeological material there was that confirmed details of the Megillah. He also realized that 99% of the Orthodox world knew nothing about this, so he decided to collect it all and publish it as a book. (He included a text of the Megillah as well, so you can follow the Megillah with his book in your hand!)

The book includes some history. But he is aware that there are large disputes between the Sages and the conventional history, and Landy figured out a way to publish his book and publicize the visual material without taking clear positions on dates and historical identifications. After all, he reasoned, Shushan is Shushan, no matter what precise year the events occurred and whether or not Xerxes is Achashverosh. (But he does take the position that, most likely, Xerxes is Achashverosh. He does not address any issue relating to the identification of Amestris and does not mention her.)

*

Mitchell First is a personal injury attorney and Jewish history scholar. He himself has written two books related to Purim and ancient Persia: (1) *Jewish History in Conflict* (1997), and (2) *Esther Unmasked* (2015). Of course, he recommends his own two books as well![326]

---

326. *Esther Unmasked* also includes articles related to the other Jewish holidays.

9. והגדת לבנך (Exodus 13:8): What is the Meaning of והגדת?

Ve-higgadeta le-vinkha ba-yom ha-hu, "you shall tell your son on that day," is a key verse of the *Seder* night. But what exactly does *ve-higgadeta* mean? I will now present several approaches. (Note: I usually save the likeliest approach for last!)

Approach #1: **Explain the reason**. This approach is taken by S.D. Luzzatto in his commentary on our verse. He cites Judg. 14:19 where the phrase *le-haggid* is used in the context of explaining a riddle. (See also *Daat Mikra* to Ex. 13:8.)

Approach #2: **Demonstrate by action.** Rav S.R. Hirsch (commentary to Deut. 26:3) writes: "הגיד means making clear not by words but by deeds, actions..." He uses the word "demonstrated." He says something similar, although less explicitly, in his commentary to Ex. 13:8.

Approach #3: *Ve-higgadeta* is related to the Aramaic root נ-ג-ד, which means "**draw out.**" The implication may be that the telling must be in a drawn out, long way. See, e.g., *Siddur Otzar Ha-Tefillot*, p. 951, commentary *Maaseh Nissim*, and *Netziv* to Deut. 32:7. Or the implication may be *moshkhin libbo shel adam*, draw out the heart of the listener"; see the *Arukh*. Or the implication may be draw your child out so that he will ask a question. (Netziv to Ex. 13:8.)

Approaches #4 and 5: At *Shabbat* 87a, the Talmud interprets the word *va-yagged* of Ex. 19:9. Two opposite interpretations are offered, a "soft" interpretation and a "hard" interpretation. The "soft" interpretation: *she-moshkhin libbo shel adam ke-***aggadah.** This interpretation is cited by Rashi at Ex. 13:8. The "hard" interpretation: matters that are as hard as *gidin* (sinews, tendons). This interpretation is cited by *Or Ha-Chayyim* at Ex. 13:8. (See also the interesting approach of *Kli Yakar*.)

Approach #6: **Study**. *Reflections of the Rav* includes the following statement: "The word *Haggadah* connotes more than the act of 'telling' or 'narrating.' It suggests an elaborate form of study."[327] This approach of Rav Soloveitchik is based on the *Mekhilta* to Ex. 19:3 (*tedakdek immahem*) and Rashi to this same verse.

Approach #7: **Tell A Story/Elaborate/***Sippur*. The Radak, in his *Sefer Ha-Shorashim*, tells us that the implication of all the various הגד

327. PP. 212-13 (1979).

words is *sippur*.[328] He is probably deriving this from the passage in the *haggadah: mitzvah aleinu le-sapper bi-yitziyat Mitzrayim*.[329]

Approach #8: **Inform, Cause to Understand**. At *Hilkhot Chametz U-Matzah* 7:2, Rambam writes: *mitzvah **le-hodia** le-vanim... she-ne'emar ve-higgadeta le-vinkha*. (Of course, Rambam uses the word *le-sapper* as well nearby.) *Le-hod:ia* is from the root י-ד-ע.

After describing all the above approaches, it is finally time to reveal what the word *ve-higgadeta* means on its simplest level. *Ve-higgadeta* comes from the verb *le-haggid*. This word originated as להגניד. The root here, and of all those הגד words in Tanakh, is נגד, "next to." The root letter נ in the first position dropped, as is common in Hebrew.[330] The ה at the beginning reflects that the word is in the *hifil* (=causative) construct. להגיד (=להנגיד) means "to cause something to be next to someone else." See, e.g., Rav S. R. Hirsch to Gen. 3:11 and Deut. 17:10, and the concordance of Solomon Mandelkern, entry נגד. See also Radak, *Sefer Ha-Shorashim,* entry נגד. The closest English equivalent would seem to be "to present." Perhaps there was originally an implication of face-to-face conversation in the root להנגיד.[331]

I also believe that some of the sources cited above would agree with this "נגד-present" approach on a *peshat* level; they may have merely been trying to give an additional layer of meaning to the word.

---

328. "*Mekor inyan kullam inyan sippur.*" Radak makes this comment in his entry נגד, where he gathers all these הגד words. Radak also explains these words with the phrase *asapper va-ekra ha-devarim le-fanav*. To Radak, the הגד words have the implication of both *sippur* and *le-fanav* (=in front of the other person). See the continuation of my article.

329. Of course, why the author of this passage chose to use the word *sippur* is the million dollar question! Perhaps he was influenced by the use of the root at Ex. 10:2. This choice by the author of the *haggadah* has had a tremendous influence in the way the *mitzvah* has been understood over the centuries. This *haggadah* passage is the earliest source to use the verb *sippur* in connection with the *mitzvah*. See D. Henshke, *Mah Nishtanah? Leil Ha-Pesach Be-Talmudam Shel Chakhamim* (2016), pp. 32-33. Henshke dates the passage to the time of the Babylonian Geonim.

330. See my article: "Searching for Omitted *Nuns.*"

331. See, e.g., *heiasfu* [=gather] *ve-aggidah lakhem...* (Gen.49:1).

I had always made the common assumption that the word *haggadah* derived from the phrase *ve-higgadeta le-vincha*. Indeed, this view is expressed in the 11th century by the *Arukh* (entry הגדה). But although the standard printed text at *Pesachim* 115b and 116a refers to the *haggadah*, there are some manuscripts that have *aggadah* or *ha-aggadah* here.[332] Similarly, there are Rishonim that refer to what we recite at the *Seder* as the *aggadah*. See, e.g., the *piyyut* for *Shabbat Ha-Gadol* by R. Yosef Tuv Elem (11th century),[333] the commentary to the *haggadah* of R. Eliezer b. Nathan of Mainz (12th century),[334] and Tosafot, *Avodah Zarah* 45a. Therefore it is possible that *aggadah* was the original term for the material recited at the *Seder*. Moreover, even if *haggadah* was the original term, or one of the original terms, for the material recited at the *Seder*, most likely the term was *not* derived from *ve-higgadeta le-vinkha*. Rather, the most widely held view is that the terms *haggadah* and *aggadah* originally had the same meaning[335] and the term *haggadah* did not originate as a Pesach-related term.[336]

---

332. See, e.g., the most important manuscript of the Babylonian Talmud, Munich 95, which has the latter.

333. See *The Complete ArtScroll Siddur*, p. 922. I would like to thank Sam Borodach for this reference.

334. See *Haggadah Shel Pesach, Torat Chayyim*, p. 12.

335. Most likely, *aggadah* was a secondary form of *haggadah*. See, e.g., E. Klein, p. 5. As W. Bacher explains (*Jewish Quarterly Review* 4, 1891-92, p. 429), "אגדה is an example of that common softening of הפעלה into אפעלה so frequently made in Palestine…. It is merely an Aramaised form of the original Hebrew word…." Other examples of Aramaised forms cited by Bacher are: אזכרה, אבטחה, אונאה, and אדלקה .

Undoubtedly, the root of the Hebrew word הגדה is נ-ג-ד=next to. A reasonable explanation for the original meaning of הגדה is that an idea was being placed next to someone else.

If *aggadah* was the Palestinian form of *haggadah*, this would imply that in Babylonia what was read at the *Seder* was originally called the *haggadah*, while in Palestine it was called the *aggadah*.

But perhaps *aggadah* was not the Palestinian form of *haggadah*, and perhaps *aggadah* was the original term for what was read at the *Seder*. In this scenario, *aggadah* could have derived from an Aramaic root נ-ג-ד that has a different meaning than the Hebrew root נ-ג-ד. Or perhaps it derived from the Hebrew and Aramaic root א-ג-ד. These scenarios cannot be ruled out.

336. See Henshke, p. 17, n. 1. I would like to thank Rabbi Jay Goldmintz for this reference.

But over time the word *haggadah* came to be associated mainly with Pesach, based on Ex. 13:8 and statements such as the one made by the *Arukh*.

*

Mitchell First is a personal injury attorney and Jewish history scholar. He used to stand up and present face-to-face lectures. Now he enjoys reclining and writing for the *Jewish Link of New Jersey*.

10. Some Interesting Words of the *Seder*

- סדר: A word with this root appears only one time in Tanakh, at Job 10:22 (סדרים). As we would expect, it means "order."
- חרות: The root ח-ר-ת only appears one time in the Tanakh, at Ex. 32:16. It means "engraved,"[337] so we have to look elsewhere for the origin of חרות as "freedom."

  One approach is to relate it to חור, "nobleman." This word appears many times in Tanakh (always in the plural). That this is the origin of the word חרות for freedom is the approach taken by R. Joshua b. Levi at Mishnah *Avot* 6:2. Here the word חרות from Ex. 32:16 is cited (*charut al ha-luchot*) and then the following statement is made: "*ein lekha* בן חרין *ella mi she-osek ba-Torah*." Of course, the statement is a homiletical one, so the etymological connection may have been meant homiletically as well.

  It is also noteworthy that the phrase בני חרין appears in the *haggadah* with the meaning "free men."

  A different approach to חרות =freedom derives it from an Aramaic root ח-ר-ר that means "to be or become free."[338] This root appears in forms such as חרר and שחרר.

---

337. There is also a biblical root ח-ר-ט that means something like "engrave." See Ex. 32:4 and Isa. 8:1. As to the word *chartumim*, this is likely a foreign word. See the article "Some Interesting Words in *Parashat Miketz*."

338. See, e.g., E. Klein, p. 231. It has been suggested that חור=nobleman derives from this Aramaic root ח-ר-ר. See E. Klein, p. 211. In such a case, we do not really have two different approaches to the origin of חרות =freedom. But many alternative suggestions for the origin of חור=nobleman have been suggested.

Finally, Professor Louis Feldman once mentioned to me the suggestion that חרות derived from the Greek word χείρ = hand, arm,[339] and referred to a hand/arm motion made to free slaves.[340]

The word in the Tanakh for freedom is דרור (occurring 7 times). It is interesting that the text of the *Kiddush* uses the word חרות instead of the word דרור.

- כרפס: This word appears in the Tanakh only 1 time, at Est. 1:6. There it means "fine fabric, linen." In the Mishnah, Tosefta, and Talmud, it has the meaning of a plant, or celery/parsley, but it is never used in connection with the *Seder*.

  It is only in the Geonic period that we first find *karpas* (in the form כרפסא) used in connection with the *Seder*. It is mentioned as one of the permissible options for the *borei pri ha-adamah* at this stage. The earliest such reference to *karpasa* at the *Seder* is a Geonic responsum published in Louis Ginzberg's *Ginzei Schechter*, vol. 2 (1929), pp. 252-260.[341] For another early reference to *karpasa* at the *Seder*, see *The Complete ArtScroll Siddur*, p. 922 (citing an eleventh-century *piyyut*).

  We are all misled by the introductory *kaddesh u-rechatz piyyut* to view the word *karpas* as integral to the *Seder*. But many other such introductory *piyyutim* have come to light, and many of them do not include the word *karpas*. This stage of the *Seder* is there in these *piyyutim*, but it is represented by a different word or words. Some of these other *piyyutim* are collected at Menachem Kasher, *Haggadah Shelemah* (1967, 3rd edition), pp. 77-82.

- מצה: The etymology of this word is much debated. The simplest approach observes that the verb מ-צ-ץ means "to suck" and the related verb מ-צ-ה means "to drain out."[342] Because it was flat and dry, unleavened bread was viewed as bread in which the normal texture and moisture was sucked out or drained out.[343]

---

339. This is the basis for the English word "chiropractor."
340. To date, I have not seen this suggestion in writing anywhere.
341. This interesting responsum describes the *Seder* as including only two *mah nishtannah* questions: matzah and dipping. I have discussed this responsum further in the article "Mah-Nishtanah: The Three Questions."
342. The word מיץ (juice), found in Tanakh three times (in Proverbs), is surely related. S. Mandelkern lists it with the root מוץ but comments that perhaps it belongs with מצץ.
343. See Mandelkern, who lists it with the root מ-צ-ץ. See also Koehler-

227

But many scholars find the above unsatisfying and propose alternatives. There was a Hebrew root א-ו-ץ that meant "urge" or "hasten."[344] There may even have been a Hebrew root נ-צ-ה that meant "hasten."[345] The word מצה could have been derived from these and meant "that which was made in haste."[346] Another suggestion points to an Arabic word *mazza* that means "to be tasteless."[347] Perhaps there was a similar Hebrew word at one time.

Another approach points out the similarity between the Hebrew *matzah* and the Greek *máza*, "barley dough, barley bread/cakes." The suggestion is then made that our Hebrew word מצה is related to this word and is not a Semitic word. Perhaps this non-Semitic word came from some other language in the region and influenced both Hebrew and Greek.[348]

Baumgartner, p. 621,which mentions " מ-צ-ץ=suck" as a possibility. E. Klein, p. 374, believes that the word probably derives from this root and means "that which is sucked up, or "that which is drained out."

There is a diacritical dot in the Bible inside the צ of מצה. One of the functions of such a dot is to indicate that a root letter is missing. This would support the idea that the root was מצץ (or perhaps נצה). But all the dot really indicates is that the post-talmudic Masoretes thought that a root letter was missing.

344. See, e.g., Koehler-Baumgartner, p. 23, E. Klein, p. 13, and the root א-ו-ץ in the Even-Shoshan and Mandelkern concordances.(In his definition of the root, one of the Latin words that Mandelkern uses is *festinare*, which means "hurry.")

345. The suggestion is based on the word נצו at Lam. 4:15. But there are other ways to understand this word. Klein also points out that there is a word in Arabic, *naḍā*, that means "hastened forward."

346. E. Klein mentions the suggestion of נ-צ-ה .

But query whether *matzah* should be understood as fundamentally relating to the idea of "haste." *Matzah* is mentioned in many places in Tanakh that are not related to the Exodus. In response, it has been suggested that *matzah* was a standard food served when preparation was hurried. See, e.g., Gen. 19:3, where Lot serves *matzot* to his unexpected guests and Judg. 6:19 where Gideon serves *matzot* to an angel that comes to speak with him. Perhaps (as humorously suggested to me by Judy Heicklen) *matzah* was the equivalent of the "fast food" of the time! (We had this conversation in a "fast food" place!)

347. See Koehler-Baumgartner, p. 621. S. Mandelkern also mentions this possibility.

348. *Theological Dictionary of the Old Testament*, vol. 8, p. 495. Koehler-Baumgartner also raises the possibility that it is a non-Semitic loanword.

That of course, would be the irony of ironies, that *matzah*, the bread that symbolizes our liberation from the slavery of ancient Egypt, would be a non-Semitic loan word. But one does not have to take such speculation seriously. The Hebrew word, or earlier Semitic word, could have led to the Greek *máza*.

Finally, I cannot resist mentioning the creative approach found in Matityahu Clark's *Etymological Dictionary of Biblical Hebrew*. He has an entry for a Hebrew root נ-צ-ה that he defines as "resist; oppose sporadically." We are all familiar with this root.[349] He includes מצה in this entry (implying that it derives from an original מנצה) and defines it as "non-fermenting bread." In other words, he views it as bread that resists fermentation. Of course this is clever, but it is farfetched.[350] There is no struggle going on within the *matzah*!

Please forgive me for mixing in a *chametz*-related word now. The contrasting word חלה probably derives from the root ח-ל-ל, "empty space." A reasonable explanation is that חלה in ancient times may have been a "pierced" or "perforated" cake, with an empty area in the middle (like pita). [351]

- מרור: The word *maror* in the singular appears nowhere in Tanakh. The word used in Tanakh is the plural: *merorim*. It appears three times: in the commandment of *Pesach* (Ex. 12:8), in the commandment of *Pesach sheni* (Numb. 9:11), and at Lam. 3:15 (*hisbiani va-merorim*, "he has filled me with bitterness.") Almost certainly, the original formulation of the *mah nishtannah* question described the herb in the plural, *merorim*.[352] In Rabbinic Hebrew, the singular refers to only one of the five herbs with which one can fulfill one's obligation. See Mishnah *Pesachim* 2:6.

---

349. See, e.g., Ex. 21:22.

350. Clark's book is based on the commentaries of Rav S.R. Hirsch, but Clark sometimes offers suggestions that are not found in Rav Hirsch. I did not see this particular suggestion in the commentaries of Rav Hirsch himself.

351. See E. Klein, p. 217. Koehler-Baumgartner agrees that it comes from חלל=hollow and defines it as "ring-shaped bread."

352. See, e.g., *Siddur Rav Saadiah Gaon*, p. 137, and Rambam, *Hilkhot Chametz U-Matzah* 8:2. In the *haggadah* text included in the standard printed *Mishneh Torah*, the reading is מרור. But the Frankel edition points out that some versions read מרורים here.

It is interesting that the Torah never tells us why *merorim* are to be eaten with the *Pesach* and *Pesach sheni* sacrifices. It has been suggested that *merorim* were merely added as a condiment to the sacrificial meat.[353] But the phrase *va-yemareru et chayeihem* is found earlier in the story (at Ex. 1:14). Therefore, it is very compelling to understand the inclusion of *merorim* in the sacrificial *Pesach* meals as symbolic of the bitterness of the slavery.

• חסל: This word, which means "finish," is used at the end of the *Seder*. The root appears seven times in Tanakh. Six times it appears as חסיל =locusts. The other time, at Deut. 28:38, it appears as *yechaslenu ha-arbeh*, "the locusts will finish it/eat it away." Most likely, locusts are called חסיל because they finish off the crops.[354]

• ספור: In Biblical Hebrew, the root ס-פ-ר means both "to count" and "to tell a story."[355] Can we find a common ground here? Interestingly, there is such a phenomenon in English as well: "to count," and "to recount" a story. Also, an "accountant" works with numbers, but a newspaper "account" is a retelling of a tale. The relationship between counting and telling a story is found in words of other languages as well.[356]

The simplest explanation for all of this is that a story is the sum of details and that, in telling a story, there has been a counting and an ordering of all the details.

Interestingly, the English word "tell" also has the connotation of "telling a story" and of "counting." (Think of a bank "teller.")

• והגדת, הגדה: I have discussed these words in the earlier article: "והגדת לבנך (Exodus 13:8): What is the Meaning of והגדת?" (There is also more on the word ספור there as well.)

• הסבה: The meaning of the word *hesebah* is ingrained in all of us. Wake any of us up from our reclining position in the middle of the night and we will tell you that הסבה means "recline." But wait

---

353. See *Daat Mikra* to Ex. 12:8.
354. Koehler-Baumgartner, p. 338 and E. Klein, p. 226. This explanation is already found in the Jerusalem Talmud (*Taanit* 3:6).
355. It means "count" in the *kal* construct. It means "tell a story" in the *piel* construct.
356. See E. Klein, p. 626.

a minute. Everyone will agree that the root of this word is ס-ב-ב, which has a meaning of "round." What is going on here? How did this root ס-ב-ב turn itself into a root meaning "recline"?

Surely the process was as follows. The root first evolved into a word for "eating a meal," since meals were eaten in a circle. Then it evolved into eating a meal with couches around the table, where the practice was to recline on the couches.[357] Eventually, it came to mean "recline," even when no couches were involved!

*

Mitchell First is a personal injury attorney and Jewish history scholar. He enjoys his freedom and his couch. There he hastily reclines and counts the number of times difficult words appear in Tanakh and recounts this material to others, all the while avoiding those all-consuming locusts.

11. *Mah Nishtannah*: The Three Questions

It is well-known that the Mishnah in the tenth chapter of *Pesachim* includes a set of *mah nishtannah*. If one opens a standard printed Babylonian Talmud (*Pesachim* 116a), one sees *four* questions in the text of the Mishnah (matzah, *maror*, roast, and dipping). But if one opens a standard printed Jerusalem Talmud, one sees *three* questions (dipping, matzah, and roast).[358] Is this one of those rare instances of a

---

357. I saw a suggestion that the root ס-ב-ב already meant "recline" in the book of Ben Sira, in pre-Mishnaic times. But I did not find the evidence convincing.

358. I will call them questions, even though some have argued that they are best understood, in the context of Mishnah *Pesachim* 10:4, as explanations or exclamations.

R. Steiner argues that the Mishnah is most properly understood as intending only *one* (long) question, i.e., "what special characteristic of this night is causing us to depart from our normal routine in so many ways?" He shows that R. Saadiah Gaon and every early medieval source understood the *mah nishtannah* as only one long question. It was not until the 13th century that a medieval source first referred to them as *she'eilot* (plural). See Steiner, "On the Original Structure and Meaning of *Mah Nishtannah* and the History of Its Reinterpretation," *Jewish Studies, an Internet Journal* 7 (2008), pp. 163-204.

disagreement between the text of the Mishnah preserved in Babylonia and the text of the Mishnah preserved in Palestine?

It turns out that it is practically certain that the original text of the Mishnah recorded only three questions: dipping, matzah, and roast. This is what the earliest and most reliable Mishnah manuscripts record. There is no distinction between a Babylonian Mishnah and a Palestinian Mishnah here.

Moreover, if one opens up a standard volume of *Pesachim* of the Babylonian Talmud and looks at the text of the Mishnah recorded in the *Rif* (R. Isaac Alfasi, 11th century) and the *Rosh* (R. Asher b. Yechiel, 13th century), one sees that they too record a Mishnah which included only the above three questions. Also, Rambam (12th century) utilized a text of the Mishnah which included only the above three questions.

Almost certainly, the familiarity of later copyists and early printers with the *maror* question from the texts of their *haggadah* led some of them to erroneously insert the *maror* question into their texts of the Mishnah.[359]

A widely quoted understanding of the *mah nishtannah* takes the position that there were always four questions, and that the roast question did not survive after the *churban*, with the reclining question substituting for it. I just showed that there were originally only three questions. It also turns out, as I will now explain, that the roast question survived in some areas for 1000 years after the *churban*.[360]

---

359. For example, the question appears in the first printed edition of the Mishnah (Naples, 1492) and in all subsequent printed editions. It also appears in the Mishnah text in the first printed edition of the Babylonian Talmud (Venice, 1520-23), and in all subsequent printed editions. Both of these first printed editions must have been relying on manuscripts that had the question. (The text of the questions differs in the Venice edition from the Naples edition, so the former was not relying on the latter.) It is also evident that Tosafot to *Pesachim* 116a (13th-14th century) had the *maror* question in the text of its Mishnah. See Joseph Tabory, "How Many Questions in the "Four Questions"?, *TheGemara.com*, April 4 2017, n. 13.

360. My discussion in this section is based mainly on the *haggadah* fragments from the Cairo Genizah included in S. and Z. Safrai, *Haggadat Chazal* (1998).

Documents from the Cairo Genizah generally date from the 10th through the 13th centuries. It is reasonable to assume that this is roughly the period of the *haggadah* fragments as well. Of course, not all of the *haggadah* fragments from the Genizah span the *mah nishtannah* section. But of those that do, **many include the roast question.**

Although most of the *mah nishtannah* fragments of the *haggadah* found in the Genizah record four questions the way they are asked today, we also find the following:

- Several record *three* questions: matzah, dipping, and roast, just like the original text of the Mishnah.
- One records the following *three* questions: dipping, matzah and reclining.[361]
- Two record *five* questions: dipping, matzah, roast, *maror*, and reclining.[362]
- Two record only the questions of dipping and roast. (There does not appear to be any reason why the matzah question would have been intentionally discontinued. Perhaps the matzah question was accidentally dropped by a scribe in one source, and further copies were later made from that source.)
- One records only the questions of dipping and matzah.

I would like to focus on this last source, which is not actually a *haggadah* fragment, but is a section of an anonymous Geonic responsum that includes an outline of the procedures at the *Seder*. It can be deduced

---

361. See M. Kasher, *Haggadah Shelemah* (Jerusalem: 1967, third ed.), p. 113, n. 11. This manuscript is MS Cambridge T-S H2.145. It is possible that this is not a legitimate variant and that the *maror* question was omitted in error by the scribe who copied this fragment.

There is also evidence of a *mah nishtannah* set of dipping, matzah, and *maror*. This does not come from the Genizah, but from additions made to a text of the *siddur* of R. Solomon b. Nathan (12th century).

362. One is T-S H2.152. See the photograph at Kasher, p. 93. The other is ENA 2018 1v. I only learned of this ENA manuscript from the 2017 article by Tabory. I was not aware of it when I wrote my article on this subject in *Esther Unmasked* (2015).

that the responsum was composed in Babylonia because it includes *avadim hayyinu*, which was not a part of the Palestinian *Seder* ritual in this period.[363] This responsum was first published by Louis Ginzberg, in his *Ginzey Schechter*.[364] Ginzberg took the position that the author of this responsum provided only an abbreviated version of the *mah nishtannah*, and listed only the first two questions, even though his practice was four. But this interpretation seems very unlikely. The whole purpose of the responsum was to spell out the procedures and text of the *Seder*. Abbreviation here would have defeated its purpose.

Shmuel and Ze'ev Safrai take a different approach to this responsum in their *Haggadat Chazal*. They write that the third and fourth questions are *chaserot be-sof he-amud*,[365] implying that these questions were originally included in this responsum but were cut off. They take this approach so that the set of questions in our responsum could then parallel the set of questions found in the other known Babylonian Geonic sources of the *haggadah* text: *Seder Rav Amram Gaon*, *Siddur Rav Saadiah Gaon*, and the *haggadah* text published in 1984 by M.R. Lehman. All these sources record the standard four questions: dipping, matzah, *maror*, and reclining.

But anyone can now view this responsum (Cambridge T-S Misc. 36.179) at genizah.org. It is clear that the third and fourth questions were never there. The first side ends with the last words of the matzah question, the next side continues immediately with *avadim hayyinu*, and there are no missing lines in between.

Assuming we reject the unlikely interpretation of Ginzberg, this source records a two-question set in Babylonia.[366] The idea that we have now been able to "excavate" such a set, evidence of a period before four questions became the universal practice there, is truly

363. Safrai, p. 50.

364. Vol. 2 (1929), pp. 258-60. It is cited in Kasher, p. 113, n. 11 with the symbol *shin*.

365. Safrai, p. 64, n. 53. See also their later English adaptation, *Haggadah of the Sages* (2009), p. 65, n. 30.

366. R. Isaac Alfasi quotes a text of Mishnah *Pesachim* 10:4 that includes only the questions of dipping, matzah and roast, and then remarks that the roast question is no longer recited. It can be argued based on this that the *mah nishtannah* at the *Seder* in his community may have only included the dipping and matzah questions.

remarkable. On a paleographical basis, the responsum has been dated to the 10th century.[367]

Regarding the issue of when the *maror* and reclining questions were added, much remains unknown. But the following are some reasonable observations:

- The *maror* question probably arose after the dipping question lost its connotation as a *maror* question. Once this happened, it was viewed as necessary to add a question relating to *maror*.
- The reclining question probably arose as a replacement to the roast question.
- Probably a desire arose at some point to fix the number of questions at four, parallel to the themes of four cups of wine and four sons.

The above an abridged version of an article published in my book *Esther Unmasked* (2015).

P.S. I cannot leave this topic without the following diversion into the modern period. The *haggadah* particularly resonated with the early kibbutz members because they felt that they were like people who had gone out of Egypt. On the other hand, they felt free to modernize the text. For example, at Kibbutz Ein Harod in the 1930's and 1940's, the Four Questions were: "Why do people all over the world hate Jews? When will the Jews return to their land? When will our land become a fertile garden? When will there be peace and brotherhood in the world?" For more on this topic, see Muki Tzur and Yuval Danieli, *Yotzim Be-Chodesh Ha-Aviv* (2004). This book includes extracts from hundreds of kibbutz *haggadaot* written between the late 1920's and 1960's.

*

Mitchell First is a personal injury attorney and Jewish history scholar. He too wants to create some new *mah mishtannah* questions.

---

367. This is the opinion of Dr. Edna Engel of The Hebrew Palaeography Project at The National Library of Israel, in correspondence to me. She also opines that the script is Oriental, i.e., from Egypt, Palestine or Syria. Since the responsum reflects the Babylonian ritual, perhaps the last is most likely. The surviving responsum may be a copy of an earlier responsum.

12. ארמי אבד אבי: Uncovering the
Interpretation Hidden in the Mishnah

As children, we all grow up thinking that the phrase *arami oved avi* refers to Lavan seeking to destroy Jacob. After all, this is what we are taught in the Haggadah, Targum Onkelos, and Rashi.

But when we get a bit older and start learning commentaries like Rashbam and Ibn Ezra, we realize that this is not a plain sense interpretation. אבד (=*oved*), if it is a verb here, would be in the *kal* construct. But in the *kal*, the root א-ב-ד is **in**transitive.[368] This means it cannot act on an object. For the root א-ב-ד to be transitive, it needs to be in the *piel* or *hifil* constructs.[369]

Thus, Lavan cannot be destroying anyone with an intransitive א-ב-ד. Rather, the subject of the verse is *avi*, and *arami oved* is a description of *avi*. The meaning of the phrase is "my father was a homeless/wandering/lost Aramean." Of course, the plain sense commentaries did not agree on whether "my father" was a reference to Abraham (Rashbam) or to Jacob (Ibn Ezra).[370]

For almost all of us, this was how we understood the history of the interpretation of the phrase. The early Sages, we believe, understood the phrase one way, while the plain sense Rishonim provided a different interpretation.

But now I am going to turn the tables on you and show you that the interpretation expressed by the plain sense Rishonim was not a new one. Rather, they were just resurrecting what was the mainstream interpretation in the time of the Tannaim.

Mishnah *Pesachim* 10:4 includes the following statement: *Matchil be-genut u-mesayyem be-shevach, ve-doresh me-arami oved avi ad she-hu gomer et kol ha-parshah*, "One begins with *genut* and one finishes

---

368. An example of the root א-ב-ד in the *kal* construct is found in the *Shema*: *va-avadtem meheirah*. This is not a statement that we will destroy someone quickly. Rather, it is a statement that we will lose our land quickly. Fundamentally, the root א-ב-ד means to lose something. But when used in the *piel* and in the *hifil*, it refers to causing someone else to lose something.

369. As examples, the *piel* third person present is *me'abbed* and third person past is *ibbed*. Here, the root א-ב-ד is transitive.

370. A very reasonable alternative approach is suggested by S. D. Luzzatto. "My father" is a reference to all the forefathers in one composite figure. As suggested by Luzzatto, one can read this approach into the Rashbam as well.

with *shevach* and one is *doresh* from *arami oved avi* until one finishes the entire section."

The Talmud records an Amoraic dispute between Rav and Shmuel about the meaning of the word *genut* (disgrace, shame). But neither of the two seem to consider the *arami oved avi* section (Deut. 26:5-9) as relating to the *genut* referred to in the Mishnah.

But what if we would consider the Mishnah on our own? The Mishnah instructs one to begin with an exposition of *genut* and end with one of *shevach*. It then refers immediately to Deut. 26:5-9, a section that can easily be understood as beginning with *genut* and ending with *shevach*. This can be mere coincidence, but much more likely the adjacency suggests that Deut. 26:5-9 is the *genut-shevach* section referred to.

We all know the first four of these five verses from our *Seder*. Deut. 26:5-9 reads: "(5) You shall speak and say before the Lord thy God: "*Arami oved avi*, and he went down to Egypt, and sojourned there, few in number; and he became there a nation, great, mighty and populous. (6) The Egyptians dealt ill with us, and afflicted us and laid upon us hard bondage. (7) We cried out to the Lord, the God of our fathers, and the Lord heard our voice and saw our affliction and our toil and our oppression. (8) The Lord brought us forth out of Egypt with a mighty hand, and with an outstretched arm, and with great awe, and with signs and with wonders. (9) He brought us to this place and gave us this land, a land flowing with milk and honey."

A very reasonable approach to understanding the Mishnah is that the *genut* referred to focuses on the phrase *arami oved avi* and the *shevach* referred to focuses on verse 9. This *shevach* can be either the implicit praise of our ancestors for becoming worthy of being given the land, or the praise of God for giving it to them. A *genut* of "my father was a homeless/wandering/lost Aramean" contrasts perfectly with this *shevach*. Moreover, a statement that "Lavan was trying to destroy my father" does not, on the simplest level, amount to a *genut*; it is merely a statement about an attempt to make our ancestor into a victim. Thus, the Mishnah itself is implicitly adopting the "my father was a homeless/wandering/lost Aramean" understanding.[371]

371. Scholars who have taken this position include Y. Tabory and D. Henshke. For Tabory, see his "*Al Nusach Ha-Haggadah Be-Zeman Ha-Bayit*," *Sinai* 82 (1978), pp. 97-108, and his *Pesach Dorot* (1996), p. 358. For Henshke, see

Of course, one can argue that being ill-treated, afflicted and put to hard work in Egypt is the *genut*, and being taken out (and brought to Israel) is the *shevach*. But in this interpretation, the *genut* does not begin until verse 6, וירעו. Moreover, verse 6 only describes what the Egyptians did to us; it does not call us *avadim* or directly assign to us a negative status. Reading the *genut* as focusing on the first few words of the section referred to, words that do clearly portray a *genut* in the non-Lavan understanding, seems to be the simplest understanding of the Mishnah.

Of course, we are assuming that verse 9 was part of the *Seder* ritual at the time of the Mishnah. But this assumption is a compelling one.[372] The Mishnah describes the section to be expounded as running through *kol ha-parashah*. To read the Mishnah as implying that only up to verse 8 was expounded is farfetched. Verse 9 is a direct continuation of the capsule history of verses 5 through 8; the Mishnah would have had to be more specific to indicate that verse 9 was not part of the ritual. Moreover, Mishnah *Bikkurim* 3:6 specifies a ritual in the *bikkurim* context that begins with *arami oved avi* and continues through *kol ha-parashah*. It is evident from Deuteronomy 26 that verse 9 was part of the ritual recitation there.

(Regarding the word ודורש, although we are used to it as indicating an extended exposition, or a resort to midrashim or hermeneutical principles, this was probably *not* the meaning of this root at the time of the Mishnah. All that ודורש meant was that some explanation above and beyond the mere recital of the verses was being suggested.)

his "*Midrash Arami Oved Avi,*" *Sidra* 4 (1988), pp. 33-51, and more recently his *Mah Nishtanah? Leil Ha-Pesach Be-Talmudam Shel Chakhamim* (2016), pp. 431-39.

372. It is adopted by many scholars. See, e.g., D. Goldschmidt, *Haggadah Shel Pesach* (1960), p. 14, Y. Tabory, *Pesach Dorot*, p. 35, and D. Henshke, *Mah Nishtanah? Leil Ha-Pesach Be-Talmudam Shel Chakhamim*, pp. 427-430. It is also adopted by R. David Zevi Hoffman, in his *Melammed Leho'il* (1926-32), vol. 3, sec. 65, and by Rav Joseph B. Soloveitchik. For the latter, see, e.g., *Reflections of the Rav* (1979), pp. 210-211. Of course, there are those who disagree. See, e.g., S. and Z. Safrai, *Haggadat Chazal* (1998), p. 33.

Admittedly, verse 9 is not found in any surviving *haggadah* text. But our earliest *haggadah* texts are only from the Geonic period (from Babylonia and from Palestine/Egypt), long after the period of the Mishnah. Our position is only that verse 9 must have been part of the *Seder* ritual at the time of the Mishnah.

In sum, reading the *genut* as focusing on the first few words of the Deut. 26:5-9 section seems to be the simplest understanding of the Mishnah. If the *genut* is to be located in these words, the Mishnah almost certainly understood *arami oved avi* to mean "my father was a homeless/wandering/lost Aramean." The assumption that verse 9 was part of the *Seder* ritual at the time of the Mishnah is a compelling one. A *genut* of "my father was a homeless/wandering/lost Aramean" contrasts perfectly with this *shevach.*

Our approach to Mishnah *Pesachim* 10:4 is very satisfying since we are no longer forced to take the position that the widespread interpretation of the Sages was a grammatically problematic one. We now understand that the non-Lavan interpretation was the widespread interpretation of the Sages, as evidenced by the interpretation assumed in the Mishnah.

Over the centuries, due to the influence of Targum Onkelos and the *haggadah*, and due to the interpretations of *"genut"* expressed by the Amoraim, the way the Mishnah originally understood *"arami oved avi"* was forgotten. It seems that it did not occur to almost all the Rishonim who argued for the homeless/wandering/lost Aramean interpretation that they were advocating the interpretation already implied in this Mishnah! (The one exception: the little-known R. Judah Ibn Balam.)

Of course, the next question is what motivated the ungrammatical Lavan interpretation found in Targum Onkelos and in the *haggadah*? Also, what motivated Rav and Shmuel to deviate from the plain sense of the Mishnah that the *genut* is found in the *arami oved avi* verses? Are there other understandings of the statements of Rav and Shmuel? Many answers to these questions have been suggested and I refer you to my longer article in *Ḥakirah*, vol. 13 (2012) (available on line at hakirah.org) or to the slightly revised version in my *Esther Unmasked* (2015).[373]

*

Mitchell First, a Non-wandering Attorney, can be reached at his desk at MFirstAtty@aol.com.

---

373. Regarding the statements of Rav and Shmuel, see most recently D. Henshke, *Mah Nishtanah? Leil Ha-Pesach Be-Talmudam Shel Chakhamim,* pp. 439-449.

The Meaning of the Word *Hitpallel* (התפלל)[374]

It is clear from the many places that it appears in Tanakh that התפלל connotes praying. But what was the original meaning of this word? I was always taught that it meant something like "judge yourself." Indeed, the standard ArtScroll Siddur (*Siddur Kol Yaakov*) includes the following in its introductory pages:

> The Hebrew verb for praying is מתפלל; it is a reflexive word, meaning that the subject acts upon himself. Prayer is a process of *self*-evaluation, *self*-judgment....[375]

More recently, when I searched Jewish sites on the internet for the definition that was offered for *hitpallel* and *mitpallel*, I invariably came up with a definition similar to the above. Long ago, Rabbi S.R. Hirsch (d. 1888) and R. Aryeh Lieb Gordon (d. 1912) also gave definitions that focused on prayer as primarily an action of the self.[376]

---

374. This article was originally published online at seforim.blogspot.com on Aug. 29, 2016. I have made only very minor revisions here. I would like to thank my son Rabbi Shaya First for reviewing and improving the draft of the original article.

375. P. xiii.

376. The edition of Rav Hirsch's Pentateuch commentary translated by Isaac Levy includes the following (at Gen. 20:7):

> התפלל means: To take the element of God's truth, make it penetrate all phases and conditions of our being and our life, and thereby gain for ourselves the harmonious even tenor of our whole existence in God.... [התפלל is] working on our inner self to bring it on the heights of recognition of the Truth and to resolutions for serving God...

Prior to this, the commentary had pointed out that the root פלל means "to judge" and that a judge brings "justice and right, the Divine Truth of matters into the matter...."

R. Aryeh Lieb Gordon explained that the word for prayer is in the *hitpael* form because prayer is an activity of change on the part of the petitioner, as he gives his heart and thoughts to his Creator; the petitioner's raising himself to a higher level is what causes God to answer him and better his situation. See the introduction to *Siddur Otzar Ha-Tefillot* (1914), vol. 1, p. 20.

I would like to share a different interpretation offered by some modern scholars, one based on a simple insight into Hebrew grammar. This new and compelling interpretation has unfortunately not yet made its way into mainstream Orthodox writings and thought. Nor has it been given proper attention in academic circles. For example, it did not make its way into the widely consulted lexicon of Ludwig Koehler and Walter Baumgartner.[377] By sharing this new interpretation of התפלל, we can ensure that at least the next generation will understand the origin of this critical word.

There are two issues involved in parsing this word: (1) what is the meaning of the root פלל? And (2) what is the import of the *hitpael* stem, one that typically implies doing something to yourself?

    With regard to the root פלל, its meaning is admittedly difficult to understand. Scholars have pointed out that the other Semitic languages shed little light on its meaning.[378]

    If we look in *Tanakh*, the verb פלל is found 4 times:[379]

The *Encylcopaedia Judaica* is another notable source that uses the term "self-scrutiny" when it defines the biblical conception of prayer. See 13:978-79.

    It would be interesting to research who first suggested the self-judge/self-scrutiny definition of prayer. I have not done so. I will point out that in the early thirteenth-century Radak viewed God as the one doing the judging in the word התפלל. *See his Sefer Ha-Shorashim*, root פלל.

377. *The Hebrew and Aramaic Lexicon of the Old Testament* (1994). The authors do cite the article by E.A. Speiser (cited in the next note) that advocates the interpretation. But they cite the article for other purposes only. The interpretation of התפלל that Speiser advocates and that I will be describing is nowhere mentioned.

378. For example, E.A. Speiser writes that "[o]utside Hebrew, the stem *pll* is at best rare and ambiguous." See his "The Stem *PLL* in Hebrew," *Journal of Biblical Literature* 82 (1963), pp. 301-06, 301. He mentions a few references in Akkadian that shed very little light.

    There is a verb in Akkadian, *palālu*, that has the meaning: "guard, keep under surveillance." See the פלל article in *Theological Dictionary of the Old Testament*, vol. 11, p. 568 (2001), and Koehler-Baumgartner, entry פלל, p. 933. This perhaps supports the "assess" and "think" meanings of the Hebrew פלל.

379. Various forms of a related noun, פלילי, פלילים, פללים and פליליה, appear 6 times. The meanings at Deut. 32:31 (*ve-oyveinu pelilim*), Job 31:11 (*avon pelilim*), and Job 31:28 (*avon pelili*) are very unclear. The meaning at Is. 16:3 (*asu pelilah*) is vague but could be "justice." The meaning at Is. 28:7 (*paku*

- It seems to have a meaning like "think" or "assess" at Gen. 48:11: *re'oh fanekha lo filalti,* "I did not think/assess that I would see your face."[380]

- It seems to have a meaning like "intervene" at Ps. 106:30: *va-ya'amod Pinḥas va-yefalel, va-te'atzar ha-maggefah,* "Pinchas stood up and intervened and the plague was stopped."[381]

- It seems to have a meaning like "judge" at 1 Sam. 2:25: *im yeḥeta ish le-ish u-filelo elokim,* "If a man sins against another man, God will judge him...."[382]

- It also appears at Ezek. 16:52: גם את שאי כלמתך אשר פללת לאחותך, "You also should bear your own shame that you *pilalt* to your sisters." The sense here is difficult, but it is usually translated as implying some form of judging.

What I would like to focus on in this article, however, is the import of the *hitpael* stem in the word התפלל. Most students of Hebrew grammar are taught early on that the *hitpael* functions as a "reflexive" stem, i.e., that the actor is doing some action on himself. But the truth is more complicated.

---

peliliah, "they tottered in their *peliliah*") seems to be a legal decision made by a priest. Finally, there is the well-known and very unclear *ve-natan be-flilim* of Ex. 21:22. Onkelos translates this as *ve-yiten al meimar dayanaya.* But this does not seem to fit the words. The Septuagint translates the two words as "according to estimate." See Speiser, p. 303. Speiser is unsure if this translation was based on guesswork or an old tradition, but thinks it is essentially correct.

380. Note that Rashi relates it to the word *maḥshavah.*

Sometimes the verb is translated in this verse as "hope." Even though this interpretation makes sense in this verse, I am not aware of support for it in other verses. That is why I prefer "think" and "assess," which are closer to "intervene" and "judge."

Many translate the word as "judge" in this verse: I did not judge (=have the opinion) that I would see your face. See, e.g., *The Brown-Driver-Briggs Hebrew and English Lexicon,* entry פלל.

381. *Brown-Driver-Briggs* translates ויפלל using a similar verb: "interpose." See their entry פלל. Alternatively, some translate ויפלל here as "executed judgment."

382. It has been suggested that the "judge" meaning is just a later development from the "intervene" meaning.

One source I saw counted 984 instances of the *hitpael* in Tanakh.[383] It is true that a large percentage of the time, perhaps even a majority of the time, the *hitpael* in Tanakh is a "reflexive" stem.[384] Some examples:

- "station oneself"; the verb יצב is in the *hitpael* 48 times in *Tanakh* (e.g., *hityatzev*)
- "strengthen oneself"; the verb חזק is in the *hitpael* 27 times in *Tanakh* (e.g., *hithazzek*)
- "sanctify oneself"; the verb קדש is in the *hitpael* 24 times in *Tanakh* (e.g., *hitkaddesh*)
- "cleanse oneself"; the verb טהר is in the *hitpael* 20 times in *Tanakh* (e.g., *hitaher*)

But it is also clear that the *hitpael* transforms meanings in other ways as well. For example:

- At Gen. 42:1 (*lamah titrau*), the form of *titrau* is *hitpael* but the meaning is likely: "Why are you looking at one another?" This is called the "reciprocal" meaning of *hitpael*. Another example of this reciprocal meaning is found at 2 Chron. 24:25 with the word *hitkashru*; its meaning is "conspired with one another."
- The root הלך appears in the *hitpael* 46 times in Tanakh, e.g., *hithalekh*. The meaning is not "to walk oneself," but "to walk continually or repeatedly." This is called the "durative" meaning of the *hitpael*. There are many more durative *hitpaels* in Tanakh.[385]

383. The exact number given varies from study to study. I have also seen references to 946, 780 and "over 825." See Joel S. Baden, "Hithpael and Niphal in Biblical Hebrew: Semantic and Morphological Overlap," *Vetus Testamentum* 60 (2010), pp. 33-44, 35 n.7.

384. We must be careful not to assume that the *hitpael* originated as a reflexive stem. Most likely, the standard Hebrew *hitpael* is a conflation of a variety of earlier t-stem forms that had different roles. See Baden, p. 33, n. 1 and E.A. Speiser, "The Durative Hithpaʿel: A tan-Form," *Journal of the American Oriental Society* 75 (2) (1955), pp. 118-121.

385. See the above article by Speiser. For example, with regard to the *hitpael* of אבל, the implication may be "to be in mourning over a period of time." With regard to התמם (the *hitpael* of תמם: e.g., 1 Sam. 22:26 and Ps.18:26), the implication may be "to be continually upright." Some more examples: משתאה at Gen. 24:21 (continually gaze), תתאוה at Deut. 5:18 (tenth commandment; continually desire), ויתגעשו at Ps. 18:8 (continually shake), and התעטף at Ps.

Now let us look at a different word that is in the *hitpael* form in Tanakh: התחנן. The root here is חנן which means "to be gracious" or "to show favor." חנן appears in the *hitpael* form many times in *Tanakh* (התחנן, אתחנן, etc.). At 1 Kings 8:33 we even have a *hitpael* of פלל and a *hitpael* of חנן adjacent to one another: והתפללו והתחננו. If we are constrained to view התפלל as doing something to yourself, then what would be the meaning of התחנן? To show favor to yourself? This interpretation makes no sense in any of the contexts that the *hitpael* of חנן is used in Tanakh.

Rather, as recognized by modern scholars, the root חנן is an example where the *hitpael* has a slightly different meaning: to make yourself the object of *another's* action. (This variant of *hitpael* has been called "voluntary passive" or "indirect reflexive.") Every time the root חנן is used in the *hitpael*, the actor is asking *another* to show favor to him. As an example, one can look at the beginning of *Parashat Vaethannan*. Verse 3:23 states that Moshe was אתחנן to God. אתחנן does not mean that "Moshe showed graciousness to himself." Rather, he was trying to make himself the object of *God's* graciousness.

Let us now return to our issue: the meaning of התפלל. Most likely, the *hitpael* form in the case of התפלל is doing the same thing as the *hitpael* form in the case of התחנן: it is turning the word into a voluntary passive/indirect reflexive.[386] Hence, the meaning of התפלל is *to make oneself the object of God's* פלל *(assessment, intervention, or judging)*. This is a much simpler understanding of התפלל than the ones that look for a reflexive action on the petitioner's part. Once one is presented with this approach and how it perfectly parallels the *hitpael's* role in התחנן, it is very hard to disagree.[387]

142:4 (continually be weak/faint). Another example is the root נחל. When it is in the *hitpael,* the implication may be "to come into and remain in possession."

386. See T. Lambdin, *Introduction to Biblical Hebrew* (1971), pp. 249-250, and Speiser, *The Stem PLL*, p. 305.

387. Rav Hirsch views התחנן as "to seek to make himself worthy of concession." See his comm. to Deut. 3:23. This is farfetched.

Hayim Tawil observes that there is an Akkadian root *enēnu,* "to plead," and sees this Akkadian root as underlying the Hebrew התחנן. He views the *hitpael* as signifying that the pleading is continuous (like the import of the *hitpael* in *hithallekh*). See his *An Akkadian Lexical Companion For Biblical Hebrew* (2009), pp. 113-14. But there is insufficient reason to read an Akkadian root into התחנן, when we have a very appropriate Hebrew root חנן.

Some Additional Comments

1. It is interesting to mention some of the other creative explanations for התפלל that had previously been proposed (while our very reasonable interpretation was overlooked!):

- The root is related to a root found in Arabic, *falla*, which means something like "break," and reflected an ancient practice of self-mutilation in connection with prayer.[388] Such a rite is referred to at 1 Kings 18:28 in connection with the cult of Baal ("and they cut themselves [=*va-yitgodedu*] in accordance with their manner with swords and lances, until the blood gushed out upon them").[389]
- התפלל is derived from the root נפל (fall) and reflected the ancient practice of prostrating oneself during prayer.[390]
- התפלל did not originate based on a three-letter root, but was a later development derived from a primary noun תפלה. In this approach, one could argue that התפלל is not even a *hitpael*. (This approach just begs the question of where the word תפלה would have arisen. Most scholars reject this approach because תפלה does not look like a primary noun. Rather, it looks like a noun that would have arisen based on a verb such as פלל or פלה.)

2. There are other examples in Tanakh of words that have the form of *hitpael* but are either voluntary passives (like התפלל and התחנן) or even true passives, as the role of the *hitpael* expanded over time.[391] Some

---

388. See *Theological Dictionary of the Old Testament*, vol. 11, p. 568, Ernest Klein, *A Comprehensive Etymological Dictionary of the Hebrew Language for Readers of English* (1987), p. 511, *Brown-Driver-Briggs*, entry פלל, and Koehler-Baumgartner, entry פלל, p. 933.

389. The Soncino commentary here remarks that this was "a form of worship common to several cults with the purpose of exciting the pity of the gods, or to serve as a blood-bond between the devotee and his god."

390. See *Theological Dictionary of the Old Testament*, vol. 11, p. 568, Klein, p. 511, and Koehler-Baumgartner, entry פלל, p. 933.

391. One scholar claims to have located as many as 68 such instances in Tanakh, but does not list them. For the reference, see Baden, p. 35, n. 7. Baden doubts the number is this high and believes that the true number is

examples:[392]

- Gen 37:35: *va-yakumu khol banav ve-khol benotav le-nahamo, va-yemaen **le-hitnahem**....* The meaning of the last two words seems to be that Jacob refused to let himself be comforted by others or refused to be comforted; the meaning does not seem to be that he refused to comfort himself.
- Lev. 13:33: ***ve-hitgallah.*** The meaning seems to be "let himself be shaved by others."
- Num. 23:9: *u-va-goyim lo **yithashav**.*
- Deut. 28:68: ***ve-hitmakkartem*** *sham le-oyvekha la-avadim ve-li-shefahot....* It is unlikely that the meaning is that the individuals will be selling themselves.
- Ps. 92:10: ***yitpardu*** *kol poalei aven.* The evildoers are not scattering themselves but are being scattered.
- Is. 30:29: *ke-leil **hitkadesh** hag...* The holiday is not sanctifying itself.
- Prov. 31:30: *ishah yirat Hashem hi **tit'hallal***
- Jonah 3:8: ***ve-yitkassu*** *sakim ha-adam ve-ha-behemah....* Animals cannot dress themselves!
- **2** Kings 8:29 (and similarly 2 Kings 9:15, and 2 Chron. 22:6): *va-yashav Yoram ha-melekh **le-hitrappei** ve-Yizre'el....* The meaning may be that king Yoram went to Jezreel to let himself be healed by others or to be healed.

3. As we see from this article, understanding the precise role of the *hitpael* is important to us as Jews who engage in prayer. Readers may be surprised to learn that understanding the precise role of the *hitpael* can be very important to those of other religions as well.

---

much lower. Baden would dispute some of the examples that I am giving.

*Hitpael*s with true passive meanings are found more frequently in Rabbinic Hebrew.

The expansion of the meaning of the *hitpael* stem to include the true passive form took place in other Semitic languages as well. See O.T. Allis, "The Blessing of Abraham," *The Princeton Theological Review* (1927), pp. 263-298, 274-278.

392. These and several others are collected at Allis, pp. 281-83. For a few more true passives, see Kohelet 8:10, 1 Sam. 3:14, Lam. 4:1, and 1 Chron. 5:17.

A passage at Gen. 22:18 describes the relationship of the nations of the world with the seed of Abraham: והתברכו בזרעך כל גויי הארץ. (The phrase is found again at Gen. 26:4.) Whether this phrase teaches that the nations of the world will *utter blessings* using the name of the seed of Abraham or *be blessed* through the seed of Abraham depends on the meaning of the *hitpael* here. Much ink has been spilled by Christian theologians on the meaning of the *hitpael* in this phrase.[393]

Whoever suspected that grammar could be so interesting and profound!

חזק חזק ונתחזק!

(Does the last word mean "let us strengthen ourselves," "let us strengthen one another," or "let us continually be strengthened"? I will leave it to you to decide!)

---

393. See, e.g., Allis, and Chee-Chiew Lee, "Once Again: The Niphal and the Hithpael of ברך in the Abrahamic Blessing for the Nations," *Journal for the Study of the Old Testament* 36.3 (2012), pp. 279-296, and Benjamin J. Noonan, "Abraham, Blessing, and the Nations: A Reexamination of the Niphal and Hitpael of ברך in the Patriarchal Narratives," *Hebrew Studies* 51 (2010), pp. 73-93.

The Root of the Word מבול: A Flood of Possibilities[394]

A common assumption is that the word מבול means "flood." This is how the word is translated in the ArtScroll Stone *Chumash*, in the Hertz Pentateuch, and in the Koren Tanakh. But in order to truly understand the meaning of a word, we must determine its three letter root.

The word מבול has four letters, the first of which is a *mem*. Usually, a *mem* at the beginning of a noun is not a part of the root. It is what is added to turn a verb into a noun. Thus, an initial thought might be that the root of מבול is בול.[395]

But there is no evidence for a verb בול in Biblical Hebrew. Therefore, the *vav* is probably not a root letter here and one of the three original root letters probably dropped out. The *dagesh* in the *bet* of מבול also implies that a root letter dropped out. Our task is to determine what that letter was.

One possibility is that the original root was בלל and that the dropped letter was a *lamed*.[396] In this view, the original noun was perhaps מבלול. If the original root was בלל, the fundamental meaning of the word מבול would be "mixture/intermingling/confusion."

---

394. This article was originally published online at seforim.blogspot.com on Oct. 11, 2014. Perhaps some minor substantive revisions are warranted. Nevertheless, I merely reprinted the original article (with some minuscule revisions). I would like to thank Rabbi Avrohom Lieberman and Sam Borodach for reviewing the draft of the original article.

395. Also, no Hebrew root begins with the two letters *mem* and *bet*. See Eduard Yechezkel Kutscher, *A History of the Hebrew Language* (Jerusalem: Magnes Press, 1984), p. 7:

> It is also instructive that [in a Semitic language] in the first two positions, not only are identical consonants excluded (the patterning AAB being non-existent except in Akkadian) but even homorganic consonants (produced by the same organ) do not occur in this position.

Mem and *bet* are homorganic consonants. (Kutscher admits that there are some exceptions to the rule he stated.)

396. See, e.g., R. Abraham Ibn Ezra to Gen. 6:17, who makes this suggestion. He also suggests נבל as the root.

The fact that the story of *migdal Bavel* follows shortly after the story of the מבול gives some credence to this approach. The root בלל is a main theme of the *migdal Bavel* story (see Gen. 11:7 and 11:9). But the *dagesh* in the *bet* of מבול implies that the dropped letter was the first letter of the root.[397]

Therefore, a more likely possibility for the root of מבול is נבל.[398] The verb נבל has the meaning of "fall, decay, destroy."[399] The root letter *nun* often drops as the first letter of the root. In this approach, the original noun was מנבול.

The problem with claiming that the root נבל underlies the word מבול is that נבל is typically used in the context of a **gradual** destruction, such as in the context of leaves and flowers.[400] See, e.g., Is. 28:1: *ve-tziz novel*, Is. 34:4: *ki-nevol aleh mi-gefen*, and Is. 40:7: *naval tzitz*. It seems to mean "wither" and "decay," rather than "destroy." There is one instance in the Tanakh where the root נבל is applied to the world. See Is. 24:4: *navlah ha-aretz... navlah tevel*. But even here the implication may be one of gradual decay.[401]

---

397. Of course, all the *dagesh* really shows is that whoever inserted this *dagesh* believed that a letter was dropped. But most likely, the vocalization was based on the pronounciation at the time, which presumably reflected a tradition that the word was pronounced *mabbul*, and not *mavul*. This suggests that there was once a root letter preceding it.

398. See, e.g., Ibn Ezra, Seforno, and S.D. Luzzatto, on Gen. 6:17. Those who take this approach can point to the fact that the word מבוע (Ecc. 12:6), also with a *dagesh* in the *bet*, undoubtedly comes from the root נבע.

399. Seforno writes that נבל means *mappalah ve-hefsed* and Luzzatto writes that נבל means *nefilah ve-hashchatah*. Seforno points to the use of the word משחיתם (=destroy them) at Gen. 6:13 as evidence that *mabul* probably has this meaning as well.

Very likely, the roots נבל and נפל are related.

400. R. Samson Raphael Hirsch argues that this is precisely the point. By using the term מבול, the Torah was implying that on some level the event was only of a mild character. I do not find this argument convincing. Although Noah and his family remained in the Ark for one year and ten days (see Gen. 6:11 and 7:14), the implication of verse 7:23 (*va-yimmach et kol ha-yekum...*) is that every living thing was destroyed decisively in the first 40 days.

401. See, e.g., the translation in the Soncino edition. The Hebrew root בלה also connotes gradual decay. See, e.g., Deut. 8:4 (clothes), 29:4 (shoes), and Gen. 18:12 (Sarah). It may be related to the root נבל.

Radak agrees that the root of מבול is נבל, but takes a different approach.[402] In his approach, the fundamental meaning of the root נבל is "fall."[403] But the word is *not* being used to describe the *effects* of the flood (earthly items falling and being destroyed). The word is being used to describe something that is *itself falling* from the heavens. In Radak's view, anything that falls from the heavens (e.g., snow, hail and fire) can be called a מבול.[404]

A third approach to the root of מבול is that it is יבל.[405] This seems to be the most likely approach. In this approach, the original noun was מיבול, but the *yod* dropped.[406]

In Akkadian, the root *nabulu* may have more of a connotation of destruction than the Hebrew root נבל. See, e.g., the concordance of S. Mandelkern, entry מבול, and Ernest Klein, *A Comprehensive Etymological Dictionary of the Hebrew Language for Readers of English* (New York: MacMillan, 1987), p. 311. This would give more of a basis to interpret מבול as deriving from נבל.

402. In addition to his comm. to Gen. 6:17, see his *Sefer ha-Shorashim*, entry נבל.

403. In Rabbinic Hebrew, a נובלת is an unripe fruit that falls off of the tree.

404. Both *San.* 108b and *Zev.* 116a refer to a *mabbul shel esh*. Radak also points to the phrase *nivlei shamayim* at Job 38:37, where the context indicates that the phrase refers to falling rain. But it seems more likely that נבלי there means "vessels," i.e., the clouds that hold the rain.

It has been suggested that מבול is related to the "vessel" meaning of נבל. In this view, the meaning of מבול is "a receptacle that holds water." See, e.g., Hayim ben Yosef Tawil, *An Akkadian Lexical Companion for Biblical Hebrew* (Jersey City: Ktav, 2009) p. 196, who mentions such a suggestion. Probably, the origin of the "vessel" meaning of נבל is that vessels were often made from the skin of a fallen animal (=a נבלה.)

נבל also has the meaning "disgusting," probably because withering and falling things become disgusting. But it seems farfetched to connect מבול with this meaning of נבל.

405. See, e.g., Moses David Cassuto, *Peirush al Sefer Bereshit* (Jerusalem: Magnes, 1953), vol. 2, p. 45, *Daat Mikra* (comm. to Gen. 6:17), Menachem Tzvi Kadari, *Millon ha-Ivrit ha-Mikrait* (Ramat Gan: Bar Ilan Univ., 2006), p. 575, and Tawil, p. 196.

The *Daat Mikra* commentary to Gen. 6:17 (p. 177, n. 52) points out that all three sons of Lemekh have a name derived from the root יבל: *Yaval, Yuval,* and *Tuval Kayin.* See Gen. 4:20-22.

406. Some other examples of words whose initial *yods* dropped are: מצע (Is. 28:10, from יצע) and מסד (I Kings 7:9, from יסד). See *Daat Mikra* to Gen. 6:17. There is a *dagesh* in the middle letter of both of these words.

Throughout *Tanakh*, יבל is a root relating to movement and flow.[407] See, e.g., Ps. 60:11: *mi yovileini ir matzor* (who will lead me into the fortified city?), Is. 53:7: *ka-se la-tevach yuval* (as a lamb is led to the slaughter), and Is. 55:12: *u-ve-shalom tuvalun* (and you will be led out with peace).

Another example of the root יבל relating to movement is in the context of the jubilee year. At Lev. 25:10, we are told: *yovel he tiheyeh lachem ve-shavtem ish el achuzato...* יובל means "ram" in several places in Tanakh.[408] Based on the statement in Lev. 25:9 that the *shofar* is blown to proclaim the jubilee year, Rashi believes that *yovel* must mean ram at Lev. 25:10, and that the reference is to the blowing of the horn of the ram. But the plain sense accords with the view of the Ramban that the meaning of *yovel* at Lev. 25:10 is "being brought back," i.e., a time of being brought back to one's land.[409]

---

407. The word also has the related meaning of "carry." See, e.g., Psalms 76:12: *yovilu shai* (carry presents).

In the *Shema*, the word יבולה is used to mean the produce of the land. Most likely, it has this meaning because produce must be carried in from the land. (See similarly, the word תבואה, which also means produce, and comes from the root בוא. See Klein, p. 689.) Alternatively, the word יבולה means produce because produce flows from the land.

408. *Yovel* means ram at Ex. 19:13 and throughout the sixth chapter of the book of Joshua. (That *yovel* means ram at Ex. 19:13 is evident from Josh. 6:5. It is also suggested by Ex. 19:16.)

409. Ramban defines *yovel* as הבאה. R. Hirsch also takes this approach to this verse. See also the commentaries of R. Saadiah Gaon, Ibn Ezra, and Hizzekuni.

R. Hirsch also makes the suggestion that when *yovel* is used in the context of a sound being made, we can translate *yovel* as "home-calling signal," based on the verb יבל. Despite the brilliance of this suggestion, a comparison of Ex. 19:13 with Josh. 6:5 suggests that, in the sound contexts, *yovel* is merely short for *keren ha-yovel* (=the horn of the ram).

Is there a connection between the "movement/bringing" meaning of *yovel* and the "ram" meaning? R. Hirsch makes the following interesting suggestion:

> [T]he ram, is the leader of the flock, the one who "brings" them to their pasturage, perhaps quite specially, who goes in front, and the flock following him, "brings them home."

See similarly Klein, entry יובל (p. 256): "leader of the flock, bellwether."

Also, the root יבל is connected to water in several verses. See Is. 30:25 and 44:4: יבלי מים (streams of water) and Jer. 17:8: יובל. See also Dan 8:2 (אובל).

Hayyim Tawil's *An Akkadian Lexical Companion for Biblical Hebrew* contributes to our understanding and supports our suggestion that the root of מבול in Biblical Hebrew is יבל. Tawil points out that there is a word in Akkadian *bubbulu,* which means something like a flood of water.[410] Most probably, this word is related to the Hebrew word *mabbul,* since Hebrew and Akkadian are related languages, and *m* and *b* often interchange. Since *bubbulu* is used in the context of water, this suggests that the root of מבול is יבל, and not נבל or בלל.

The issue of the root of the word מבול is not just an etymological one. Philosophically, what we are asking is: was the מבול a force meant to cause intermingling/confusion? a force meant to cause things to fall/decay/be destroyed?[411] or more neutrally, a force of flowing water? Most likely, the root is יבל and the last is correct.[412]

Interestingly, Rashi conducts practically the same analysis of the word מבול that we did. In his explanation of the word at Gen. 6:17, he writes:

> she-**bilah** et ha-kol, she-**bilbel** et ha-kol, she-**hovil** et ha-kol min ha-gavoha la-namukh....

בלה means "destroy and wear down," similar to נבל. בלבל means "mix," the equivalent of בלל. הוביל means "move" and is from the root יבל.[413] But Rashi seems to believe that the word מבול was purposely chosen to convey all three connotations.

---

410. Tawil, p. 196. The standard word in Akkadian for flood is *abūbu.*
411. Or, according to Radak, a force of falling water.
412. It is interesting to note that in the Septuagint the word מבול was translated as κατακλυσμός = down-cleansing. (The ArtScroll Tehillim commentary to Psalms 29:10, p. 354, refers to the *mabul* as a "cataclysmic" upheaval. Surely, this is just coincidence!) But the Greek-speaking Egyptian Jews had a very limited understanding of the structure of Hebrew words. Surely, they did not see the root יבל in the word.
413. For further elaboration, see the *Siftei Chakhamim* and ArtScroll's Sapirstein edition of Rashi. The three-pronged interpretation expressed in this Rashi seems to be his own.

Additional Notes

1. Outside of the 12 times the word מבול appears (in various forms) in *Parashat Noach*, the only other time the word appears in Tanakh is at Psalms 29:10: *Hashem la-mabbul yashav*. Many assume that the meaning here is something like "God sat enthroned at the Flood,"[414] but the prefix *la-* is difficult in this approach.

An interesting interpretation is provided by Tawil. He cites a scholar who claims, based on a parallel in Akkadian, that למבול here means "**before** the Flood," i.e., "from time immemorial." The phrase *Hashem la-mabbul yashav* would then parallel the subsequent phrase *va-yeshev Hashem melekh le-olam*.[415]

Many other interpretations of *la-mabbul yashav* have been suggested.[416] Most creative is the suggestion of Naphtali Herz Tur-Sinai that the reference is to God having dried up the waters of the *mabbul* and that ישב here is just a methathesized form of יבש![417]

2. An analysis similar to the one we have conducted on the word מבול can also be conducted on בול, the pre-exilic name for the month of *Marchesvan*.[418] Is בול named for some activity in the month relating to mixing (בלל)? relating to withering (נבל)? or relating to moving/gathering produce (יבל)? All have been suggested.[419] Because בול may

---

414. See, e.g., the ArtScroll Siddur. See also Rambam, *Moreh Nevukhim*, part I, chap. 11.

415. See Tawil, p. 196.

416. For example, the *Daat Mikra* commentary to Psalms 29:10 cites a suggestion that מבול here means "throne," based on a resemblance to a word in Arabic. The suggestion is made by Jacob Nahum Epstein in "*Mabbul*," *Tarbitz* 12 (1940), p. 82. But the Arabic word that Epstein bases his suggestion on is pronounced מנבר; Epstein must assume that there was a switch of *resh* and *lamed*. (The *Daat Mikra* comm. to Gen. 6:17 states that the relevant word is in Akkadian, but this is an error.)

The Anchor Bible translates: "has sat enthroned *from* the flood" (=from the time of the flood) and argues that the reference is not to the מבול of the time of Noah, but to some other water-related Divine victory.

417. See his *Peshuto shel Mikra*, vol. 4, part 1 (Jerusalem: Kiryat Sefer, 1967), p. 56.

418. See 1 Kings 6:38.

419. See, e.g., J. Talmud Rosh ha-Shanah 1:2, *Daat Mikra* to I Kings 6:38, and Ludwig Koehler and Walter Baumgartner, *The Hebrew and Aramaic Lexicon*

have typically been a rainy month, a derivation from the word מבול has also been suggested. See, e.g., Radak to 1 Kings 6:38.

Interestingly, a statement at *Midrash Tanchuma, Noach,* sec. 11, explains the word מבול as based on the fact that the Flood spanned 40 (מ) days in the month of בול![420]

3. I focused above on determining the root of מבול in Biblical Hebrew. If we rephrase the question and ask what the root of the word was in proto-Semitic, the answer changes slightly. The answer would be ***vav-bet-lamed***. The prevailing scholarly view is that most Hebrew roots with an initial *yod* derive from earlier Semitic roots with an initial *vav*.[421]

---

of the Old Testament (Leiden-New York-Köln: Brill, 1994), vol. 1, entry בול. (The connection to בלל seems least likely.)

Of course, because the word בול lacks a *mem* at the outset, there is less reason to suspect that an initial root letter such as *nun* or *yod* was dropped. But the בול of Job 40:20 surely comes from יבול.

420. See Gen. 7:11-12.

421. Support for this in our case is that there is a word in Arabic, *wabala,* to bring down rain. See Cassuto, vol. 2, p. 45. See also Tawil's reference (p. 196) to the Akkadian word *(w)abālu.*

Of course, it is possible that מבול is a non-Semitic word that happened to make its way into the Tanakh and we are completely misguided in our search for its origin and meaning in Biblical Hebrew and the other Semitic languages. But it is a noun that begins with *mem* and this is a typical Biblical Hebrew form. Moreover, the parallels in the other Semitic languages support our conclusion that the origin of the word is a Semitic one and that its root is *vav-bet-lamed/yod-bet-lamed.*

Corrections

P. 35: *old* should be *od*

P. 42: Here I wrote that an origin of for the prayer *Ha-Noten Teshuah* in pre-expulsion Spain was unlikely. It turns out that the prayer did have its origin in pre-expulsion Spain. In fact, the earliest reference we have for it is a prayer for King Ferdinand V, the king who later expelled the Jews. See Aharon Arend, *Pirkei Mechkar Le-Yom Ha-Atzma'ut* (1998), p. 182.

P. 76: The reference to the Letter of Aristeas should be removed. The passage should read: "Also, the Septuagint is preferable because of the tradition about the miracle that occurred: the translators translated separately, but. . . . " I thank Michoel Chalk for pointing out my error to me.

P. 100: In discussing the root חלם, I stated that there are two times in *Tanakh* that there are words from this root that mean something like "healthy" and "strong." I would like to add that the word חלמיש, found five times in *Tanakh*, also perhaps derives from this root. It means "hard stone." Other examples of nouns in *Tanakh* that have *shin* added as a suffix include: חרמש, עכביש and רטפש. See S. Mandelkern, pp. 398 and 1090.

P. 144: Here I implied that שאול with its "netherworld" meaning was not found in other ancient languages unless they were derived from Hebrew. I was basing myself in part on *EJ* 2:996 which has: "The term does not occur in other Semitic languages, except as a loan word from the Hebrew *She'ol*. . . . "

But in 1967, at Deir Alla (= probably the biblical "Succot," about eight kilometers east of the Jordan River), archaeologists found an inscription describing visions of a "Bilam son of Beor," who is described as a *chozeh* (seer) of the gods. Its language is a dialect with a mix of Aramaic and Hebrew. The text can be dated to around 800 BCE. Here the reading שאול has been conjectured two times. In one, we have part of the word. The other is a conjecture based on its proximity to the other.

P. 160: "Yet in other ancient sources they are called "Chaldeans." This should be: "In Akkadian, these people are called *kaldu*."

P. 202: "Esau" should be "Jacob." I thank Jonathan Tavin for pointing this out to me.

P. 227: Here I erroneously assumed that *matzah* in early biblical times was flat and dry. But before we can determine the etymology of the word, we must determine, to the best of our ability, what matzah would have looked like in its earliest form when the name for it would have arisen. I thank Michoel Chalk for pointing out my error.

P. 243, n. 385: I retract what I wrote that תתאוה meant "continually desire." I have given a much better explanation for the *hitpael* in the article on the root חמד in *Links to Our Legacy*.

Mitchell First
February 2021